Love, Hate, an

MW00720870

Edited by Richard Cavell

In Canada, the Cold War had a distinctly cultural dimension because it raised issues of national self-representation that went beyond international political tensions related to capitalistic versus communistic regimes. The prevailing atmosphere of the Cold War in Canada was anti-communist, but it was also anti-American in many ways. The essays in this volume present a Cold War different in many respects from the familiar one of anti-communist hysteria that characterized the Cold War period in the United States. Drawing on a number of disciplinary approaches, and exploring what Michel Foucault calls the 'discursive practices' of the period, the contributors examine the intersection of the personal and the political in Canada's Cold War, as, for instance, in the state's attempt to regulate sexuality in pulp fiction, in film, and in public spaces.

A major theme emerging from *Love, Hate, and Fear in Canada's Cold War* is that many of the political issues and cultural processes associated with the Cold War in Canada actually preceded the fall of the Iron Curtain and continue to haunt us today. This has become particularly apparent after the terrorist attacks of September 2001, when politicians began employing the rhetoric of the 'War on Terror' and invoking issues of border security, immigration and refugee quotas, and 'harmonization' of policies. Representing many areas of research, this collection of essays presents challenging new documentation and interpretation that shed light on a subject of burgeoning interest.

RICHARD CAVELL is a professor in the Department of English and the founding director of the International Canadian Studies Centre at the University of British Columbia.

The Green College Thematic Lecture Series provides leading-edge theory and research in new fields of interdisciplinary scholarship. Based on a lecture program and conferences held at Green College, University of British Columbia, each book in the series brings together scholars from several disciplines to achieve a new synthesis in knowledge around an important theme. The series provides a unique opportunity for collaboration between outstanding Canadian scholars and their counterparts internationally, as they grapple with the most important issues facing the world today.

PREVIOUSLY PUBLISHED TITLES

Richard Ericson and Nico Stehr (eds): *Governing Modern Societies* (2000)

Sima Godfrey and Frank Unger (eds): *The Shifting Foundations of Modern Nation States* (2004)

 The Green College Thematic Lecture Series

Love, Hate, and Fear in Canada's Cold War

Edited by Richard Cavell

UNIVERSITY OF TORONTO PRESS
Toronto Buffalo London

© University of Toronto Press Incorporated 2004
Toronto Buffalo London
Printed in Canada

ISBN 0-8020-3676-7 (cloth)
ISBN 0-8020-8500-8 (paper)

Printed on acid-free paper

National Library of Canada Cataloguing in Publication

Love, hate, and fear in Canada's Cold War / edited and
introduced by Richard Cavell.

(Green College thematic lecture series)
Lectures originally given during the 2000–2001 academic year.
Includes bibliographical references.
ISBN 0-8020-3676-7 (bound).   ISBN 0-8020-8500-8 (pbk.)

1. Social control – Political aspects – Canada – History – 20th
century.   2. Cultural industries – Political aspects – Canada – History –
20th century.   3. Canada – Foreign relations – 1945–   4. Political culture –
Canada – History – 20th century.   I. Cavell, Richard, 1949–   II. Series.

FC95.4.L69 2004   971.063'3   C2003-907022-0

University of Toronto Press acknowledges the financial assistance
to its publishing program of the Canada Council for the Arts and
the Ontario Arts Council.

University of Toronto Press acknowledges the financial support for
its publishing activities of the Government of Canada through the
Book Publishing Industry Development Program (BPIDP).

Financial support for the publication of this volume has been provided
by the Brenda and David McLean Chair in Canadian Studies and
the International Canadian Studies Centre, University of British Columbia.

Contents

III: Love

Love, Hate, and Fear in Canada's Cold War

Introduction:
The Cultural Production of
Canada's Cold War

RICHARD CAVELL

June 19, 1948

For this is a conspiratorial age. Power is running in new channels. This is still only true of half the world, but will that half corrupt the other? Is this one of the clues to what is going on around us? Where there is power there is also conspiracy? Perhaps this has been true in the most respectable parliamentary democracies, but there are conspiracies and conspiracies. What faces us now is something secret, violent, and fanatical, calling on all the excessive will – the inhuman, single-track obsession – which can apparently be found in the most commonplace men. The professor turned communist – the prostitute turned spy – the public-school boy turned secret agent. Could this not become a new form of excitement as necessary to the nerves as smoking? ... Is a new pattern developing? Is this a by-product of the omnipotent state? Does it not go on under ministries where the civil servants increasingly control the lives of nations? Is part of our rage against communism the rage of Caliban at seeing his own face in the glass?

Charles Ritchie, *Diplomatic Passport*[1]

During the cold war the world was divided into the First, Second and Third Worlds. Those divisions are no longer relevant. It is far more meaningful now to group countries not in terms of their political or economic systems or in terms of their level of economic development but rather in terms of their culture and civilization.

Samuel P. Huntington, 'The Clash of Civilizations?' (1993)[2]

I

· The chapters in this book began as a lecture series at Green College in the University of British Columbia during the 2000–1 academic year. Originally intended as a way of examining issues underlying cultural production in Canada during the 1960s, a subject on which a number of colleagues and I had collaboratively taught a course in the Canadian studies program, the series, we decided, should focus specifically on the Cold War, and, reflecting Green College's support of interdisciplinary research, should do so from a number of disciplinary directions. The areas represented in this volume are political science, history, sexuality studies, sociology, women's studies, cultural studies, American studies, queer theory, film studies, and Canadian studies. While we gave our speakers free reign in their individual discussions, the series title, 'Love, Hate, and Fear in Canada's Cold War,' encouraged our contributors to explore political phenomena in terms of personal ones, and this politicization of the personal is one of the major themes to emerge from the collection, as Robert K. Martin accentuates in his coda to the volume. A number of the chapters (those by Gary Kinsman, Mary Louise Adams, and Tom Waugh) analyse how the Cold War sought to politicize the personal in terms of regulating sexual behaviour and expression, be it in pulp fiction, film, or public spaces. This regulation took a number of forms, including outright censorship as well as institutional homophobia. Gender was likewise an area of regulatory interest on the part of the state, as Franca Iacovetta and Valerie Korinek demonstrate in discussions of the moral panic occasioned by 'romantic' refugees, and of the role women were encouraged to play on the domestic front. Even religion was a site which the state sought to regulate, as Steve Hewitt brings out in his account of RCMP surveillance of United Church members. Underpinning this regulatory zeal was a much broader process of 'othering,' and this leads to the next major thematic strain in these essays, that the cultural processes associated with the Cold War in Canada *preceded* the fall of the Iron Curtain and *survived* the collapse of the Berlin Wall. Indeed, readers will find that many of the issues raised in these chapters are uncannily present, post-September 11, when politicians of all stripes employ the rhetoric of the 'War on Terror' and invoke the concomitant issues of border security, immigration and refugee quotas, and 'harmonization,' connections which Reg Whitaker explores in the opening chapter. The regulation of sexuality which came to the political forefront during the Cold War is an issue that is likewise still with us, as the cross-border trials involving Little Sister's bookstore and the court challenges to gay marriage demonstrate. Finally, as the title suggests, these chapters demonstrate that Canada's Cold War was not simply an extension of the one waged in the United States; ours had a particularly cultural dimension because it raised issues of national self-representation that went beyond Cold War tensions related to capitalistic versus communistic regimes, and it is this particular dimension of Canada's Cold War that I explore in the introduction, which seeks to set up a scaffolding for the chapters that follow.

The essays in this volume thus present a Cold War different in many respects from the overly familiar one of anti-communist hysteria that characterized the Cold War period in the United States. As Reg Whitaker and Gary Marcuse argue in their landmark study, *Cold War Canada: The Making of a National Insecurity State, 1945–1957*, Canada's Cold War differed from its U.S. counterpart by reason of the greater control which Canada's centralized power structure had over its effects: 'In this era at least, the Liberal élites governing from Ottawa were more centralized and exercised greater control over the society than their counterparts in Washington. Through them the state could manage the transition to a Cold War and national-security footing with many fewer of the uncontrolled effects that took place in the United States.'[3] As a statist phenomenon, the discourse of the Cold War in Canada was concerned with complex issues of national self-representation; if the Canadian state was anti-communist in many of its activities, it was also anti-American. This latter element is especially strong in one of the major cultural documents of the period, the Massey Report of the Royal Commission on National Development in the Arts, Letters and Sciences (1951), which emerged out of, and in many ways was a response to, the climate of the Cold War. In fact the first director of the Canada Council, which was created upon the recommendation of the Massey Report, was the former minister of defence.[4] As Jody Berland comments, 'the 1951 Massey Report made an explicit connection between autonomous culture and national defence ... The analogy was presented in pointed connection with the Canadian-American border, in protest against what the report called the "American invasion" ... Nationalism was a precondition to cultural autonomy.'[5]

The situation in Canada was unlike that in postwar Europe, where culture was encouraged to move in directions different from the nationalistic one that wartime events had deeply tainted. The Massey Report in effect recommended that culture in Canada should be a bulwark of national security.[6] The coincidence of the Cold War and the Massey Report can be said to have set in motion a certain discourse about culture during this period (and beyond it, in many ways, to the present day),[7] and this notion of what Michel Foucault has called discursive practices[8] arches over the various and varied contributions that follow. Discursive practices identify regimes of cultural production which are at once sites for the exercise of power and for resistance to that power. One of Foucault's most profound insights was that sexuality is itself a product of these discursive dynamics – that sexuality is a site of regulation – and one of the major contributions that this volume brings to the study of the Cold War in Canada is its articulation of the intersections of sexuality, cultural production, and state regulation that politicized the personal.

To state that Canada's Cold War was 'culturally' produced is to assert, broadly, that it was not a 'natural' outgrowth of our contiguity with the United States or of our European ties, but that it was actively produced here and not just passively received from somewhere else – its roots lying deep in the historical substrata of the nation. For example, a recent collection of essays entitled *Whose National Security?* has traced Cold War ideologies to the early history (1914–39) of the RCMP, as well as to contemporary events such as the aftermath of the APEC protest at UBC in 1997.[9] As the editors put it in their introduction, 'Cold War paranoia is not sufficient – except as an excuse – to account for the extent of the secret monitoring of Canadians in the twentieth century by their own government' (1); they add that 'national security was not only about state regulation, but also included a broader form of social and moral regulation and attempts to define "'proper Canadian subjects"' (3). And whatever else they might be, these 'proper' subjects were born in Canada; as Gregory S. Kealey remarks in *Whose National Security?*, 'from its inception the RCMP has equated dissent with the foreign-born' (18), a history taken up by Franca Iacovetta in the present volume. To state that the Cold War was culturally produced also implies, more specifically, that the cultural dimension of this production is as significant a historical phenomenon of the period as other dimensions more often examined. This specific domain of cultural production is examined in the chapters by Adams (pulp fiction), Korinek (the magazine), Iacovetta (the romance genre), Waugh (film), Cavell and Martin (literature). The more general sense of culture as a site of national self-definition informs the chapters by Whitaker, Hewitt, and Kinsman.

Frances Stonor Saunders uses the phrase 'the cultural cold war'[10] to describe her account of the CIA's underwriting of cultural production in western Europe during a period extending from the 1950s through to the end of the 1960s, with the goal of promoting the 'American' way of life (as opposed to the communistic one). Her study is a useful reminder that one of the major areas of Cold War activity was precisely in the camp of culture. Serge Guilbaut has explored this issue more broadly in his classic materialist history, *How New York Stole the Idea of Modern Art: Abstract Expressionism, Freedom, and the Cold War* (1983),[11] where he writes that 'culture had become politicized and important in a world sharply divided between the forces of good and evil' (4), though the complexities surrounding the notion of politics were such that a number of the artists Guilbaut writes about adopted the tactic of a 'political apoliticism' such that they were able to 'preserve their sense of social "commitment" … while eschewing the art of propaganda and illustration' (2). The war itself had been seen as a cultural battle between civilization, represented by the allies, and barbarism, represented by the Nazis; in the postwar period, the terms of the battle shifted to capitalism versus communism (a shift that is crucial to Guilbaut's theory about New York's 'theft' of cultural hegemony during this period), but the goal was still 'the Mind of Europe.'[10] The results were decisive: 'American art moved first from nationalism to internationalism and then from internationalism to universalism' (174). The direction of this movement was counter to the one that cultural policy took in Canada, however. Whereas for postwar America, '[t]he first important item on the agenda was to get rid of the idea of national art, which was associated with provincial art and … no longer corresponded to reality, much less to the needs of the Cold War' (174), in Canada, the cultural Cold War was waged as an extension of state regulatory power. The 'war' that the following chapters delineate, thus, was for nothing less than control of national self-representation, including norms of gender and sexuality (noted by Mary Louise Adams and Valerie Korinek in their separate ways in the chapters that follow). As Whitaker and Marcuse put it, the *'Cold War debates … were struggles for control of the symbols of legitimacy in Canadian society'* (CWC 24, emphasis in original). It is this very broad notion of culture as a set of strategies of representation that I am invoking throughout this introduction, while bearing in mind that the definition of 'culture' is itself contested terrain. As Don Mitchell brings out in *Cultural Geography* (2000),[13] there are multiple and variate meanings of the term 'culture,' all of which intersect at certain points. Culture refers to artistic production, both 'high' and 'low.' It extends further to embrace the signifying habits of a people, including their language, music, architectural styles, religion, family structures, and values (*CG* 13). It can be divided into realms, such as the economic, political, and social, with the latter including issues of gender and sexuality. It is both material and symbolic. It expresses relationships of power and is thus contestatory and ultimately political.

Considerable reticence prevails to this day in Canada about political aspects of cultural production generally,[14] let alone with reference to an 'event' – the Cold War – which was fundamentally concerned with the politicization of the cultural life of the nation. These aspects of cultural production were complicated by a strong strain of anti-Americanism in the Canadian cultural milieu, especially as codified in the Massey Report, and this complication provides another major reason why Canada's Cold War, while within the orbit of the Red Scare and McCarthyism, nevertheless has its own shape and is worth studying as a distinct phenomenon.[15] Indeed, among the effects of the Massey Report was the production of a cultural isolationism[16] that was closely linked to attempts to depoliticize the cultural milieu, and these effects were exacerbated by Cold War tactics. The most telling example of these linked effects were the purges at the National Film Board of Canada, which rendered 'the innovative and sometimes left-wing voice of Canadian documentary film ... effectively isolated and ... politically toothless. Thus the internal Cold War itself helped stifle a potentially distinctive and independent Canadian outlook on the world' (*CWC* 19).

The reticence remaining to this day around Cold War regulation in Canada can be gauged by the fact that Steve Hewitt's lecture for the series on which this book is based was reported on the front page of the *Vancouver Sun* – so 'shocking' was the revelation that the Canadian state had sought to regulate even religious expression and the peace movement during the heyday of the Cold War.[17] This reticence is all the more curious, given that the Cold War as spectacle began in Canada with the 1945 defection in Ottawa of Soviet cipher clerk Igor Gouzenko and his revelations about vast spy rings that Russia had deployed in the West. The spectacle was elaborated through the Kellock-Tachereau report of the Royal Commission set up to investigate Gouzenko's claims, an advance copy of which Winston Churchill read before delivering his 'Iron Curtain' speech in Fulton, Missouri.[18] Gouzenko turned to writing novels after his defection, and, in one of the most unambiguously political moves in Canadian cultural history, his novel *The Fall of a Titan*[19] won the Governor General's Award for fiction in 1954 – this for a novel rumoured to have been ghost-written by an RCMP interpreter.[20] (Charles Bruce's *The Channel Shore* was also published in 1954, as was Mordecai Richler's *The Acrobats*, Robertson Davies' *Leaven of Malice*, and Ethel Wilson's *Swamp Angel*.) The blurb inside the jacket of the U.S. edition (a Book-of-the-Month Club selection) makes very clear the context in which the book was being read: 'the novel is, in Clifton Fadiman's words, "an insider's demonstration of the absolute corruption of the Soviet hierarchy."'[21] In effect, the novel is the prequel to the story that Gouzenko revealed when he defected in 1945, telling us (in 629 turgid pages) how a Russian academic becomes a spy. Its plot focuses on the role of culture in the production of statist ideologies: Novikov, an agent of the Soviets as well as dean of history at Rostov University, seeks to prevent the aged and respected revolutionary writer Mikhail Gorin (based on Maxim Gorky) from writing an anti-regime novel (which would have the effect of exposing the sham of the communist experiment as played out under Stalin).[22] In effect, Gouzenko's novel becomes the book that Gorin was thwarted from writing, Gouzenko demonstrating the importance of culture in the shaping of the Soviet regime (and, by implication, of other regimes as well).

It is the notion of culture's role in the production of nationalist ideology that grants a degree of contemporary interest to this novel, as the following passage indicates:

After brilliantly completing his course in the Faculty of History, Novikov was sent to the University in his own town of Rostov, to do postgraduate work as a lecturer. Feodor went to work with redoubled zeal, cherishing anew the old hope of breaking away from secret work. He thought that now his chances were greater. But again, at a secret meeting [with agents of the secret police], he was given to understand what was required of him.

'All these old Intellectuals are untrustworthy,' he was told. 'We must keep a sharp eye on them. That will be your task. You must become a good postgraduate and, who knows, you may go a long way. Do your best, and it won't be our fault if you don't rise – we will help you.'

Feodor understood then that to become simply a scholar was not for him. He accepted his defeat and decided not only to resign himself to it, but to squeeze the most out of the situation. He did his very best.

In 1932 Novikov became a professor. He attained this spectacular step up in his career by using his talents and his peculiar position. He wrote an original work on the ancient Slavs. He felt, before anybody else, where the trend in Party policy was leading in the sphere of history. The indications were minor and not yet clear, but he came to one definite conclusion: the trend was in the direction of Russian nationalism.

At that time Novikov had no idea how sweeping this policy would be. He merely felt the stirring of a faint breeze and decided to move with it. Only several years later did it become the all-embracing idea of propaganda for everything Russian – not only in the sphere of history, but in all fields of knowledge without exception: science, industry, agriculture, art, everything. (75–6)

Novikov's place in this system is to influence Gorin to write a work that will justify, from a historical standpoint, the ways of Stalin to man. Gorin finally decides (with a good deal of subtle help from Novikov) upon a historical drama based on the life of Ivan the Terrible, at once positing him as the true forerunner of Stalin and as someone deeply maligned by history – 'the Tsar-Reformer' (376). The play is an enormous success and Novikov awaits his next assignment – to Ottawa, perhaps?

An important theme emerging out of Gouzenko's novel is the role of the media in constructing the Stalinist state, which should alert us to the parallel development of the Cold War and the rise of the mass media as a cultural and political force. Surely part of Joseph McCarthy's power (and, ironically, part of the reason for his downfall) was the fact that his hearings were telecast into the very homes under whose beds 'commies' were potentially lurking. As Whitaker and Marcuse remind us, the 'era that spawned the indelible TV image of Senator Joseph McCarthy pointing the finger of accusation at alleged Communist subversives was precisely the era in which TV made its entry into Canadian life' (CWC 19). These questions of media and Cold War politics were of contemporary interest to Marshall McLuhan and Edmund Carpenter,[23] who were making pioneering forays during the 1950s into what would become 'media studies.' Editing the journal *Explorations* (with a Ford Foundation grant) from 1953–9, they sought to research the effects of the new media on Soviet Russia. As Carpenter, an anthropologist, recalls: 'I wrote to Russian linguists, asking for articles on the effect of electronic media, especially TV, on Marxist theory and practice ... I wanted to know if, or how, anyone thought Marxism, so clearly a product of print, could possibly survive an electronic storm. So I wrote and wrote, suffered Soviet and RCMP visitors, and in the end only got the party line. I printed these depressing Soviet articles only because the 1950s belonged to McCarthy, even in Canada, and any dialogue seemed better than no dialogue.'[24] One such article, 'The Soviet Press' by Arthur Gibson, argued that Pravda was nothing but an advertisement for the Russian state.[25]

McLuhan's take on the electronic fate of the Soviet republics differed somewhat from Carpenter's; writing in the eighth number of *Explorations* (1957; item 2, unpaginated), he argues that the 'intense individualism and even more ferocious nationalism that is born out of ... print-processing is just now being discovered in the Soviet area. It will eventually splinter the Soviet area as effectively as it splintered England and Europe in the sixteenth century.' McLuhan's cultural significance for the Cold War period lies in his development of the terms 'hot' and 'cool' as descriptors of media effects.[26] The terms were very broadly applied; as Moira Roth has argued, the notion of 'cool' became the characteristic response of liberal American artists to McCarthyite politics. Such artists 'found themselves paralysed when called upon to act on their convictions, and this paralysis frequently appeared as indifference.'[27] Roth contends that 'McLuhan's *The Mechanical Bride* [1951] ... was an early announcement of this new tone of indifference ... [A] study in advertising manipulations, [the *Bride*] was written in a cool rather than indignant manner' (34). Roth associates this aesthetic with artists such as Marcel Duchamp (on whose *Bride Stripped Bare by Her Bachelors, Even* McLuhan's *Bride* is an extended meditation), Cage, Cunningham, Rauschenberg, and Johns. Yet McLuhan's use of the word 'cool' was counter-intuitive: cool media were *more* involving because they required a degree of completion on the part of the reader/producer; hot media, however, presented themselves in a 'finished' state and afforded little opportunity for involvement. Understood in these terms, as Jonathan Katz writes in a response to Roth's article, the work of cool artists 'is considered and dissident, powerfully resistant and hardly indifferent.'[28] This notion of resistance has been particularly important in (re)assessing Cold War cultural production as well as the politics of marginalized groups (as Kinsman and Martin bring out).[29]

Resistance of the sort Katz identifies was made in response to the 'culture of containment' (Andrew Ross) and the 'crisis of masculinity' (Robert Corber) which accompanied it in the postwar gender settlement (as Waugh puts it). The 'crisis of masculinity' emerged out of the unmooring of gender and sexual 'norms' occasioned by the Second World War.[30] Men were placed in the homosocial milieu of the army, and women took on new economic roles in the factory, as exemplified most enduringly by Norman Rockwell's 1943 portrait entitled *Rosie the Riveter*. Seated during her lunch break against a backdrop of the Stars and Stripes, Rosie, in coveralls – her sleeves rolled up to reveal huge biceps – balances an immensely phallic riveter's gun on an upraised knee, her foot trampling a copy of *Mein Kampf*. The painting captures the contradictions and uncertainties of a period which postwar politics sought to stabilize by luring women back to domesticity (the ambiguities of which Valerie Korinek's essay in this volume details) with a profusion of appliances, and men back to the factories to build them (the world critiqued in *The Mechanical Bride*). But the unease of this enterprise was captured in contemporaneous films such as the 1948 classic *The Best Days of Our Lives* (William Wyler, 1946), and, more broadly, in *film noir* (one notable example, *Kiss Me Deadly*,[31] ending with an atomic explosion), where the mysteries that are never satisfactorily solved point toward the broader uncertainties that characterized this period of the *femme fatale* and the rootless shamus who seeks to solve the mystery of her identity (while ignoring the mystery of his own). As Patrizia Gentile has written, 'One of the greatest anxieties [of the period] was the fear that women would refuse to go back into the home and that "[they] would achieve sexual independence outside the parameters of marital/familial relations." The notion of "deviance," then, was a way to identify not only gays and lesbians but also women who resisted or challenged the gender norms and social order prescribed by political and medical experts.'[32] These notions were brought together in the then-current idea that women who refused to stay in their suburban homes and be 'mothers' would turn their sons into homosexuals, as Robert Corber has suggested.[33]

Corber's *Homosexuality in Cold War America: Resistance and the Crisis of Masculinity* (1997) sets up the political and cultural dynamic of the period by referring to Leslie Fiedler's 1958 essay 'The Un-Angry Young Men,' which argues that the intellectual vacuum of the 1950s created by left-wing intellectuals had been filled up by gay male writers, whose shocking scenarios were the last cudgel with which the bourgeoisie could be beaten. As Corber notes, the threat that gay male writers posed was the politicization of areas of experience – primarily sexuality – that had up to then been considered apolitical. As such, this politicization of the personal became a site through which Cold War paranoia could be enacted, the invisibility of the gay male mirroring the invisibility of the communist, a conflation powerfully made through the cliché of the communist under the bed of an unsuspecting America.

As Corber writes, 'Cold War political discourse tended to position Americans who protested the rise of the "organization man" or who rejected the postwar American dream of owning a home in the suburbs, as homosexuals and lesbians who threatened the nation's security ... The politicization of homosexuality was crucial to the consolidation of the Cold War consensus. The homosexualization of left-wing political activity by the discourses of national security enabled Cold War liberalism to emerge as the only acceptable alternative to the forces of reaction in postwar American society' (2–3). Homophobia, in other words, ensured that the discourse of the Left would be rendered ineffectual in the face of the occluded project of the Right to re-stabilize the social contract. This was the politics of containment; as Corber puts it, 'the homosexualization of left-wing political activity provided Cold War liberals with a mechanism for containing the demands of women, African Americans, and other historically disenfranchised groups for greater access to the American dream in exchange for their contributions to the war effort' (3–4). In Canada, this culture of containment was translated into a culture of regulation (as Gary Kinsman has classically summarized it)[34] and was characterized by the purging (through the use of the notorious 'fruit machine')[35] of the federal civil service of thousands of suspected homosexuals – by 1967 there were 8,200 files on suspected homosexuals, of whom circa 3,000 were in the public service (CWC 184).

A classic example of this form of regulation in the Canadian civil service is the case of diplomat and scholar Herbert Norman, and precisely because of the reticence still surrounding it. Although Norman's sexuality never figured overtly in the events leading up to his suicide, it has figured covertly in historical accounts and much more openly in literary works based on Norman's life. Norman committed suicide in 1957 after being hounded for years by the RCMP and FBI about his possible connections to communism. While Whitaker and Marcuse end Cold War Canada with a chapter on Norman that refutes any suggestion that he was a spy, what they don't consider is the possibility that the underlying discourse on sexuality that the present volume seeks to bring out played a role in Norman's death.[36] The one reference they make to Norman's sexuality is attributed to a New York anti-communist journalist and is judged to be an example of the 'sleazy' quality of intelligence amassed on Norman (487 n16). Yet both the journalist's comment and the book's response to it downplay the extent to which homosexuality (treated elsewhere in CWC as an important aspect of the Cold War period) was not only a major issue in Cold War politics but fundamental to the larger intersections of culture, politics, and national self-representation.

As recounted by Charles Taylor in one of the chapters of *Six Journeys: A Canadian Pattern*,[37] Norman was born in Japan to missionary parents and schooled in Canada, where he flirted with Epicurean thought and Marxism. Postgraduate work at Cambridge in the fall of 1933 led to his encounter with the intellectual Left, many of whose members (including Anthony Blunt and John Cornford) called themselves communists, and by 1935 Norman had entered the party. The following year found Norman at Harvard, where he was studying Japanese history, eventually earning a PhD. He learned there of the death of Cornford, his closest Cambridge friend, in the Spanish Civil War: 'I not only respected him and his gifts, both intellectual and political, but loved him' wrote Norman (as quoted by Taylor 118–19).[38] Cornford's death confirmed Norman's commitment to Marxism, as it did Anthony Blunt's, Miranda Carter has recently suggested. Writing in *Anthony Blunt: His Lives*,[39] she states that 'Cornford was a Galahad figure: nineteen years old, a poet, single-minded, charismatic, a little humourless, and utterly devoted to building the Party' (121). Cornford 'lived publicly with a working-class girl called Ray' and Blunt was 'glamorized' by Cornford's 'spare young beauty.' Carter goes on to note that 'for Blunt's generation of homosexual men, friends in innumerable ways provided a support network in a hostile world, and defended the individual against the state. They kept one's secrets. Against the vitality of love, of friendship, of honesty ... was opposed the dead hand of the state' (179). The conflation of Marxism and homosexuality here is unmistakable, and unmistakably the inverse of statist constructions of homosexuality as providing access to the mass threat of communistic culture.

Norman became a highly respected scholar of Japan; he was hired by External Affairs in 1939 and cleared the ritual security test. Although he came under the suspicion of the FBI through association with his Harvard Marxist study group, he went on to an illustrious postwar career in Tokyo, under the direct command of General MacArthur, where he interrogated and classified political prisoners, tutored a royal prince, and pursued his scholarship in Japanese history. But by 1950 he was back in Ottawa, and placed under suspicion of having broken his oath of secrecy to the Canadian government. 'Refusing all interviews,' writes Taylor, 'Norman declined to answer the charges *except to refute one specific, minor allegation that was demonstrably false*' (140, emphasis added). It is reticence such as this that has made Norman's case one of continuing interest, both for what it has to tell us about Norman as well as about the underpinnings of the Cold War. Posted to Cairo in 1956, Norman soon found himself in the midst of the Suez crisis. Having befriended Nasser, it was he who persuaded the leader to permit UN soldiers on Egyptian territory, paving the way for peace (and for Lester Pearson's Nobel Prize). In 1957, however, Norman's name once again surfaced in the U.S. State department, and again he was accused of being a communist. On 4 April, Norman jumped to his death from a Cairo apartment block.

Norman's death has fascinated Canadian author Timothy Findley, who revisits it at the opening of his Second World War novel *Famous Last Words* (1981).[40] He revisits Norman himself in his play *The Stillborn Lover* (1993)[41] with an obsessiveness that finds a number of parallels in Tony Kushner's epic play about the Cold War, *Angels in America* (1993–4),[42] where the homosexuality of Senator McCarthy's legal assistant, Roy Cohn, becomes the hinge on which Kushner articulates his examination of Cold War culture in the United States. Findley has likewise stressed in his writings the connections between war and sexuality, beginning with *The Wars* (1977), war being in his view the inevitable result of a refusal to legitimate the power of homosocial bonding except through the carnage of battle. Thus the suicide of the character at the beginning of *Famous Last Words* provides the leitmotif for the bloody turmoil that is to follow and gives a powerfully psychosexual dimension to the notion that with the Second World War, Europe itself committed suicide.

The Stillborn Lover is important in this regard because it is Findley's attempt to extend this psychosexual notion to the era of Cold War diplomacy. Harry Raymond, who, as the play has it, worked with Herbert Norman[43] in postwar Japan (46), has been taken to a 'safe house' near Ottawa, where he is questioned about his past and about the death of a Russian youth found murdered in a Moscow hotel room.[44] The youth is rumoured to have been Marian Raymond's lover, and Harry is said to have murdered him, necessitating his immediate removal from Moscow since any scandal could hurt External Affairs minister Michael Riordan's chances of winning his party leadership and becoming the next prime minister.[45] Harry, however, confesses to his daughter, Diana, that the youth was in fact *his* lover. Raymond's plight thus becomes not communism, but homophobia: 'You say "who gives a damn" if I'm homosexual. *I do*. My *work* does. My government does' (56), remarks Raymond to his daughter, who has been stunned by his (self)deception. It is Marian herself, Harry's wife, who procured Mischa for her husband, as she had procured boys for him in Cairo. Diana asks, 'Why did you bring him ... men?' and Marian replies, 'Love, Diana, does what it must' (77). What Findley seeks to show is that deceptiveness and intrigue characterize both the communists and the RCMP who have been sent to interrogate Raymond, and that this deceptiveness is founded upon sexual duplicity.

If the official responses to the postwar climate represented here by Findley were the 'hot' ones of red-baiting and witch-hunting, the response from the gay and lesbian communities was 'cool,' an obliquely represented 'oppositional consciousness' (4), as Corber puts it. In Canada this consciousness found one of its most telling expressions in NFB documentaries generally, and in the work of Norman McLaren specifically, as Waugh's essay demonstrates. Corber's comment that '[f]ilm noir was fairly explicit in its opposition to the postwar reorganization of masculinity' (9) can likewise be ascribed to documentary film; indeed, such films noir as *The Naked City* (Jules Dassin, 1948) were structured as documentaries. The most powerful element they had in common was their genesis within the milieu of war. As John Grierson writes in 'The Film at War,' 'I knew very well that ... in Hollywood was one of the greatest potential munition factories on earth. There, in the vast machinery of film production, of theatres spread across the earth with an audience of a hundred million a week, was one of the great new instruments of war propaganda.'[46]

Waugh's essay shows that the battle in postwar Canadian film was waged over the regulation of desire, and here it must be noted that the regulation of sexuality had its counterpart in what would become one of the most regulated cultural economies in the developed world (thanks in large part to the establishment of the Canada Council). The movement toward containment also characterized the cultural economy of the United States during this period, as Andrew Ross has argued.[47] Here, the cultural dynamics were complicatedly organized around the 'threat' of mass culture, which was identified with the collectivist thrust of Soviet domestic policy, and the broader notion that individuality was actively militated against by the Soviet system (and by fascism before it). Within the American context, the collectivist threat was posited in popular cultural movements (be they kitsch or fluoridation), the antidote to which became, in practice, a form of cultural elitism (class, as opposed to mass). This was the era, par excellence, of the public intellectual, of Clement Greenberg, Dwight MacDonald, Lionel Trilling,

Harold Rosenberg (and a number of other authors at *The New Yorker*), and of the anomalous Canadian Marshall McLuhan.

Ross places McLuhan precisely within the 'mass/class' nexus, arguing that McLuhan simply rewrote the equation in terms of (tele)visual and print media. McLuhan is anomalous in this regard, however, because he worked out this equation counter-intuitively, such that (tele)visual culture[48] was deemed to be *more* involving (and thus 'cool'), while print culture was understood to be passive ('hot'). It is this theoretical chiasmus that puzzles Ross, who tries to account for the fact that McLuhan was at once a 'corporate intellectual' and a 'pop intellectual' who was profoundly influential on the counter-cultural movements of the period. Equally disturbing was the fact that McLuhan swam against the current of contemporary American thought, critiquing, in *The Gutenberg Galaxy* (1962), those aspects of print culture which had produced individualism. Instead, as Ross notes, McLuhan posited 'vanguardist' (116) qualities in popular cultural movements, arguing that television watchers were not simply passively watching the tube but actively involved in an immense psychic ritual, first hinted at during the televised funeral of John F. Kennedy, whose mourners are given a double-page spread in *The Medium Is the Massage* (1967).[49]

McLuhan was at the height of his popularity in the 1960s, when Canada was 'the most "wired nation on earth"' (Ross, 131), and this factor, as well as a political tradition of 'postnationalism,' as Northrop Frye had put it at the end of *The Modern Century* (1967),[50] must inevitably cause us to read Canada's Cold War differently from the way in which we read the phenomenon in the United States. If the Cold War was part of an ideology which was seeking to preserve a national identity in the face of a foreign threat, then for Canada that threat was coming from south of the border rather than from the Soviet Union – it is noteworthy that Glenn Gould made a triumphant concert tour of Moscow in 1957.[51] As Whitaker and Marcuse note, 'America represented a cultural threat ... because America was the engine of *mass culture*. [Vincent] Massey's idea [in the Massey Report] of national culture was *high culture* that educated citizens for their task of defending civilization' (*CWC* 228). High culture, however, in the context of the Massey Report, was profoundly European in its orientation, and thus merely exchanged one form of colonization for another. As Grierson had put it, 'the *graphiti* [sic] of the people were never more important than now' (*GD* 161). Hence the paradox of the purges at the National Film Board, which in effect shut down a distinctively indigenous cultural entity in the name of a Cold War produced within the context of American mass culture. Whitaker and Marcuse put it succinctly: 'National security was invoked, but the real beneficiary of the purge was the powerful private-sector movie lobby, centred in Hollywood and extending into Canada through the American-owned theatre and distribution chains. The loss was an indigenous Canadian film industry' (*CWC* 229).

Grierson headed the NFB during the war years, turning a propaganda engine into an unparalleled film production unit by the war's end, when he resigned as the NFB's commissioner, noting that his efforts to promote a 'new internationalism' (*CWC* 230) at the board were not expended without criticism.[52] One such critic was Watson Kirkconnell, who denounced the NFB's 'constant Communist propaganda' (*CWC* 308). In Grierson's wake there was a purge of many filmmakers at the NFB, and a perceptible turn to the right. Nor was the nascent film industry alone in being purged. In 1951, the Toronto Symphony Orchestra, under Sir Ernest MacMillan, purged six of its members when they were denied entry into the United States because they were deemed security risks. Among these six was the stellar violinist, Steven Staryk; despite protests from artists such as A.Y. Jackson, Staryk and his colleagues were not reinstated (*CWC* 291–2). Looking back on the event forty years later, Staryk states that he 'performed for a lot of ethnic and religious groups – Ukrainian, Polish, Jewish, Macedonian, etc., in halls, in churches, and for any organization where music was supposedly appreciated,'[53] and it was the association of such groups with communism that may have led to his coming under suspicion.

The most powerful literary evocation of this period is Earle Birney's novel *Down the Long Table* (1955).[54] Like Patrick Anderson, about whom Robert Martin writes in the coda to this volume, Birney was drawn to communism in the prewar years, becoming an organizer for the Trotskyists in Toronto and travelling to Norway to interview Trotsky himself.[55] The plot of *Down the Long Table* focuses – more or less autobiographically – on Gordon Saunders, a Canadian academic who has been teaching in the United States for a number of years (as had Birney, briefly, at the University of Utah). During the mid-1950s, Saunders is investigated for his association with communism in 1932–3, and the novel is structured through Saunders's attempts to understand his past in terms of his present. As the book jacket states, 'Dr. Birney has written a powerful and searching book in which both the professor's and the committee's questions are answered – not as the committee would have them answered, and not as Gordon himself could have answered them twenty years before, but as the novelist can answer if he has the insight, the honesty, and the technical ability that are demanded of him ... Students of politics and the social scene should find much to interest them in the story of Communist, Trotskyist and other organizations that formed and operated in Canada during the long years of poverty, unemployment and unrest.'

The novel is far more introspective and philosophical than the jacket blurb would suggest, however. Saunders (who is deeply relieved that the inquiry is not to be televised) is at the outset asked about his 'moral code' and whether he had violated it while teaching in Utah in the summer of 1932. Replying that his code has something to do with philosophy or religion he is further asked whether this code 'include[s] loyalty to the Government of the United States' (4):

'Certainly.' No, for godsake be honest today, if ever in your life. 'That is – in so far as I have a na-national loyalty.' Why must I stumble over it? I am not afraid ...

The Senator took his time, regarding the room impassively. 'And how far is that, Dr. Saunders? Just how much of our form of government do you believe in? ... Three years ago you became, at last, an American citizen, at which time you swore loyalty to our government, and yet when I ask you if you are loyal to it you begin to qualify.'

His tone convinces. Perhaps he's no hypocrite at all? 'I believe that it is good for humanity, myself included, to' – don't get pompous – 'to keep hoping for, and keep thinking toward a peaceful federation of all countries, whose citizens will owe their first loyalty to the – well, to the world.' (The Senator is bouncing his pencil on the pad.) 'In so far as the United States Government is working toward that goal, I am loyal to it.' ...

'But,' the word seemed to smack the table, 'your first loyalty is to internationalism?' (4–5)

After this opening gambit, the senator moves on to the dreaded question: 'Are you, Doctor Saunders, a member of the Communist Party?' (6), which occasions the flashback that comprises the remainder of the novel, some chapters of which are written newspaper style, with double columns, headlines, and boxed articles. This graphic reminder of the numerous contradictory forces at work in the 1930s, together with the Canada/U.S. dynamic evident in the passage just quoted, permeates the novel. The nuance given to 'international' is particularly complicated in the multilayered context of Canada's anti-Americanism, of the cultural cosmopolitanism advocated by poet and critic A.J.M. Smith, and, later, of the global village theorized by McLuhan.[56]

The issue of sexuality (in a work uncharacteristically frank for its time) is raised early on in the novel; indeed, it becomes a metonym for communism when Saunders first learns that his appointment at Utah is to be terminated. When he asks the reason, Saunders is told that he 'had been reading rather, well, ... sexy poems in one of [his] classes' (18). In fact, Saunders is having a secret affair with the wife of an eminent colleague as well as dating the daughter of the university's president, though this doesn't prevent people from suggesting that he and his roommate are 'pansies because we don't go steady with women' (47). When he returns to Toronto to complete his doctorate, Saunders finds himself, one day, at a communist rally. Apprehended by a plainclothes policeman, he is brought up to date on the Canadian political scene: 'Perhaps you didn't know the Communist Party was supposed to be underground in Canada? ... There's eight of the top boys taking a five years' rest in Kingston penitentiary. Yeah. And there's a few agitators still creeping around under phoney names, running cover organiza- tions like this fake unemployed outfit today. *And* we've got our eye on a few young punks in the University' (57). Birney portrays the Toronto communists as a group of rabble rousers and misfits to whom Saunders is drawn out of loneliness more than anything else, though his overly intellectual approach to the cause gets him labelled a Trotskyist fascist (84) and he is very quickly expelled into the sphere of the Barstow family, who wish to convert him to social democracy by having him join their discussion group on 'proletarian literature' (112):

> 'But where the devil does the artist fit into all this?' Gordon asked.
> 'Our times can only make an artist by accident,' Ronnie answered, 'and even then by a kind of waste of a good revolutionary.'
> 'Waste!'
> 'O yes,' Ronnie went on. ... 'I think a great writer could be quite good at other things; I don't think he's all that limited.'
> 'Limited!' Gordon felt professionally outraged. He would not let this humorless youth shake his whole hierarchy of values.
> 'Rosa Luxembourg was a great writer too,' Thelma [Barstow] said then.
> Jack snorted and Ronnie skirted the remark tactfully. 'P-political writer, yes.'

'She didn't live in Canada in any case,' Sather interjected. 'Let us distinguish between Writing, which even Canadian college professors find time for, and Literature, which is carried on in other countries by persons who inherit money or marry it, or who die young.' (113)

This discussion brings out the extent to which ideological issues found a home in arguments around the role of culture in the state both before the war and after; the sardonic reference to Canada is likewise a reminder of how these discussions were inflected by Canada's colonialist heritage. The way Birney represents the discussion, communism means the end of art as individualist expression – a 'surrendering [of] ... identity' (160) – and it also means a form of neo-colonization as well. Birney's representation of these issues as being part of a 'family romance' (Thelma is Gordon's love interest) is brilliant, and is a theme which recurs in the stories told by Franca Iacovetta in her chapter in this volume. In these stories, as in Birney's novel (where Gordon is completing a dissertation entitled 'Carnality and Idealism in the Fifteenth Century Scottish Chaucerians'), the political economy is shadowed throughout by a libidinal one.

Hopping freight trains from Toronto to Vancouver,[57] Gordon seeks to prove himself to Thelma by establishing a communist cell there, though the further he gets from her the more he doubts the viability of this enterprise. 'Perhaps he would never know himself well enough to be sure where, in the tangle of his emotions, love and fear of his fellowmen ended and desire and distrust of Thelma began – nor how he might have disentangled either from love of himself' (185). Ironically, at the very moment when Gordon signs up twenty-six members to his Vancouver communist cell, he receives a letter telling him that Thelma has eloped, and the Vancouver organization likewise implodes soon after, thanks to a police spy who had infiltrated the group. When Hughes, one of Saunders' fellow Marxists, murders the informer and appears to have set up Gordon to take the fall, Gordon flees to the home of his mentor, Professor Channing, and renounces politics:

'Doc, ... I've stopped being a Marxist, ... and I never can be one again. Not even a fellow traveller. I don't believe any more in the New Atlantis. ... What I've wanted all along was love, but that was the very thing I stopped giving – except to people who didn't want it. I ran away from marriage and children, because I confused them with bourgeois sterility and prole-

tarian misery. ... And what did I do instead! I got myself mixed up with a
bunch of starry-eyed juvenile delinquents who had repudiated honest
childlikeness and who started me out playing blindman's bluff and then
drifted off, leaving me wearing the bandage.' (282–3)

Saunders subsequently gets married and has a child. The critiques that
the present volume makes of heteronormativity and its connections to
the regulatory state render this conclusion highly ironic; yet Birney's
novel is valuable both as a historical document and for its exposure of
the libidinal element within the radicalism of the time. And in Saunders'
fear that his senatorial proceedings might be televised we are afforded a
glimpse of the ultimate irony of the Cold War as spectacle – that it
should come to an end not through the effects of the bomb but through
the effects of television.

II

Four years after the fall of the Berlin Wall, Samuel P. Huntington
argued in his essay 'The Clash of Civilizations?'[58] that the fall of the
Wall did not so much put an end to the Cold War as reinscribe it in
specifically cultural terms. As Huntington puts it, 'It is my hypothesis
that the fundamental source of conflict in this new world will not be
primarily ideological or primarily economic. The great divisions among
humankind and the dominating source of conflict will be cultural'
(22). While this realization of the role culture plays in political events
is rather belated, especially in the context of the current 'War on
Terror,' it does, however, highlight an implicit theme of the present
volume, namely, that this cultural turn can be glimpsed in Canada's
Cold War, owing both to its post-national status within the theatre of
world powers in the postwar period, and to the cultural needs for
identity production and protectionism vis-à-vis the United States,
which, in combination, have led us to the current cultural moment,
paradoxically founded upon identitarian fluidity and social and cultural over-regulation.

   Reg Whitaker's contribution to *Love, Hate, and Fear in Canada's Cold
War* explores this broad notion of a Cold War whose identifying charac-
teristics both preceded the Second World War and lingered long after
the fall of the Berlin Wall, only to be exacerbated by the events of 11
September 2001. Focusing specifically on defence and on immigration
policies over the last decade, Whitaker's chapter, '"We know they're

there": Canada and Its Others, with or without the Cold War,' notes both the continuities and discontinuities in these areas of national *in*security with the Cold War practices that preceded them. Of particular importance in the aftermath of the Cold War as spectacle is the disappearance of an easily identified 'enemy,' together with the rise of 'non-state actors.' (It is important to note that Whitaker was delivering this lecture in September of 2000.) In this political context, 'othering' (in the form of undocumented immigrants and bogus asylum-seekers, for example) takes on a new and powerful role, the 'Communist menace' having given way to the 'terrorist/criminal menace.'

The conflation of communist with religious 'others' is the subject of Steve Hewitt's chapter, 'Sunday Morning Subversion: Organized Religion and Canadian State Security in the Cold War.' Hewitt provides an overview of Cold War analyses and their reliance on the 'espionage' model, whereby the Cold War is constructed as 'a noble battle to protect the nation state against the operations of foreign intelligence services.' Drawing on extensive archival research, Hewitt disputes this model, noting, like Whitaker, that the 'othering' processes which so characterized the Cold War period actually had their beginnings during the First World War. In support of his position, Hewitt then turns to the example of religious 'subversives' who came under suspicion because their humanitarian interests (such as nuclear disarmament) appeared to align them with Canada's enemies. Targets of this campaign included Dr Lotta Hitschmanova (and it was this revelation that garnered front-page attention from the *Vancouver Sun* for Hewitt's lecture) as well as the United Church of Canada, which came under suspicion for encouraging a 'Marxist-Christian dialogue' with the People's Republic of China.

It is the sexual 'other' that concerns Franca Iacovetta's chapter, 'Freedom Lovers, Sex Deviates, and Damaged Women: Iron Curtain Refugees in Early Cold War Canada'; it thus introduces a central theme of the present volume. Iacovetta powerfully draws out the libidinal elements which underpinned the political 'romance' of the freedom 'lovers' who escaped – often daringly – the exigencies of life under communism for the freedom of the West, and the ironies attendant upon the cultural differences which rapidly recast these freedom lovers as sexually deviant others out of step with the moral regulation of the period. Iacovetta situates her discussion in the context of current social histories of the Cold War which have sought to link notions of sexual misconduct with the national insecurities of the period as manifested in terms of 'moral panic' and concomitant attempts at containment. Given the 'romantic' element underpinning the representations surrounding this culture of moral panic, Iacovetta is particularly sensitive to the discursive practices of the period (and to the gender differences within these practices), especially as they appeared in the newspaper copy which retailed this panic to an avid readership.

The element of regulation likewise characterizes the material researched by Gary Kinsman for his chapter, 'The Canadian Cold War on Queers: Sexual Regulation and Resistance.' Kinsman emphasizes, however, that there was resistance to these regulatory efforts as well. Based on extensive interviews with gay and lesbian survivors of the 'national security regime,' Kinsman's chapter details the surveillance activities which the RCMP directed toward homosexuals during the Cold War period, when all homosexual acts were criminalized. This was the era of purges, informants, demotions, and the notorious 'fruit machine.' Kinsman takes a revisionist approach to the period in seeking to 'disrupt and de-centre the master narrative of heterosexual Cold War Canadian history' by arguing that the hunt for communists was a spectacle meant to occlude the ongoing regulation of sexual 'deviants.' Kinsman thus seeks to bring together his concern that theory not be divorced from the discourse of the period as evidenced in the experiential material he derived from the interviews he conducted. And it is precisely here, in these interviews, that the discourse of resistance most powerfully emerges.

Publishing was a particular site of moral regulation during the Cold War, as Mary Louise Adams details in her account of censorship during this period, 'Margin Notes: Reading Lesbianism as Obscenity in a Cold War Courtroom.' The 1952 trial of the National News Company for obscenity cited a number of periodicals as well as novels, including Women's Barracks, which was deemed to be obscene because of its lesbian content. The two days of the trail devoted to this novel represent one of the rare entries into public discourse in this period of the taboo subject of female homosexuality. Adams positions this discourse – which she examines minutely – in opposition to the heteronormative one of family and home which characterized the Cold War period, a period whose increasingly material benefits masked an anxiety about the world beyond Canada's borders, the world of the unknown, of the other. Among such others were homosexuals, who in 1952 were designated by Canadian immigration laws as undesirables, a sign of the powerful displacement of the national anxiety about identity from the political realm to the sexual one. The representation of homosexuals in publications that were increasingly accessible (this was the heyday of the pulp novel) underlines the role the mass media played in the Cold War era, and it was on this terrain that the censorship battle around *Women's Barracks* was fought, the court transcripts providing invaluable insights into the representation of 'deviant' sexualities during this period, as does the fact that the Crown won its case.

Although *Chatelaine* was not on the Crown prosecutor's list of objectionable publications, Valerie Korinek's chapter reveals that it was a crucially important site for the production of a discourse that juxtaposed love, women, suburbia, and Cold War anxieties about house and home, marriage and family. In '"It's a Tough Time to be in Love": The Darker Side of *Chatelaine* during the Cold War,' Korinek examines women's popular culture through the discourses produced in *Chatelaine* during the period from 1950 to 1969, when the magazine, unlike many of its U.S. counterparts, took a highly politicized stance toward Cold War issues. Addressing her chapter to the circa 20 per cent of the magazine that was devoted to editorials, Korinek notes that they addressed both local and international politics (and increasingly so in the 1960s), especially as these related to second-wave feminist issues. Among the political issues most consistently addressed were progress and the space age, nuclear weapons, and the communist 'other'; it was in this context that Svetlana Gouzenko was interviewed, and that Doris Anderson travelled to Moscow in 1959 to explore the situation of Russian women under communism, which in some ways she found to be decidedly better than that of Canadian women under capitalism.

The most significant achievements in Canadian cultural production during the Cold War period were arguably made in film (and, through film, television), as Tom Waugh demonstrates in 'Monkey on the Back: Canadian Cinema and Queer Others in Canada's Cold War.' Waugh's central concern is the insecurity which characterized both geopolitics and gender and the ways in which a 'Canadian cinematic imaginary' engaged with these anxieties – perhaps paradigmatically in Norman McLaren's 1952 film *Neighbours*. Waugh also discusses a number of films by Gudrun Parker, including her 1953 *A Musician in the Family*, which riffs on Sinclair Ross's classic story 'Cornet at Night.' Waugh notes the paradox that many films of this era portrayed bachelorhood in all its permutations, despite the heteronormativity of the period, and this leads him to his central concern: the absent presence of homosexuality in the films of this period. In McLaren's case, only his last film,

Narcissus (1983), finally gives voice to this silent topic, and it does so in testamentary fashion.

Waugh's chapter is structured as a reminiscence about his school-teacher, Miss Davies. Robert Martin's comments in the Coda to this volume likewise contain reminiscences of that 'scoundrel time.' Martin is particularly sensitive to the cultural codings that characterized the period, when an aesthetic of the 'national' and the 'natural' was in conflict with an aesthetic of beauty and artifice, discourses of politics and sexuality underpinning both. Martin cites the Canadian literary scandal which grew up around the awarding of the 1946 Governor General's prize for poetry to Robert Finch, whose 'dandified' poetry was read as both anti-nationalist and unmasculine. A more extreme case in which communism and homosexuality were conflated was that of Patrick Anderson, whose verse 'challenges the assumption of modernism as a renewed masculinity.'

III

I take great pleasure in thanking here the colleagues who contributed to the lecture series on which this volume is based: Stephen Hugh Lee (history and international relations), Dianne Newell (history), John O'Brian (art history), Becki Ross (sociology and women's studies), Scott Watson (critical studies in sexuality), and Rhodri Windsor-Liscombe (interdisciplinary studies). I am very grateful to Green College, and to its former principal, Richard Ericson, for providing the space, the intellectual milieu, and much of the wherewithal, that made the series and this book possible. The UBC Program in Canadian Studies, and the International Canadian Studies Centre, through the Brenda and David McLean Chair in Canadian Studies, were equally generous. Douglas Todd provided priceless front-page coverage in the *Vancouver Sun* of one of the lectures in the series. Part of the editing of these lectures was done while I was lecturing at Meiji Gakuin University, Tokyo, and I thank Professor Ayako Sato and her colleagues for their generous hospitality while I was there. Katja Thieme processed the edited chapters, and Peter Dickinson was, as always, inestimably supportive.

At the end of Gary Kinsman's lecture in the series, a member of the audience stood up to announce that he was one of those persons who had been purged from the federal civil service during the height of the Cold War; this was the first time in his life that he felt he could acknowledge that fact in public. This tells me that *Love, Hate, and Fear in Canada's Cold War* has served a vital, communitarian purpose through the excellence of research its contributors have brought to it, as well as through their personal commitment to forms of scholarship which acknowledge the importance of experiential as well as theoretical learning. It also reminds me of another way in which, for many Canadians, the Cold War has not yet come to an end.

Notes

1 Charles Ritchie, *Diplomatic Passport: More Undiplomatic Diaries, 1946–1962* (Toronto: Macmillan, 1981) 37–8.

2 Samuel P. Huntington, 'The Clash of Civilizations?' *Foreign Affairs* 72.3 (1993) 22–50.

3 Reg Whitaker and Gary Marcuse, *Cold War Canada: The Making of a National Insecurity State, 1945–1957* (Toronto: U of Toronto P, 1994) 286. Hereafter *CWC*.

4 See Jody Berland, 'Nationalism and the Modernist Legacy: Dialogues with Innis,' in Berland and Shelley Hornstein, *Capital Culture: A Reader on Modernist Legacies, State Institutions, and the Value(s) of Art* (Montreal & Kingston: McGill-Queen's UP, 2000) 21.

5 Jody Berland, 'Marginal Notes on Cultural Studies in Canada,' *University of Toronto Quarterly* 64.4 (1995) 514–25; this quote 517.

6 As Berland (2000) notes, p. 16.

7 As Berland (2000) comments, the 'Massey Report has been implicated in every positive and negative development in Canadian culture and cultural administration for nearly half a century' (15).

8 I am thinking particularly of the opening section in Foucault's *The History of Sexuality, Volume 1: An Introduction*, trans. Robert Hurley (1978; New York: Vintage, 1990).

9 Gary Kinsman, Dieter K. Buse, and Mercedes Steedman, eds., *Whose National Security? Canadian State Surveillance and the Creation of Enemies* (Toronto: Between the Lines, 2000).

10 Frances Stonor Saunders, *Who Paid the Piper? The CIA and the Cultural Cold War* (London: Granta, 1999): 'During the height of the Cold War, the US government committed vast resources to a secret programme of cultural propaganda in western Europe ... The centrepiece of this covert campaign was the Congress for Cultural Freedom, run by CIA agent Michael Josselson from 1950 to 1967 ... Its mission was to nudge the intelligentsia of western Europe away from its lingering fascination with Marxism and Communism towards a view more accommodating of "the American way"' (1).

11 Serge Guilbaut, *How New York Stole the Idea of Modern Art: Abstract Expressionism, Freedom, and the Cold War*, trans. Arthur Goldhammer (Chicago: U of Chicago P, 1983). The term 'materialist history' is the one Guilbaut uses to describe his book (12); he reminds us that the Cold War was the era in which U.S. Senator George Dondero made the statement, 'modern art equals communism' (4).

12 The phrase is Stephen Spender's, uttered in 1948 and quoted by Guilbaut, 173.

13 Don Mitchell, *Cultural Geography: A Critical Introduction* (Oxford: Blackwell, 2000). Hereafter *CG*.

14 See Kenneth C. Dewar's fine discussion of this issue in his entry 'Intellectual History,' in *Encyclopedia of Canadian Literature*, ed. W.H. New (Toronto: U of Toronto P, 2002) 528–34.

15 Four years before the publication of the Massey Report, Watson Kirkconnell, a professor at and later president of Acadia University, co-authored *The Humanities in Canada* (1947), arguing that humanistic research in Canada had to take as its major goal the battling of totalitarian regimes. That same year, Kirkconnell anonymously wrote a 40-page anti-communist tract distributed by chambers of commerce across Canada (*CWC* 277). Kirkconnell's association with the Humanities Research Council of Canada, of which he was a founder and first president, was likewise motivated by anti-communist zeal. After his tenure there (1943–7), Kirkconnell turned his attention to fluoridation, arguing that 'fluoridation is a Communist plot to make Canadian brains susceptible to domination' (*CWC* 279).

16 This was Frank Underhill's contemporaneous critique of the Massey Report: 'It is too late now for a Canadian cultural nationalism to develop in the kind of medieval isolation in which English or French nationalism was nurtured. These so-called alien American influences are not alien at all; they are just the natural forces that operate in the conditions of twentieth-century civilization' (37). See 'Notes on the Massey Report,' in *Our Sense of Identity: A Book of Canadian Essays*, ed. Malcolm Ross (Toronto: Ryerson P, 1954) 33–9.

17 Douglas Todd, 'Mounties Spied on Lotta Hitschmanova: Famed children's advocate – and others – were watched for signs of communist sympathies,' *Vancouver Sun* (19 April 2001): A1, A2, where the headline is 'Documents show RCMP spied on religious groups.' Hewitt's chapter should be read in the context of Whitaker and Marcuse's detailing of James Endicott's persecution in connection with his involvement in the Canadian Peace Congress. See *CWC* 364–83.

18 Laurence Hannant remarks that an advance copy of the 733-page Kellock-

Taschereau Royal Commission Report was given to Churchill while he was preparing the speech in which he would use for the first time the phrase 'the Iron Curtain' to describe the rift between the 'free' world and that of communism. See 'Igor Gouzenko and Canada's Cold War: The Man with the Bag over his Head,' *The Beaver* 75.5 (Oct.–Nov. 1995): 19–23.

19 Igor Gouzenko, *The Fall of a Titan*, trans. Mervyn Black (New York: Norton, 1954). In 1951, A.M. Klein had published *The Second Scroll* (New York: Knopf), which can be productively read as a Cold War novel, especially in its concerns with Marxism, the dialectic, and Hegelian notions of master and slave (to which Charles Ritchie also alludes in the first epigraph to this introduction).

20 See James Doyle, 'Gouzenko Controversy,' in W.H. New, ed., *Encyclopedia of Literature in Canada* 445–6. Nor was this the last time when the political substrate of cultural production erupted in Canada; see Stephen Henighan's account of the awarding to Josef Skvorecky of the Governor General's award for fiction in 1984 (for *The Engineer of Human Souls*), the circumstances of which eerily parallel those surrounding the Gouzenko award (*When Words Deny the World: The Reshaping of Canadian Writing* [Erin, Ont.: Porcupine's Quill, 2002] 27.

21 See Guilbaut on Fadiman's role in the early years of the war as a popularizer of its unifying influence (57).

22 As Guilbaut notes, the seventh congress of the Komintern (1935) created the notion of a 'popular front' to which were recruited artists and writers who would create for communism 'a strong and credible image, the image of a united and dynamic front' (17); the term is used by Waugh and Martin in their chapters that follow.

23 See also Richard Cavell, *McLuhan in Space: A Cultural Geography* (Toronto: U Toronto P, 2002).

24 Edmund Carpenter, 'Remembering *Explorations*,' in *Canadian Notes and Queries* 46 (Spring 1992) 3–14; this quote 3–4.

25 Arthur Gibson, 'The Soviet Press,' in Edmund Carpenter and Marshall McLuhan, eds., *Explorations in Communication: An Anthology* (Boston: Beacon P, 1960) 200–6.

26 Daniel Belgrad argues McLuhan's centrality to the postwar discourse of 'spontaneity,' which is the focus of his book *The Culture of Spontaneity: Improvisation and the Arts in Postwar America* (Chicago: U of Chicago P, 1998).

27 Moira Roth, 'The Aesthetic of Indifference,' in *Difference/ Indifference: Musings on Postmodernism, Marcel Duchamp and John Cage* (Amsterdam: G and B Arts, 1998) 33–47; this quote 34.

28 Jonathan Katz, 'Identification,' in *Difference/ Indifference*: 49–68; this quote

68. Compare Guilbaut's argument about the 'political apoliticism' (2) of the era, and see Waugh's chapter.

29 In the context of Kinsman's chapter, it is important to note that, as Katz argues, Cage, Cunningham, Rauschenberg, and Johns work within a gay aesthetic.

30 The notion of the 'crisis of masculinity' has been developed over the last two decades through a broad number of studies; Corber cites Barbara Ehrenreich, *The Hearts of Men: American Dreams and the Flight from Commitment* (New York: Doubleday, 1983); Elaine Tyler May, *Homeward Bound: American Families in the Cold War Era* (New York: Basic Books, 1988); Elizabeth Long, *The American Dream and the Popular Novel* (Boston: Routledge and Kegan Paul, 1985); Lynn Spigel, *Make Room for TV: Television and the Family Ideal in Postwar America* (Chicago: U Chicago P, 1992); Elizabeth Traube, *Dreaming Identities: Class, Gender, and Generation in 1980s Hollywood Movies* (Boulder: Westview P, 1992); and David Savrin, *Communists, Cowboys, and Queers: The Politics of Masculinity in the Work of Arthur Miller and Tennessee Williams* (Minneapolis: U Minnesota P, 1992). See also the chapters by Iacovetta and Waugh that follow.

31 *Kiss Me Deadly*, directed by Howard Meeker (1955).

32 Patrizia Gentile, '"Government Girls" and "Ottawa Men": Cold War Management of Gender Relations in the Civil Service,' in Kinsman et al., eds., *Whose National Security?* 131–41. Gentile quotes from Annalee Gölz, 'Family Matters: The Canadian Family and the State in the Postwar Period,' *Left History* 1.2 (Fall 1993), 10–13.

33 Robert Corber, *Homosexuality in Cold War America: Resistance and the Crisis of Masculinity* (Durham: Duke UP, 1997), 2–3.

34 Gary Kinsman, *The Regulation of Desire: Homo and Hetero Sexualities*, 2nd ed. (Montreal: Black Rose, 1996).

35 The fruit machine was a chair rigged electronically to determine the sexual identification of its victim with pictures flashed before the victim's eyes; see CWC 184–5.

36 I am not arguing that Norman was a homosexual; I am arguing that the discourse on sexuality continues to be marginalized in accounts of the Cold War in Canada.

37 Charles Taylor, *Six Journeys: A Canadian Pattern* (Toronto: Anansi, 1977). Whitaker and Marcuse also discuss the Norman case at length in CWC 402–25.

38 Compare Harry Raymond's love for Francis Oliver in Timothy Findley's *Stillborn Lover*, discussed below.

39 Miranda Carter, *Anthony Blunt: His Lives* (New York: Farrar, Straus and Giroux, 2001).

40 Timothy Findley, *Famous Last Words* (Toronto and Vancouver: Clarke, Irwin, 1981).
41 Timothy Findley, *The Stillborn Lover* (Winnipeg: Blizzard Publishing, 1993).
42 Tony Kushner, *Angels in America, A Gay Fantasia on National Themes. Part One: Millennium Approaches* (New York: Theatre Communications Group, 1993); *Part Two: Perestroika* (New York: Theatre Communications Group, 1994).
43 An indication of Findley's obsession with Norman in a play putatively about the fictional character Harry Raymond is the error, repeated a number of times in the play, whereby Findley refers to 'the Norman household' (e.g., p. 43) when he means to refer to the 'Riordan household.'
44 There are resonances here, as well, with the case of John Watkins, brilliantly fictionalized by Ian Adams in *Agent of Influence: A True Story* (Toronto: Stoddart, 1999). Watkins, ambassador to Moscow, was picked up for interrogation in Montreal in the fall of 1964; three days later he was dead under circumstances not yet explained. Adams leaves no doubt that Watkins's gay lifestyle was a factor in his coming under suspicion and that his friendship with Herbert Norman was a deciding factor in his persecution by the RCMP. In 2003, Adams' novel was made into a movie by CTV; press accounts made no mention, however, of Watkins' sexuality. See, for example, Alison Cunningham, 'Political Intrigue: Christopher Plummer helps shed light on a gripping tale in *Agent of Influence*,' *Vancouver Sun TV Times* (11 April 2003): 'Although the RCMP held Watkins, it's clear that the CIA – which suspected not just Watkins but even then-prime minister Pearson of being in bed [sic] with the communists – was dictating the events' (4). See also *CWC* 184.
45 Findley treads rather indelicately on highly controversial ground here; 'Mike' was Lester Pearson's nickname and his wife's name was Marion. Working in Egypt during the Suez crises, Herbert Norman paved the way for Lester Pearson's successes as Minister for External Affairs, for which the latter was awarded the Nobel prize.
46 John Grierson, 'The Film at War,' in *Grierson on Documentary*, ed. Forsyth Hardy (London: Collins, 1946) 152–5, hereafter *GD*. Grierson headed the NFB throughout the Second World War.
47 Andrew Ross, 'Containing Culture in the Cold War,' *No Respect: Intellectuals and Popular Culture* (New York: Routledge, 1989).
48 McLuhan, in fact, understood television to be an audile-tactile medium, rather than a visual one pure and simple; he made this comment long before touching screens became a commonplace.
49 Marshall McLuhan and Quentin Fiore, *The Medium Is the Massage: An Inventory of Effects* (New York: Random House, 1967).

50 Northrop Frye, *The Modern Century* (Toronto: Oxford, 1967).

51 See Otto Friedrich's comments in his biography *Glenn Gould: A Life and Variations* (Toronto: Lester and Orpen Dennys, 1989) 62–4: 'Gould ... was the first classical musician from North America to be invited behind what was persistently called the Iron Curtain' (62).

52 See Grierson's references in his article 'Searchlight on Democracy' to 'the international viewpoint' and 'international understanding,' *GD* 165. These references to internationalism should be read in the context of similar arguments made by A.J.M. Smith about the international element in Canadian literature. For further elaborations see my 'Material *Querelle*: The Case of Frye and McLuhan,' *Essays on Canadian Writing* 68 (2000): 238–61.

53 Len Scher, *The Un-Canadians: True Stories of the Blacklist Era* (Toronto: Lester Publishing, 1992) 32. Scher also details blacklisting at the CBC and at the NFB; there are contributions from Al Purdy, Ted Allan, Harry J. Boyle, Eric Koch, Lou Applebaum, Irving Layton, Pierre Berton, and Larry Zolf, among others.

54 Earle Birney, *Down the Long Table* (Toronto: McClelland and Stewart, 1955). Another, lesser known response to the Cold War is Laurence Hyde's *Southern Cross: A Novel of the South Seas* (Los Angeles: Ward Ritchie P, 1951). Told completely with engravings, the novel failed to find a publisher until championed by Rockwell Kent, the illustrator and storyteller long associated with the communist Left in the United States. Kent writes the introduction to the novel, which focuses on the effects of postwar atomic testing in the South Seas.

55 In 1948 Birney was one of those named publicly in a BC 'red scare.' See Elspeth Cameron, *Earle Birney: A Life* (Toronto: Viking, 1994) 341. See Guilbaut's *How New York Stole the Idea of Modern Art* on Trotsky's role in the dialogue of art and politics that took place on the eve of the war (27–9).

56 See my article 'Material *Querelle*,' noted above. Guilbaut's discussion of 'globalism' indicates the importance of the concept in this period (77–80).

57 Whitaker and Marcuse comment that British Columbia was 'especially subject to the political passions' of the Cold War era (*CWC* 287).

58 See also Samuel P. Huntington, *The Clash of Civilizations* (New York: Simon and Shuster, 1996). The phrase was quoted by Prime Minister Chrétien in a speech he delivered in Chicago in February 2003 urging the United States to defer to the United Nations in its plans for an Iraqi invasion. See also Tariq Ali, *The Clash of Fundamentalisms: Crusades, Jihads and Modernity* (London: Verso, 2002).

Part I: Fear

1

'We Know They're There': Canada and Its Others, with or without the Cold War

REG WHITAKER

A few years ago, I co-authored a book on Canada's Cold War in the 1940s and 1950s.[1] But the Cold War is over now. Everyone knows this. Why dwell on what has passed into history? My answer, as a political scientist, is that history is important not only as a record of the past but also as a guide to the present. We need to know where we have come from in order to better understand where we are heading. The Cold War has been over for more than a decade, but Canada in the early twenty-first century still bears the distinctive marks of Canada half a century ago, when the Cold War was falling into place.

I propose to look at continuities and discontinuities in the Cold War and post–Cold War eras. I will focus on two areas of 'national security' – or national *in*security as I prefer to call it – namely defence and immigration policies, each of which has undergone apparently sharp discontinuities in the transition from the Cold War a decade ago, yet on closer examination discloses strong continuities as well. Each turns crucially on Canada's relationship with the United States. This is the thread connecting the two eras. During the Cold War, Soviet communism was the Enemy; in the post–Cold War era, communism has collapsed and the Soviet Union has imploded. For Canada, the United States remains our significant Other. Although never indeed our Enemy, not at least since the war of 1812 (which a recent poll indicates is still considered one of the most significant events in Canadian history), the precise nature of the relationship remains problematic. To put the matter in a somewhat enigmatic nutshell, the United States is the ambiguous Other that defines the threatening Other.

U.S. and Them

In the 2000 Republican presidential primary election campaign in Iowa, George W. Bush is reported to have said: 'When I was coming up, it was a dangerous world, and you knew exactly who They were. It was Us vs. Them, and it was clear who Them was. Today, we are not so sure who the They are, but we know They're there.' With Mr Bush, words are sometimes a bit elusive. But this does get at something very important about the meaning of the Cold War and the break with the post–Cold War world.

The Cold War was many things – an international alignment along diplomatic, military, economic, and ideological/cultural lines; a system of power exercised among states and within states; a confrontation of destructive weaponry that threatened the planet itself. Yet, paradoxically, the Cold War preserved peace between hostile superpowers for almost a half-century because it was, above all, a system of international order. Like all balance-of-power systems it was potentially unstable, but proved surprisingly long lasting in practice, no doubt because the nuclear alternative was too terrible to contemplate. However, part of the basis of its stability lay beyond the dynamics of international relations, as such. For the Cold War contributed to the internal stability of the protagonists, as well as to the internal stability of the two blocs. To take the case of the United States, one can point to the following factors that generally held at least until the 1970s and 1980s:

1 *Economic stabilization*: 'Military Keynesianism' at home legitimated the regulatory role of the national government, while America's global reach facilitated the growth of export markets for U.S. goods and capital;
2 *Class integration*: Defence-led industrial activity provided relatively high levels of employment;
3 *Regional development*: Defence dollars were allocated to industrially underdeveloped areas, spurring the growth of the 'sunbelt' in the west and southwest;
4 *Cultural integration*: Anti-communism provided an ideological framework for integration of immigrants and refugees;
5 *Bipartisan consensus in national policy*: not only foreign and defence policy, but important parts of the domestic agenda were largely, although never entirely, subject to consensus;
6 *American diplomatic and military hegemony in the Western bloc:* The

anti-Soviet alliance provided a largely consensual framework for allied discipline.

The foregoing list applies mainly to the United States as superpower and chief antagonist of the Soviet bloc. Washington's North American ally, Canada, was, both internationally and domestically, part of this Cold War consensus. However, not all the features alluded to above applied in equal measure to Canada. Military Keynesianism could not be sustained in Canada much past the end of the Korean War, and by the late 1950s and early 1960s gave way to more of a welfare than a warfare state. With the decline of military spending, the regional integration characteristic of the U.S. experience was less in evidence, leading to greater regional disparities and more overt politicization of regional antagonisms. Class integration was also weaker, leading to higher levels of unionization and greater strike activity by the 1960s. And of course, Canada experienced American leadership differently from the senior partner in the alliance, a point to which I will return shortly. However, the Cold War framework did provide North America with an ideological consensus constructed around the fear of a common enemy.

There were limits to this consensus, nevertheless. In the United States, Cold War cultural integration failed to encompass the African-American minority. Racial tensions building in the late 1950s erupted in the 1960s and continued to erode the sense of common citizenship to the end of the Cold War. In Canada, a somewhat equivalent problem surrounded the Québécois national minority. Francophone Quebec was one of the principal partners in the anti-communist consensus when that community was still dominantly Roman Catholic and politically conservative in the 1940s and 1950s. Following the 'Quiet Revolution' of the early 1960s, however, Quebec nationalism took a radical turn. By 1970, violent Quebec secessionists replaced communists as the principal internal security threat to the Canadian state. After the suppression of its terrorist wing, the parliamentary secessionist movement became the chief threat to national unity, drawing away attention from the external threat that had loomed so large in earlier decades.

The Vietnam War, along with racial strife, helped break down ideological consensus in the United States in the latter half of the 1960s and early 1970s. And in Canada, Canadian nationalism, which had been largely latent in the 1950s, began to more openly question American leadership in the 1960s and 1970s. Despite these challenges to the Cold

War consensus, the underlying basis remained strong enough so that, in the Reagan years (the 1980s), there was a renewal of superpower antagonisms, an accelerated arms race, and a revival of some of the domestic features of the Cold War. Canada under Conservative Party rule in the latter half of the 1980s took a less critical approach to American leadership than its Liberal predecessors had done from the 1960s to 1984, and indeed negotiated the bilateral free-trade agreement with the United States that was the predecessor to NAFTA. Yet even at the height of what has been termed the second Cold War, two major departures were being prepared. First, the renewed arms race had the intended effect of spending the Soviet Union into submission. One of the main factors involved in the end of the Cold War was the Soviet bloc's incapacity to meet the Western military build-up while its own economies were near collapse. Second, the effect of Reaganite and Thatcherite neoliberal economic policies was to abrogate the domestic Cold War consensus of class integration. In other words, the second coming of the Cold War in the 1980s actually laid the groundwork for the Cold War's final demise.

The most significant transformation of the end of the Cold War has been the disappearance of a permanent, identifiable, widely agreed-upon Enemy. It is an exaggeration to argue, as some have, that Western capitalist democracies are now without enemies.[2] Non-state actors (terrorist and criminal networks organized on a global scale) have replaced states as enemies of democracy. One might reformulate the thesis such that democracies no longer face enemy states. But this too would be an exaggeration, given the role of small, so-called rogue states in provoking the two major military confrontations in which the West has been involved in the post–Cold War era, the Gulf war and the Kosovo intervention, and the alleged role of state sponsorship of terrorism. A further refinement would be to specify that democracies no longer face superpower state enemies. This is not unimportant, for it profoundly changes the international balance of power. But it leaves open the question of what stance the only remaining superpower, the United States, will take when small state and non-state antagonists have replaced its main adversary.

From the point of view of North American societies, the Cold War was always very much about *identity*, about who We were, and who They – the Other that defined 'Us' – were and what they purportedly wanted of us. As the leaders of the 'Free World,' the Americans were always at the epicentre of the Cold War, and the identity of 'Us' was thus relatively straightforward. To consider the Cold War as a Canadian phenomenon is to immediately embark upon a more ambiguous task. Most often, we Canadians were enjoined to think of ourselves as partners, allies, part of 'us / U.S.' After all, we did have a common enemy. But if the Other defined Americans in their own eyes, this could not quite do the trick for Canadians. Not that, by and large, we did not agree that Soviet communism was the great antagonist. Opinion polls are a bit sketchy on the early days of the Cold War, but what data there is suggests that Canadians tended to identify Joseph Stalin as the successor to Adolf Hitler even earlier than Americans recognized this new post-Nazi threat. It was a source of both puzzlement and a certain perverse pride to Canadians that the first public notice of the Cold War had taken place in, of all places, Ottawa, where the Gouzenko affair revealed that the Soviets had been spying on this most inoffensive of their wartime allies, and using Canadians sympathetic to communism and the USSR to do so. Nor is there much evidence through the many subsequent decades that Canadians ever grew more friendly to, or less suspicious of, Soviet communism than their neighbours to the south. Despite popular belief to the contrary, there is good evidence that Canadians were just as ready as Americans to show intolerance toward communists, or alleged communists, or those associated with communists, or those considered sufficiently left-wing to be labelled pro-communists or 'fellow travellers' or communist 'sympathizers,' to use the invidious terminology of the times. The only reason why Canada did not produce the level of anti-communism that reigned to the south in the late 1940s and early 1950s was because the British parliamentary system of government, with its greater executive dominance and deference to Crown authority, choked off would-be McCarthys (like national Conservative leader George Drew) from taking anti-communism out of the careful control of the state sector and making it a divisive and destructive partisan issue. But on the fundamental question of the Cold War enemy, Canada was at one with the United States.

The problem came with the next question after the identification of the Enemy: what do We do about Them? It was as apparent then as it is now that the answer to this question implies different things in the United States and Canada.

Defending North America with the Cold War

The threat of Soviet nuclear attack by manned bombers over the polar region (before bombers were replaced by land and sea-based missiles as the delivery means of choice) required – for America – early warning and effective air defence systems, necessitating command over Canadian air space. Hence the NORAD treaty, which is still in effect. A U.S.-Canada partnership to defend North America against the common threat would seem unexceptionable except for two facts, uncomfortable to Canadians, but unnoticed by Americans. First, the huge disparity in military, but also economic and political, weight of the two countries means that 'common defence' necessarily involves Canadian subordination to American strategies, priorities, and standards. Canadians were used to this, of course. Through two world wars, Canadian forces had been subordinated to British command. (The most tragic example of this was the senseless sacrifice of thousands of Canadian servicemen by Lord Mountbatten at Dieppe.) There was a change in command with the Cold War, but the relationship remained the same. We could live with that. The second fact was more uncomfortable. If the Soviet bombers bearing their deadly nuclear payloads were to be brought down before delivering them to American targets, it would be over Canadian soil, and Canadian population centres. This became more uncomfortable yet when the American military, through NORAD, began insisting in the early 1960s that the BOMARC anti-aircraft missiles stationed in Canada be fitted with nuclear warheads. The reluctance of external affairs minister Howard Green, backed by sections of Canadian public opinion as well as some officials in his department, was countered by the pro-nuclear enthusiasm of Defence Minister Douglas Harkness, in turn backed by his military brass and by other sections of the Canadian public. The refusal, or inability, of Prime Minister John Diefenbaker to decisively adjudicate this division led to the collapse of the Conservative government, and its subsequent defeat at an election in 1963 that featured a more or less overt American intervention,[3] and to the election of a Liberal government committed to nuclear warheads on Canadian soil. This was the context in which philosopher George Grant wrote his classic *Lament for a Nation: the Defeat of Canadian Nationalism*.

We might note one further implication of this perhaps less-than-ennobling story. Canadian integration into American military strategies and structures, and especially Canada's acceptance, albeit transitory, of nuclear weapons, narrowed the margin for Canada to take an independent role as diplomatic peacemaker in the game of nuclear brinksmanship played by the Americans and the Soviets, which reached its most dangerous point ever during the Cuban missile crisis of 1962. This was a role especially prized, ironically, by the man who acceded to office in 1963 on a pro-nuclear platform, Lester Pearson (the recipient in 1957 of the Nobel Peace Prize and the inventor of Canada's now cherished role as international peacekeeper). The problem was that the closer Canada stood under the shadow of U.S. power, the more difficult it was to pretend to be an honest broker. Canada's desire to play this latter role did not arise from any refusal to recognize the Soviet Union as a threatening power requiring global containment. Pearson was always very clear on this point. But as a middle power, Canada sought negotiation and compromise, a diplomatic means in preference to military muscle-flexing. The identity of the enemy was the same, but Canada preferred diplomatic over military means of containment, whereas the United States, having the most powerful military in the world, preferred the latter. Pearson himself felt this acutely when he vainly tried to bring about a negotiated settlement to the Korean War, in the face of the public hostility of the U.S. secretary of state. In his memoirs, Pearson referred to a 'difficult negotiation between Corporal Pearson and General Acheson.'[4] For his pains, Pearson became a target of the FBI and U.S. congressional witch-hunters seeking Soviet agents of influence within Western councils. The distinguished diplomat and scholar Herbert Norman took his own life when relentlessly pursued as a stalking horse for Pearson. Later, Pearson provoked the wrath of President Lyndon Johnson for daring to voice mild public criticism of America's tactics in Vietnam. Later yet, Prime Minister Pierre Trudeau drew insults from State Department officials for his forlorn one-man mission to promote nuclear disarmament, despite his government's controversial agreement to permit U.S. testing of the Cruise missile over Canadian territory.

Agreement on a common enemy and acceptance of a military role, however modest, in collective Western security under American leadership did not entirely resolve Canada's identity crisis, even as the Cold War imposed meaning and purpose on an America forsaking isolationism and assuming global leadership. Indeed, it may even have made it more acute, highlighting certain contradictions that otherwise went unnoticed in the day-to-day business of international affairs. To return to the wisdom of President George W. Bush: we knew who the Them was. But we were not in agreement on what to do about Them, and whenever we did try to adopt a moderately independent course, we were pulled in the wake of the great American battleship.

Defending North America without the Cold War

The contemporary American answer to the question of what to do about the threatening Them has already antagonized the Russians and the Chinese, deeply unsettled the Europeans, and raised alarms in Canada. The projected National Missile Defence (NMD),[5] which was under active consideration by the Clinton administration until it was put on hold pending the coming of a new administration in 2001, is warmly supported by the Republican Bush administration, and is a direct fall-back on Cold War thinking – the discredited 'Star Wars' project of the Reagan administration[6] – and constitutes an isolationist Fortress North America defence strategy. Costing between $60 and $200 billion[7] by best estimates, unproven (and beset by criticisms of allegedly faked tests), and, in some respectable scientific opinion, unworkable in theory, NMD risks the entire structure of hard-won arms limitation and anti-ballistic missile treaty (ABM) progress, alienating allies and potentially driving the former Cold War adversaries, Russia and China, back into intransigent and aggressive stances. The threat that NMD is supposed to counter is that of a missile-launched nuclear attack to the continental United States. Stretching credulity to breaking point, this threat was alleged to emanate from rogue states like North Korea and Iraq, and perhaps from terrorists. The Clinton administration subsequently dropped the 'rogue' appellation in exchange for new terminology: 'states of concern.' Even though diplomatic initiatives with North Korea appear to have made the removal of any missile threat from that state a matter for negotiation, the NMD enthusiasts, including the new Bush team, have responded by simply emphasizing other potential threats. In the end, the means proposed, and their consequences, seem so radically out of proportion to the threat that the origins of the policy must be sought not in the stated policy rationales but elsewhere.

Elsewhere, in this case, points back to the functionality of the Cold War. The economic logic that spurred the military-industrial complex has by no means disappeared. The same interests that would have profited from Star Wars simply bided their time and have now returned behind NMD. Equally important is political support in Congress, especially from those districts that most benefited from Cold War military spending and its careful distribution on a regional basis. Here one might note how President Bush was a former governor of the state of Texas, a long-time beneficiary of federal defence largesse. Finally, there is a comforting rhetorical return in NMD to the quasi-isolationist thinking of the 1950s such that American know-how and business/engineering acumen can keep the threatening outside world at bay, definitively preventing any more Pearl Harbors. The imagined security of the impregnable fortified homeland vanished with Sputnik in 1957 and the subsequent emergence of a Soviet missile threat. Reagan tried in vain to appeal to a nostalgia for strong military defence with Star Wars. Now it has returned once again with NMD, bizarrely enough in the aftermath of the conclusion of the very conflict that gave rise to nuclear insecurity in the first place.

There are obvious implications of NMD for Canada as America's northern neighbour. With the decision to go ahead, there will be little or no opportunity for Canada to opt out. A Fortress America that excludes the northern half of the continent makes little sense, although it is conceivable from the American point of view. NMD requires neither land-based northern early warning systems, nor American air defence bases on Canadian soil. Yet the consequences for Canada opting out of NMD would likely entail the end of the NORAD treaty, now over four decades old, and with it, Canada's formal role as joint partner in hemispheric air defence. As one observer has written, the consequences to Canada would be serious indeed: 'If NORAD were to go, Canada's long-term standing as a close ally whose views on matters of international security needed to be listened to and whose interests needed to be given most serious consideration would diminish, and not just with the U.S. military but also with the State Department, intelligence agencies, senior administration officials, and members of Congress ... Over the years, Canada would not count quite as much with the U.S. government and so would not be viewed in quite the same fashion.'[8] Yet much of Canada's present foreign policy agenda, especially the human security aspect, is threatened by the diplomatic consequences of NMD, particularly the abrogation of the ABM treaty. Not surprisingly, former foreign affairs minister Lloyd Axworthy spoke out publicly against the project, warning that the plan could 'set loose the demons' of a nuclear arms race and undermine the fragile nuclear non-proliferation regime. But his colleague Art Eggleton, former minister of national defence, spoke out strongly in favour of Canada getting in on the NMD ground floor, as it were, and in support of a Canadian contribution, typically modest in financial terms, toward a common 'homeland defence.'[9]

There is nothing new in this kind of disagreement. I have already referred to the 1962 BOMARC crisis, with the same line-up of opponents in foreign affairs and proponents in defence. But there is something more than political divisiveness at work here. There is a structural continuity over time, before and after the Cold War. Continental defence integration was put in place on a government-to-government basis, beginning during the Second World War, with the Hyde Park declaration of 1941. Once set in motion, close linkages were established at a sub-political level between the two military establishments. With increasing standardization of equipment and integration of training and operations, Canada, as the junior partner in continental defence, not surprisingly found little independent voice within the military councils at the Pentagon and White House. The Canadian military command instead grew to act as a willing conduit within the Canadian state for promotion of American military strategic perspectives. That ministers of defence have tended to act as advocates within the Canadian cabinet for American military perspectives is less a matter of personality and philosophical conviction than of representation of interest. Beyond the professional interests of the armed forces, there are Canadian industrial interests which have been plugged into American defence production through various sharing agreements and subcontracting, and these interests no doubt see potential profit in the $60–$200 billion NMD program. In the era of NAFTA and global competitiveness, these economic opportunities cannot be ignored. Recent protectionist moves in Congress to cut out foreign defence subcontractors on 'national security' grounds led to frantic lobbying by Canada to gain a Canadian exemption. This is, however, only temporary; failure to endorse NMD could well lead to a loss of the exemption.

On every occasion in the past half-century when tensions opened up between an independent Canadian foreign policy and a dependent defence policy, it is the latter that has carried the day. It is highly likely that the same will happen over NMD, now that the project has received the green light from Washington. Thus the economic forces of the private sector that push toward continental integration are reinforced by the political and bureaucratic forces that operate at the state level – and importantly, at the sub-political level, between, in this case, military professionals in both countries linked by common interests and perspectives.

Securing North America with the Cold War

Let us briefly examine a second case of Canada's continuing thin margin of autonomy. One of the ways in which the Cold War imposed its icy hand on domestic life was, and is, through security screening.

Security screening sets political and ideological standards as to who is acceptable, and who constitutes a risk to the state and must therefore be excluded. Security screening was instituted for government employees in 'sensitive' departments or positions (i.e., those with access to secret or classified information), for workers in defence industries, and in other strategic places in the private sector (such as airport security personnel today). Security screening was also imposed upon immigrants and refugees seeking entry, and upon applicants for citizenship. During the Cold War years, this meant that newcomers to our shores were tested for political reliability – which meant for anti-communism. Entry into Canada, and membership in the Canadian community, was subject to political policing. Anyone associated with communism (which could range from having been a Communist Party member to simply having relatives still residing in a country under communist rule) could be barred.

While I was researching *Cold War Canada*, I was so impressed with the impact of immigration security on the shape of Canadian society that I published a volume on Cold War immigration controls.[10] One of the striking aspects of this history was the mixture of motives that gave it impetus. While business interests sought to keep out communist labour organizers (or 'agitators,' in the parlance of the day), anti-communist immigrant groups wished to prevent their left-wing rivals in the same ethnic communities from entering Canada. And a great deal of the pressure to impose uniform anti-leftist controls on immigration came from the United States. In order to maintain its share of defending the free world, Canada had to conform to U.S. standards with regard to the political policing of the movement of people across borders.

Sometimes these pressures forced Canada into positions it might never have otherwise taken. The worst example of this is the construction of homosexuality as a Cold War security risk. Both Canada and Britain were strongly pressured by the United States to follow suit when an anti-homosexual moral panic (the 'lavender scare') in the late 1940s and early 1950s became enmeshed in the growing red scare of the McCarthy era. There is little evidence from the public records that Canada was initially interested in pursuing homosexuals as security risks, but under American pressure, homosexuality was added to the prohibited categories in the Immigration Act. While this seems never to have been enforced, the RCMP security service in the late 1950s did take up the challenge with a vengeance in its civil service screening, thus initiating a homosexual purge that peaked in the 1960s. This process, characterized by a later prime minister as 'odious,' was a shameful page in Canadian history, but without American pressures, it probably never would have reached such ugly proportions.[11]

Securing North America without the Cold War

With the end of the Cold War, and the disappearance of the communist enemy, one might naively have thought that the political policing of immigration would have wound down. Not so. New 'enemies' and potential enemies have simply taken the place of communists, and the political policing continues apace with new targets. And once again, American pressures in defining these targets call into question Canadian autonomy and sovereignty.

The end of the Cold War has transformed in a number of ways the issue of the movement of people. Refugee policies on both sides of the Atlantic were deeply conditioned by Cold War ideology from the immediate postwar period right through to the end of the 1980s. Movements from communist countries were viewed with relative equanimity, since these countries were defined as oppressive, refugee-producing states. On the other hand, refugees fleeing oppressive anti-communist regimes were viewed with suspicion as security risks.[12] With the end of the Cold War, security criteria have become more diffuse and ambiguous, with no single organizing principle commanding widespread public support.[13] Indeed, the targeting of people of certain national origins as inherently risky, due to conflicts in their homeland involving groups willing to use violent means to further their aims, inevitably rouses ethnic tensions in a multicultural society where numerous immigrant groups are represented.

Security and policing agencies have focused on movements of people for reasons of post–Cold War threat targeting. The major non-state actors seen as posing security threats are terrorist groups and global mafias engaged in money-laundering, cyber crime, corruption of governments, drugs and illegal arms traffic, and the sex trade. In most cases these activities rely heavily on the illegal movement of people. In another twist, illegal migration has begun to rely on the services of criminal networks to evade stricter border controls. In other words, movements of people across borders have been defined as inherently risky from a security standpoint, and thus are subject to heavy, and increasingly high-tech, mechanisms of surveillance and control. States are the main agents of enforcement, with private sector organizations such as air carriers coerced into assisting state policing, sometimes under threat of financial sanctions for non-compliance.

There is another reason why Western democracies are turning to stiffer border controls in the post–Cold War era. The collapse of the ideological consensus formed around the Cold War perception of a common enemy has contributed to a legitimacy problem for governments that can no longer rely on automatic assent to foreign and defence policy initiatives. The legitimacy problem has been further deepened by the ascent of neoliberalism and the decline of the old social contracts that fostered class integration in the earlier Cold War era. Governments no longer feel free to promise or to deliver social programs on the scale they once could offer. In many cases, states have felt compelled to roll back social programs and to discourage any idea of recovery of lost ground. In this context, states look to alternative means to enhance legitimacy. One is to promise citizens, especially those most directly affected by the rollback of the welfare state, that governments will protect them against the competition of non-citizens – 'outsiders,' foreigners, undocumented aliens, illegal immigrants, bogus asylum-seekers, etc. – who would seek to enter and take unfair advantage of scarce job opportunities and shrinking social entitlements.

Although condemning racist anti-immigrant movements and insisting that neo-fascist parties must never be allowed to enter office, centre-right and centre-left governments in Europe have in effect played upon many of the same populist (and sometimes racist) anxieties in seeking to strengthen their own legitimacy. Many observers have spoken about the construction of a 'Fortress Europe' with free movement across borders within, but high fences against entry from outside. In Fortress Europe, despite certain security agreements such as those of Trevi, Dublin, and Schengen, the relative success of efforts toward the construction of supranational institutions on political and economic matters (Maastricht and the Euro) has not been matched by success in constructing supranational institutions to support Europe's 'third pillar' on immigration and security.[14] This has not proven necessary, owing to the legacy of the Cold War. Cooperation was already closer in security and policing than in other areas. Intelligence exchange had already been institutionalized as an aspect of the conduct of the Cold War; a common enemy and acceptance of American leadership produced common security standards and common databases. Moreover, much if not most of this close cooperation occurred at the sub-national level. Transnational communities of interest and function sprang up among police, security, and intelligence agencies from allied countries, with relatively thick webs of direct relationships tested by experience, often with minimal input from the political leadership.[15] These linkages have endured the end of the Cold War and the re-targeting of security threats that has followed. The reason why Maastricht's third pillar has followed a slower track is obvious: why build supranational institutions to accomplish something already being served by existing intergovernmental cooperation, especially when this cooperation makes minimal demands on the attention of the politicians?

There are considerable differences in the ways in which the movement of people is policed in Europe and in North America. The most striking difference is the divergence of Europe from NAFTA on the issue of labour mobility. Europe is intended to form a common labour market with full internal mobility for all occupational categories. NAFTA, in sharp contrast, was always designed to promote mobility of business, technical, and professional occupational categories required for the efficiency of continental business operations, while it actively discriminated against the mobility of other occupational categories, especially low-skilled and unskilled labour. Indeed, NAFTA was sold to sceptical American voters as a means of discouraging Mexican immigration by providing low-wage job opportunities south of the American border. On the face of it, this difference might point to different policy priorities on immigration security. A politically integrated Europe with labour mobility requires a common Europe-wide policy and enforcement at all entry points into Europe, as well as common surveillance standards and practices throughout Europe to track non-citizens. Hence Fortress Europe. A politically divided North America with only partial labour mobility would seem to require only national controls over the internal movement of people. So why bother with a Fortress North America? In practice, however, the two continents have been moving on similar tracks. Anxiety surrounding the movement of people is pointing in the direction of intensified state integration as a policy response. How we have arrived at this somewhat ironic result is the subject of the last part of this paper.

Neither Us nor Them

In late 1999 Ahmed Ressam, an Algerian national illegally in Canada, was stopped at a U.S. border entry point on the west coast and was taken into custody. Ressam has subsequently been convicted of planning with others to smuggle into the United States explosives designed for a terrorist attack to coincide with the millennium celebrations. The incident set off a disturbance in U.S.-Canadian relations, inciting vigorous congressional and media demands that Canada either meet American antiterrorist and immigration security standards or face severe restrictions and controls along the 'world's longest undefended border.'

The Ressam incident would not have garnered such publicity were there not a growing anxiety in the United States that it was becoming a target of international terrorism. It is a rather startling fact that since the end of the Vietnam War, more American servicemen have died as a result of terrorist attacks than in combat, despite a number of military interventions abroad. The World Trade Center and Oklahoma City bombings in the 1990s and the attacks on American embassies in Africa raised legitimate public concerns. Extensive publicity, much of it directly inspired by agencies of the U.S. government, built up Saudi exile Osama bin Laden as a serious threat to American national security. American laws were strengthened and new statutes, such as the Orwellian sounding Anti-Terrorism and Effective Death Penalty Act, have been enacted to give the federal authorities greater powers.

While America thus has valid concerns, given its status as a primary target for terrorist actions, there is a political context to this issue which involves other agendas. There is a partisan context: Republicans made the most of any real or imagined laxity on the part of the Clinton administration toward national security. And there is another, related concern, particularly among many Republicans, namely anxiety about immigration. The international context of much terrorism provides the Republicans, as well as some conservative Democrats, with leverage to focus on immigration as a conduit for foreign terrorism, to piggyback, as it were, anti-immigrant politics onto a widely popular anti-terrorist agenda. A key figure here is a Republican from Texas, Lamar Smith, who chairs the House of Representatives immigration subcommittee, which he has turned into a platform for agitation for tougher security controls. This linkage between a more restrictive immigration policy and anti-terrorist security measures tends to gloss over some uncomfortable realities, such as the importance of home-grown terrorism with no external connections. (Oklahoma City was an all-American affair.) However, conservative politicians tend not to emphasize the threat from right-wing militia-type organizations with ideologies uncomfortably close to their own anti-government programs; far better to stress 'un-American' foreign groups whose presence in the United states can be blamed on the legacy of the Clinton administration's liberal laxity.

There is also a contextual and conjunctural oddity. At this historical moment, employment levels are relatively high in America, and business is pushing for increased entry quotas for skilled workers. Traditionally, high employment and labour shortages have resulted in stepped-up immigration levels. Consequently, as one recent news report put it, 'the national conversation about immigrants and immigration has changed dramatically.'[16] Those suspicious of high levels of immigration are unable under these circumstances to fit their concerns into the largely economic discourse of immigration policy. It appears however that anxiety about immigration has roots that go beyond economics to cultural and ethnic fears that do not move in relation to employment levels. Indeed, these anxieties may actually be spurred in periods of prosperity precisely because of the stepped-up levels of entry. Focusing on refugees and on illegal movements in terms of security offers an alternative route for anti-immigrant sentiment to find a voice in good times. This is what happened during the first postwar decade, when massive numbers of displaced persons arrived in a context of full employment and economic growth, and a widespread consensus about the positive contributions of immigration to prosperity. Yet this coincided with a red scare, and with the imposition of draconian and discriminatory controls over refugee and immigration applications. These measures facilitated the exclusion of left-wing 'subversives' from the intake, and the deportation of any who had somehow evaded the screening. A similar situation can be seen today, within a similar partisan political context. The communist menace has given way to the terrorist / criminal menace, and to the extent that particular national origins are associated with terrorist activity, with an ethnic menace as well. Hence, there is some convergence between North America and Europe on immigration / refugee controls, even though unemployment remains much higher in many European countries than in the United States.

It is in this context that the impact of the Ressam affair must be read. Even before this incident took place, concerns about the security of the Canada-U.S. border led Congress to include a section in the Illegal Immigration Reform and Responsibility Act of 1996 requiring all 'aliens' to register upon entry into and exit from the United States. This would have resulted in chaos in cross-border trade and traffic, but skilful

Canadian lobbying succeeded in postponing implementation of this provision.[17] When the National Commission on Terrorism, created by Congress, published its report in June 2000, it began its argument about the threat posed to American security by citing the Ressam arrest.[18] Lamar Smith and other politicians (all, notably, from states far away from the Canadian border) threatened Canada with border controls if it did not stop the alleged infiltration of foreign terrorists across the U.S. border. Canada was referred to derisively as a 'Club Med' for terrorists, and the weakest link in America's security screen.

It is interesting to note that the voices critical of Canadian immigration controls and Canadian security in general were by no means limited to those in the United States. When Congressman Smith held hearings in Washington on the security threat posed to the United States by Canadian laxity, some of the testimony most sharply critical of Canadian policy and practices came from Canadians, from conservative think-tanks and from private security consultants with former ties to Canadian security agencies. Behind them were public warnings issued by the Canadian Security Intelligence Service (CSIS) that Canada was a primary target for terrorist groups because of its proximity to the United States and the ease with which they could cross the Canada-U.S. border – and that Canadian resources, in terms of money, personnel, and political will, were inadequate to the task of dealing with this threat. Direct and close linkages between Canadian security intelligence and the FBI go back to the Second World War and were intensified during the Cold War. A tendency to hold a similar view of security issues has survived the Cold War; indeed, Canada's dependence on the United States for much of its foreign intelligence has, if anything, deepened the commonality of view. Right-wing politicians in Ottawa and the conservative media picked up this theme, in effect offering support to American critics of Canadian performance. In other words, this was not strictly a Canadian-American issue, but rather an issue with partisan and ideological divisions that cut across the border.

The threat of border controls, backed by earlier congressional legislation that has been held in abeyance following furious Canadian lobbying, was strongly opposed by politicians (such as the governor of Maine) representing states bordering on Canada. However, given the economic price of border controls for both sides, there was never any real interest in this option. The point was to encourage positive policy moves on the Canadian side to avoid costly and cumbersome border controls. This outcome (predictable enough from the previous history of Canadian-American Cold War cooperation) was signalled by two policy initiatives. First, the Canadian government budgeted for major spending increases by CSIS, the Royal Canadian Mounted Police (responsible for criminal security), and for immigration and border security. More important, Canadian officials had already begun floating the idea of a 'perimeter security' system for North America. This was now offered as an alternative to border controls. A common cordon around the continent would require Canada and the United States to 'harmonize' their immigration policies and visa requirements, as well as to develop common security and criminal databases and common priorities and investigative targets. Citing European precedent, one Canadian official suggested: 'we have to get at the problem before the problem gets to North America.'[19]

Given the huge power imbalance between the two countries, harmonization clearly implies Canadian adoption of American standards and priorities. Indeed, if this were not the case, the forces in the United States pushing Canada on the border security issue would not be satisfied with perimeter defence. Yet internal documents of the Canadian government reveal that a high-level inter-ministerial committee on intelligence policy had considered U.S.-style anti-terrorist measures two years earlier, and rejected them because it could not 'see the need for such a scheme.'[20] One of the first casualties of Fortress North America will be the capacity of the Canadian state to set its own independent policies. But Canada already has considerable experience from the years of the Cold War alliance with the smallness of its margin for policy autonomy in areas that matter to the senior partner. Perhaps the only difference is that the shrinkage of space in the era of globalization has reduced that margin even further; as in the Cold War era, the close and direct relationship between the policing and security agencies, largely at the sub-political level, is laying the groundwork for the harmonization of policy that will eventually require little more than a political rubber stamp.

The pressures toward integration of state security policy and administration dovetail with some powerful economic forces. Recently the Business Council on National Issues, a prestigious blue-chip corporate policy forum with a long history of influence on Canadian federal policy makers, issued a policy paper calling for an extension of free trade to allow the free movement of people across the border. Citing rising U.S. concerns with 'security issues such as terrorism, illegal immigration and illicit drugs,' the BCNI deplored increasing border tensions. 'It may make sense to combine these issues and others in a comprehensive agreement that builds on the Canada-U.S. Free Trade Agreement,' which preceded NAFTA but excluded Mexico. The BCNI was particularly concerned about the United States taking policy steps on border issues that would be inimical to Canadian interests. 'If Canada is not seen as part of the solution to their concerns, we will be treated as part of the problem.'[21] In short, what is being urged is a European-style common labour market for Canada and the United States, shorn of the occupational restrictions imposed under NAFTA. And a European-style common market would clearly require a common immigration and citizenship policy and a common security perimeter.

Although the BCNI recognized the present lack of political will on both sides for broader union, a study being prepared jointly by an American and Canadian author for the Carnegie Endowment for International Peace suggests that the border is actually on its way to becoming an 'irrelevancy' that will 'substantively disappear before any politician finds the political courage to negotiate its removal.' A gradual movement toward visa harmonization could eventually allow 'complete freedom of movement within North America.'[22] Canada has been until now 'largely insulated from America's often wild and unpredictable tilting at the windmills of foreign terrorism or illegal immigration or drug trafficking, although not without a great deal of effort and smart diplomacy.' According to the Canadian author, sovereignty concerns make it unlikely that a common visa regime like that in Europe will emerge.[23] But the logic of a disappearing border points in exactly this direction. The study does suggest the desirability of imposing common immigration controls at a non-NAFTA immigrant's first point of entry into NAFTA space, and, as an initial step, the study further suggests that Canada and the United States 'agree to a common visa regime for the widest band of countries each country could accommodate and exercise much greater care in the issuance of visas for the citizens of countries about which visa free entry could not be agreed to by the other country.' As the same authors bluntly suggest in another study: 'It may be easier and more desirable to construct a fortress North America than a fortress around either one of the individual countries.'[24]

This exposes a contradiction at the heart of NAFTA. Freer trade in the Americas is based upon deliberately differentiated labour mobility. Fortress North America, in contrast, points toward a common Canada-U.S. labour market. Although the Mexican president has raised the idea of full labour mobility among the existing three NAFTA signatories, that idea appears to be politically unattractive to the U.S. Congress and U.S. public opinion. Even less palatable would be the extension of free labour entry to further Latin American states beyond Mexico, within the projected Free Trade Area of the Americas agreed to in principle at the Quebec City meeting in April 2001. Could we then be looking at a two-tier construction, with an inner and outer Fortress of the Americas?

A U.S.-Canadian inner core would clearly imply the increasing harmonization of policies, and eventually some harmonization of institutions. The prospect of the formal political integration of Canada into the United States is, however, very unlikely for a variety of reasons. Although it has often been suggested by both critics and supporters that economic integration will lead ineluctably to political integration, the latter seems no closer in the early twenty-first century, despite the steady erosion over the years of Canadian economic autonomy. Given the underlying dynamic favouring policy harmonization in border controls, the alternative to institutional harmonization will be further piecemeal integration, without any national and democratically accountable resolution of the institutional and constitutional problems generated by this process. These problems will be felt mainly in Canada, where 'push' factors far exceed any 'pull' that Canada can exert on American policies and practices. In short, the democratic deficit that has been much discussed in Europe will be part and parcel of an emergent Fortress North America. From the Canadian perspective, it might seem like a reprise of an old American theme: taxation without representation.

While there are many areas of radical discontinuity between Canada and the United States following the end of the Cold War, in the two policy areas I have focused on it is the continuities that remain most striking. The Cold War may be over, its corpse buried, but in many ways its spirit lingers, like Banquo's ghost at the feast. So long as we require an Other, an Enemy, a Them, against which to define ourselves, the spirit of the Cold War will live on. Ironically, these attempts at self-definition have only drawn us closer to that most ambiguous Other, neither Us nor Them, the United States.

Notes

1 This paper was written prior to the terrorist attacks of 11 September 2001. A great deal has happened subsequent to that fateful date with regard to Canadian-American relations, but these developments only confirm and

deepen what I discerned before that date. With the U.S.-led War on Terrorism, the world has returned to another Cold War. President George W. Bush has now definitively discovered who the 'They' are that he was sure were there. For Canada, post–11 September is being experienced very much like a rerun of the late 1940s and early 1950s, but this time the border between us and the United States has become even more blurred.

2 An interesting case is made by Ulrich Beck, *Democracy without Enemies* (Oxford: Polity Press, 1998).

3 U.S. general and outgoing NATO commander Lauris Norstad in an Ottawa speech in January 1963 stated that Canada was reneging on its commitments by not accepting nuclear weapons for its jet fighters. Later that same month, the U.S. State Department issued a press release stating that Prime Minister John Diefenbaker had lied about this issue. During the ensuing election campaign, an American magazine, *Newsweek*, which had a wide Canadian readership, featured a scowling cover photo of Diefenbaker with an accompanying story that described Diefenbaker as more or less the equivalent of other troublesome foreign leaders whom the United States would prefer to be rid of, such as Fidel Castro.

4 John A. Munro and Alex. I. Inglis, eds., *Mike: The Memoirs of the Right Honourable Lester B. Pearson, Volume 2: 1948–1957* (Toronto: U of Toronto P, 1973), 184.

5 The Federation of American Scientists hosts an excellent website with information on NMD: <http://www.fas.org/spp/starwars/program/nmd/index.html>.

6 Frances Fitzgerald, *Way Out There in the Blue: Reagan, Star Wars, and the End of the Cold War* (New York: Simon and Schuster, 2000).

7 Elizabeth Becker, 'Missile defense may have price of $60 billion,' *New York Times*, 26 April 2000.

8 Joseph T. Jockel, 'US National Missile Defence, Canada, and the Future of NORAD,' in Maureen Appel Molot and Fen Osler Hampson, eds., *Vanishing Borders: Canada among Nations 2000* (Don Mills: Oxford UP, 2000), 89–90.

9 Allan Thompson, 'Eggleton eyes U.S. missile defence plan: Canada's backing makes sense, minister says,' *Toronto Star*, 21 April 2000.

10 Reg Whitaker, *Double Standard: The Secret History of Canadian Immigration* (Toronto: Lester and Orpen Dennys, 1987).

11 See Reg Whitaker, 'Cold War Alchemy: How America, Britain, and Canada Transformed Espionage into Subversion,' in David Stafford and Rhodri Jeffreys-Jones, eds., *American-British-Canadian Intelligence Relations, 1939–2000* (London: Frank Cass, 2000): 177–210.

12 G. Loescher and J.A. Scanlan, *Calculated Kindness: Refugees and America's Half-Open Door* (New York: Free Press 1986); Whitaker, *Double Standard.*

13 Reg Whitaker, 'Refugees: The Security Dimension,' *Citizenship Studies* 2.3 (1998): 413–34

14 Tony Bunyan, ed., *Statewatching the New Europe* (London: Statewatch, 1993); *Key Texts on Justice and Home Affairs in the European Union from Trevi to Maastricht* (London: Statewatch, 1997).

15 M. Anderson and M. den Boer, eds., *Policing across National Boundaries* (London: Pinter Publishers, 1994).

16 Somini Sengupta, 'The immigration debate: Full employment opens the door,' *New York Times*, 18 June 2000.

17 Fen Osler Hampson and Maureen Appel Molot, 'Does the 49th Parallel Matter Any More?,' in Molot and Hampson, *Vanishing Borders*, 12.

18 National Commission on Terrorism, *Countering the Changing Threat of International Terrorism.* <http://www.fas.org/irp/threat/commission.html>.

19 Andrew Duffy, 'Ottawa urges U.S. to adopt continental security ring: Anti-terrorist "perimeter" plan would mean harmonized visa rules, sharing intelligence,' *National Post*, 29 Jan. 2000.

20 Jim Bronskill, 'Ottawa rejected U.S.-style anti-terror measures in 1997: Policy group studied ways to strengthen Canada's ability to keep terrorists out,' *National Post*, 15 Feb. 2000.

21 Alain Toulin, 'BCNI urges extension of free trade,' *Financial Post*, 30 May 2000.

22 Demetrios G. Papademetriou and Deborah Meyers, 'Of Poetry and Plumbing: The North American Integration "Project,"' *Carnegie Endowment for International Peace* <http://www.ceip.org/programs/migrat/CommonBordersSummary.html>.

23 Jan Cienski, 'Canada-U.S. border will disappear, study says,' *National Post*, 17 June 2000.

24 Deborah Meyers and Demetrios G. Papademetriou, 'Walking a Fine Line: Issues in Border Management,' *ISUMA* 1.1 (Spring 2000).

2

Sunday Morning Subversion: The Canadian Security State and Organized Religion in the Cold War

STEVE HEWITT

For a generation of Canadian television viewers, the words '56 Sparks Street, Ottawa' could mean only one thing: Dr Lotta Hitschmanova was concluding a television commercial for the Unitarian Services Committee (USC) Canada, the organization that she founded in 1945.[1] In the context of the Cold War, however, these words were also – for some – the utterance of a potential subversive. How an individual internationally recognized as a humanitarian, as well as her organization, her church, and other religious institutions, such as the United Church of Canada, could be viewed as suspicious is directly attributable to the forces at work during Canada's Cold War.

Intimately connected with the activities of the Cold War was the development of the security state, the instrument used by a nation to insure its internal safety.[2] In the Canadian context this entity consisted primarily of the security branch (which had a variety of names depending on the era) of the Royal Canadian Mounted Police. It also involved components within other branches of the federal government, including External Affairs, the Department of National Defence, the Department of Citizenship and Immigration, Canada Customs, and even the Post Office. In its modern form it emerged in Canada, the United States, and the United Kingdom during or around the First World War, not at the end of the Second World War, as is widely believed.[3]

Research on the domestic operations of the security state has tended to focus on the United States, largely because its Freedom of Information Act has been in operation since 1967.[4] The field in Canada is much more recent and much smaller: academically it is dominated by the research of historian Gregory S. Kealey, on the era before 1939, and political scientist Reg Whitaker, covering the period since then. *Whose National Security?*, a recent work in the field edited by sociologist Gary Kinsman et al., is one of the first attempts to analyse comprehensively several facets of the state's security operations during the Cold War and to challenge the philosophical underpinnings of the entire system.

Whose National Security? runs counter to the current direction in analyses of security and intelligence, where the prevailing trend is to study espionage and the efforts to counter it. The publication in the fall of 1999 of *The Mitrokhin Archive*, a collection of KGB documents smuggled out of Russia by a retired spy-archivist, reflected and reinforced this trend. The media coverage of the book frequently followed a rather comforting 'what they did to us' format, which is a major source of the popularity of books about espionage and explains why British intelligence allowed the material to be published in the first place.[5] However, little effort was made to ascertain what Western intelligence agencies actually knew about the KGB activities described in the Mitrokhin book, nor, more important, what *'our side'* was doing to 'our side' during the Cold War. In addition, the media did not pick up on the irony that researchers have had earlier and more detailed access to communist archives about espionage in the Cold War than to comparable archives in the West. A similar point is made at the conclusion of *The File*, Timothy Garton Ash's search for, and examination of, the file on him held by the *Stasi*, the now extinct domestic security agency of the equally extinct German Democratic Republic. There he poses the question that so often remains unasked: what are our intelligence services doing here at home? The answer, he discovers, is quite a lot.[6]

Part of this neglected story is examined in this chapter, a case study, with wider implications, of what was being done in Canada during the Cold War by 'our side.' As such, it examines one single target of a system that collected files on over 800,000 individuals and organizations in Canada alone.[7] That target was organized religion. Why religious institutions became a target of the Canadian security state requires a multi-layered and historically contextualized answer. According to the Mounted Police, who did the spying, their work was in response to the threat represented by foreign intelligence services. However, limited evidence of such activity exists in the Mitrokhin archives, and is specifically related to KGB efforts to infiltrate the Russian Orthodox Church and the World Council of Churches.[8] This focus on espionage (the comparable current emphasis is on terrorism or the 'threat of violence')[9] is the way that the security state likes to construct its past – that it was a noble battle to protect the nation-state against the operations of foreign intelligence services. There are two major problems with this interpretation. First, the evidence currently available to researchers does not fully support it. Despite the ending of the Cold War, Western spy agencies remain reluctant to allow the release of files related to the operations of foreign intelligence services in their backyard. Second, as already noted, the security state in both Canada and the United States began during the First World War, and it began not as a means of routing foreign spies but as a way of controlling those deemed by the state to represent enemies from within. Class and ethnic prejudices inspired this security work in the state's targeting of labourers and immigrants. The systems of espionage that are emphasized in recent analyses of the Cold War and by those involved in the state system did not enter the equation in any meaningful way until after the Second World War.[10]

What did enter the discourse of the security state at end of the First World War was an idea that has largely disappeared since the height of the Cold War: subversion. Weakly defined as subverting or overturning from within, subversion emerged in the modern era as a convenient justification for directing the powers of the state against domestic targets. The use of subversion allowed the state to 'delegitimize activities and ideas opposed to the established order, and hence to legitimize the state in acting against them, even though the activities are legal.'[11] The discourse of subversion arose in the West before communism was perceived as a threat to security, and the state applied this discourse to ethnic and class organizations, as well as to those on the political left deemed by dominant elites to be 'outsiders' who were prone to radicalism and thus inherently untrustworthy.[12] The Canadian state was hardly unique in emphasizing subversion as an explanatory tool for understanding domestic discontent. For example, in his work on American domestic security, the late Frank Donner labels this assumption as 'the agitator-subversion thesis,' which 'denies the relevance of social and economic factors as the cause of unrest.'[13]

After the Second World War the emphasis on subversion and the role of individuals continued, but in a modified form, in part owing to the information carried out of the Soviet embassy in Ottawa by Igor Gouzenko in September 1945. The files Gouzenko gave to the Canadian government documented the existence of spy rings involving not the traditional ethnic and class targets of the security state – the 'usual suspects' – but civil servants, scientists, and academics, who were, in effect, members of Canada's elite. This fracturing of the construct of the nature of the threat, combined with the arrival of the main phase of the Cold War, led to an expansion of the domestic activities of the security state. In directing its operations, the Mounted Police employed an imprecise definition of what constituted subversion; indeed, into the mid-1970s, the RCMP had no operational definition whatsoever of subversion beyond the criterion that communism be involved. This looseness of terminology was combined with an ill-defined role, a lack of direction from their political masters, the limited educational backgrounds of the officers themselves, and a narrow focus derived from limited security training that emphasized communism, especially as an ideological force, as the prime security threat to Canada.[14] All of these factors contributed to a record expansion of targets in the post-1945 period, as the police sought to systematically record everything about anyone and anything with the remotest connection to communism. In 1952, for example, the RCMP began 'carding' children either because they or their parents were deemed to be involved in subversive activities, and plans were made to intern them in the event of a war with the Soviet Union.[15] Even the names of those donating money to the Communist Party were recorded, as was anyone who had a CPC lawn sign during an election.[16] The McDonald Commission reported in 1981 that during the era of the RCMP intelligence operations, files were opened on more than 800,000 individuals. In 1967 alone, 'D' Ops, the countersubversion branch of the Security Service, maintained active files on 48,000 individuals and 6,000 organizations.[17]

This expansion of targets also had a bureaucratic element, the state's security system requiring continual information if for no other reason than to justify its existence. Many police officers recognized that the road to promotion was paved with paper, and hence the desire to generate as many reports as possible, even if this involved recycling the same basic information.[18] In addition, there was a sense of intrigue intermixed with pride that drove the momentum. Frank Donner describes this mentality well in his study of American red squads when he writes of their appearances before political committees, 'preening on their cloak and dagger triumphs: the informers they had successfully run, the albums of photographs and mug shots, the literature surreptitiously acquired, the stolen diaries, maps, and financial records, followed by portentous conclusions about the conspiratorial root of it all.'[19] As Reg Whitaker and Gary Marcuse illustrate in *Cold War Canada*, the one question rarely asked by those involved in perpetuating the system, perhaps because they feared the answer, was 'So what?' To use Whitaker and Marcuse's example, did it make a difference that communists belonged to or even controlled a union? Was the union more radical than one without communist involvement? Instead of attempting to address concrete questions about social context, the state spun out a series of 'what ifs.' In fact, both the police and the communists they monitored were driven by ideology above all else.[20] Cumulatively, these were the underpinnings of a system that targeted religious organizations and individuals during the height of the post-1945 Cold War.

The initial state security interest in religious activities dates from the end of the First World War; it coalesced with police interest in labour and ethnic activities in the nationwide discontent of 1919. In the era of the Social Gospel, police informants reported on labour churches that appeared in the aftermath of the Winnipeg General Strike. In one instance, a Methodist minister who chaired a labour meeting in Saskatchewan became the subject of a police file.[21] In another instance, A.E. Smith, a minister and a strong proponent of the Social Gospel, became a member of the fledgling Communist Party of Canada in 1925 (demonstrating the appeal that communism could have for someone on the religious left early in the life of the Soviet Union), and this led to him being monitored by the RCMP.[22] Yet other early targets of the newly formed security state were Jehovah's Witnesses, primarily because they believed in the inevitably of Armageddon and were antipathetic to the state. In Alberta, several Jehovah's Witnesses were charged with possession of restricted literature, but according to the senior Mountie on hand, '[o]nly nominal fines were imposed as it was plain that these people were not propagandists, but simply religious fanatics.'[23] Jehovah's Witnesses would encounter the power of the state again during the Second World War, when they were compared by the commissioner of the RCMP to 'poison toadstools' and their religious order was banned as a subversive organization.[24] The state applied a similar attitude to Seventh-Day Adventists in the same period, when military intelligence encouraged the Mounted Police to investigate Alberta members of the church and their apparent opposition to the war. After sending a policeman into a Seventh-Day Adventist church and listening to some religious broadcasts, the RCMP concluded that while the sect was indifferent to the conflict, this was caused not by pro-German sentiments but by 'their blind religious fanaticism.'[25]

If Jehovah's Witnesses and Seventh-Day Adventists could generally be ignored in the postwar period (except, notably, in Quebec) because their religious views appeared to pose little threat to the state, this was not true of religious groups and individuals who appeared vulnerable to the appeal of communism. The leading example was the Unitarian Church, which was deemed a threat and which faced investigation, as did some of its branch organizations and clubs. The RCMP believed the Unitarian Church was a haven for 'closed-club members,' police slang for hidden Reds. It was not that the police crudely viewed the Unitarian Church as a communist organization; however, communists belonged to it, and, just as importantly, the values of the church seemed to support causes similar to those of Canada's 'enemies.' A former commissioner of the RCMP, justifying police investigations of universities, expressed the general philosophy behind the targeting of the Unitarian Church:

> It is not suggested that universities, per se, are involved in conspiratorial activities directed against our democratic system, however, it is an irrefutable fact that they do exert considerable influence on sociological issues of the day and are, therefore ripe targets for communist infiltration and manipulation. You will undoubtedly agree that a person who privately harbours Communist sympathies and who gains an influential position in a select faculty on a university, can contribute immeasurably to the Communist cause. The value of such a person to the movement is obvious as is our corresponding security responsibilities.

When it came to investigating members of the Unitarian Church, the explicit justification came after the fact. In 1966 the RCMP produced a twenty-plus-page report entitled 'Communist Infiltration of the Unitarian Church of Canada,' in which the author(s) devoted considerable space to the early history of Unitarianism in order to provide an amazing explanation of its ties to communism:

> The philosophy of the Unitarian Church embodies a crusade toward social betterment and the development of the individual self. In the process of Communism seeking to develop a rapport with religion generally, *the Unitarian Church provides a quasi-religious forum where Communism is more likely to be looked at objectively, free from the antipathies which have characterized its reception by most other organized religions*. It thus provides Communism with a foothold in a society which is chiefly hostile to Communism and all it entails. (emphasis added)

The report concluded with a warning:

> The Unitarian Church, with some 15,000 members in Canada, is a poten-
> tially fruitful area for Communist exploitation. However, Communist
> efforts to date have lacked co-ordination and direction with the possible
> exception of Ottawa. This may change as the CP of C steps up its involve-
> ment in select key sections of society of which religion is one.[26]

The final two sentences were the rationalization regularly employed to
justify continued coverage of a target when evidence of communist
involvement was lacking.

The author(s) of the report also refer to the Mounted Police's main
Unitarian target, the Ottawa branch of the Unitarian Men's Club. Employing informants who were recruited from the inside and also im-
planted from the outside, as well as undercover police officers, the
RCMP began its investigations in 1937 when an informant covered a
gathering of the Ottawa branch of the Unitarian Men's Club following a
report that civil servants were attending 'socialist meetings.' (The guest
speaker at one of the meetings was Tommy Douglas, then a federal CCF
member of Parliament.)[27] The Men's Clubs were of interest, according
to the police, 'because the aims of these Unitarian Men's Club [sic] are
to work towards peace. Although they are bona fide organizations, like
any peaceful movements attempts are made for subversive infiltration.'[28] The police coverage escalated at the end of the 1950s when the
Ottawa club resumed operations; using informants, the Mounted Police tracked suspected communists, those 'suspected of Communist
sympathies,' and hidden communists ('closed-club members'). Detailed
reports on each meeting were filed, including topics discussed and a
description of the speeches of guests such as the Soviet ambassador
(the text of whose talk the police obtained) and scholar Eugene Forsey,
whose speech, an informant decided, was in no way 'communistically
inclined.'[29] Those who asked questions were noted, along with the
amount of money dropped in the collection plate, and the contact between 'suspects' and other members of the club. While the meeting was
under way, police on the outside recorded the licence plates of those in
attendance; afterwards, on occasion, club members were followed.

Why did the RCMP make such efforts to monitor a forum devoted to
intellectual activity? As with the Unitarian Church, the club itself was
not officially deemed subversive, but its executive was believed to be
'infiltrated ... by persons ... suspected of Communist sympathies' and

those in attendance discussed 'points embarrassing to the Canadian government.'[30] An individual could be labelled a subversive with no other evidence than the assertion that he or she was a communist; what the police sought were linkages among those showing a propensity for communism and others not previously on police radar. If your car turned up at a Unitarian meeting, that in itself would not necessarily lead to the opening of a permanent file, merely a temporary one. But if that fact was combined with other information – you had repeated contact with known communists at meetings, not just through the Unitarian Church but in other forums – then another check mark would be added to your name. This put you on the road to being declared a 'suspected' communist and, finally, after enough 'adverse references,' a 'confirmed' communist, and thus a subversive. Even reaching the 'suspicious' level required that additional attention be paid to an individual, lest he or she be in a position to have a subversive influence on someone else. Here from a police report is such subversion at work:

> executive members of the U.M.C. [Unitarian Men's Club] who are of particular interest to this office apparently intermingle with other members and during each meeting are scattered throughout the hall where they attempt to cultivate friendship and instigate controversial discussions in questioning the guest speaker ... From all appearances these suspects are taking advantage of the U.M.C. as a front where these persons can introduce their friends and assess individuals whom they may consider have similar socialist ideas and possibly recruit into more confined and politically conscious groups.[31]

The underlying discourse here, and elsewhere, paralleled that which the state employed with regard to 'illicit' sexual activity: communists were represented as seeking to introduce others to their depravity and thus, in the process, corrupting them. In the United States, the head of the Federal Bureau of Investigation during much of the Cold War, J. Edgar Hoover, described the route to communism as 'perverted' and compared communists to drug addicts. The linkages in statist discourse between conversion to communism and sexual weakness or degeneracy have been noted by historian Elaine Tyler May in her landmark examination of the impact of the Cold War on the family.[32]

While the police interest in the Unitarian Men's Club of Ottawa died out in the 1960s, their interest in the better-known USC Canada continued into the 1970s; its decision to launch the examination of the USC

Canada was undoubtedly influenced by the investigation of the Boston branch of the USC in 1946–7 for alleged communist influence.[33] The founder of the USC Canada, Dr Lotta Hitschmanova, a refugee from Czechoslovakia, became a target of the RCMP in the late 1940s as part of their attempt to discover who and what was behind the committee; the investigation included scrutiny of correspondence sent to the organization, and the RCMP sought information about Hitschmanova from 'reliable contacts' (one of many police euphemisms for informants) who belonged to the Ottawa branch of the Czechoslovak National Alliance, as did she. The informants, however, were unable to turn up anything 'that would cast an unfavourable reflection on her from a political point of view.'[34]

Periodic reports on the USC Canada continued into the 1970s. In 1976 the RCMP provided a security assessment of the organization to External Affairs and later proudly noted that, partly because of information such as this, the government was applying greater scrutiny to the foreign aid that it supplied to countries such as the recently unified Vietnam.[35] The Canadian government eventually eliminated funding for this aid program, prompting the USC Canada to cancel its Vietnam project. The Mennonite Central Committee (MCC), another non-governmental organization with projects overseas, was investigated by the RCMP in 1977, after being asked for intelligence by the Canadian International Development Agency (CIDA); however, the RCMP, using its file on the MCC that they had opened in 1965, declared that the organization was not connected to foreign political interests.[36]

The RCMP also investigated targets connected to Canada's largest Protestant denomination, the United Church of Canada. The first report on the church was written in 1947 with a permanent file opened the following year. The police cross-referenced relevant church material to a variety of files, including one under the name of the church, others under church organizations or programs, and one under the heading of 'Marxist-Christian dialogue,' a title that neatly summarized one version of the subversion that the police believed they were investigating. 'Although it is inconceivable that any devoted theologian would be converted by such a dialogue,' wrote one officer, 'the mere fact that Christian leaders are willing to associate and/or discuss differences with Communists has given the Communist an appearance of respectability.'[37]

The initial decision to open a file on the United Church was based on a news report in 1948 of an annual church meeting at which a resolution was introduced that repeatedly used the word 'synthesis'; this, wrote a police analyst, 'gives away its Marxist character,' and the force opened a file on the church the same day.[38] In the 1960s the police reported on meetings, such as one held at the University of Saskatchewan on the theme of 'Christianity and Socialism,' organized to some extent by the United Church or groups connected to it. Informants relayed details to their handlers of meetings between church and party members in Toronto, and between a United Church youth group and Young Communist League members in Vancouver.[39] Particularly troubling to the RCMP was a church announcement in September 1964 stating that it intended to publish a comparative study of communism and Christianity. The police were among the first to acquire a copy of *Communist Faith, Christian Faith* when it appeared in February 1965, and they examined their files for any tidbits about its author, discovering that someone with his name had visited Hungary sixteen years earlier to attend a conference organized by the World Federation of Democratic Youth, a communist front group.[40] The Alberta School of Religion's summer courses for ministers, the majority drawn from the United Church, also came under suspicion. 'The main theme [of the education],' warned a policeman, 'was that Marxism provided the method to attain their goals and the Soviet form of government was a shiny example of the end result.' An internal police debate ensued about whether the school was just communist-infiltrated or whether attendance in itself demonstrated that one was a communist sympathizer. Of such distinctions the bureaucratic Cold War was made – for if the security state applied the second classification then all who had attended would be labelled as subversives, creating a permanent blemish on their security files.[41]

The United Church garnered attention for its activities in other areas as well. The security state became concerned in the 1960s about the church encouraging the federal government to offer diplomatic recognition to the People's Republic of China and supporting its admission to the United Nations. Church efforts included organizing and participating in conferences related to China and issuing related publications, copies of which the RCMP had its divisions across Canada acquire. Once again, underlying this investigation was the suspicion that communists were secretly behind the effort; the Mounted Police were ably assisted by External Affairs, which supplied them with materials and assessments of conferences involving External Affairs and the church. It also offered up information about United Church missionaries to China, including their addresses in Canada, and warned the RCMP about the church's policy position on China.[42] The church faced similar police scrutiny in the 1970s when it became interested in Latin American issues.[43]

Regardless of the religious group it was investigating, the RCMP's central concern was that communists would manipulate the churches in such a way as to weaken the Canadian state. Nowhere was this concern more evident than in the one area in which organized religion had the greatest potential to have a major societal impact: the peace movement.[44] The RCMP had long targeted the Canadian wing of the World Peace Council, the Canadian Peace Congress (CPC), and its head, Dr James Endicott, a former missionary to China. Influential in the CPC's birth in 1949 was another religious figure, the Right Reverend Hewlett Johnson, the 'Red' Dean of Canterbury. Controversial in the United Kingdom because of his strong support for the Soviet Union and communism, Johnson made a tour of Canada in 1948 during which he encouraged the formation of peace councils. The RCMP secretly followed him every step of the way: from the airport, to where he was staying, to his speech site, to the airport again – a pattern that was repeated across the country. The RCMP were less interested in him, however, even though they referred to him as a 'suspect,' than in those he met along the way, including other religious figures.[45]

While the rationale for the investigation of peace groups was ostensibly their susceptibility to communist infiltration and their potential for exerting political influence, the principles alone of those who belonged to the peace movement, especially religious believers, made them ready targets of the security state. Given that between 1958 and 1962 the percentage of Canadians favouring a ban on U.S. nuclear tests grew to nearly 50 per cent,[46] the authorities expanded their net of surveillance to include the Christian Peace Conference International (from which a source supplied the police with copies of documents); the Vancouver Peace Action League, which met at a Unitarian Church; and a protest against the Vietnam War organized by the United Church that was held at B.C.'s border with the U.S. in 1970, at which a police surveillance team took photos later used to identify individual protesters.[47]

Some peace groups were investigated for their potential to impair the military arm of the security state. For example, in May 1977, Major Tom Haney of the Police and Security Liaison Section of the Department of National Defence contacted the RCMP Security Service to request information about Project Ploughshares, a newly formed Mennonite peace organization at the University of Waterloo. Specifically, Major Haney asked for a determination of whether the pacifist group posed a threat to the Canadian armed forces through its potential to 'subvert' members of the military. The request arrived in headquarters in Ottawa, which passed it on to the Kitchener-Waterloo branch of the Security Service. Its members quickly determined that Project Ploughshares did not pose any more of a threat to the Canadian military than any other pacifist group. The military officer was informed of this discovery, along with the reassurance that Project Ploughshares would continue to be monitored.[48]

The failure to find evidence of subversion in the peace movement did not mean that it was necessary to stop searching. As one Mountie (the regular recipient of a newsletter from the First Unitarian Congregation of Toronto) articulated it, this 'would be to underestimate the ability of the Communist movement,' and he specifically pointed to Unitarian efforts to encourage disarmament as evidence of communist influence.[49] The investigation of the peace movement by state security continued into the 1980s, expanding in the era of President Ronald Reagan as the peace movement grew in opposition to his administration's arms policies.[50]

An ironic aspect of the Cold War era and the rapid expansion of the security net is that it also ensnared its practitioners, a part of the story that is often ignored. Not surprisingly, the focus of those studying this era has been on the targets of surveillance, not those doing the spying. Yet one major consequence of the expansion of the security state was in the area of paper work. As Richard V. Ericson and Kevin D. Haggerty have noted, 'The police face the risk of having their organization overwhelmed by ... the sheer volume of knowledge work. They have a strong sense of organizational risk and insecurity because of external demands for knowledge; a perpetual feeling of having insufficient knowledge.'[51] A 1961 time study of a single Mounted Police office found that the security and intelligence investigator spent 51 per cent of his time on office duties, of which 62 per cent involved writing reports, and the remainder handling mail and files.[52] The RCMP found itself so overwhelmed by paper work that it had to continually redefine how many 'adverse references' were necessary before an active file would be opened on an individual. The force also went through a process of crashing files because it simply could not keep up with the additional information.

The lack of clarity within the investigation process ultimately proved to be its downfall. Driven by its massive focus on communist subversion, it was unable to react quickly to the emergence of new forces, such as Quebec nationalism and the New Left. The perception among federal politicians was that in the key area of national unity, the Anglo-dominated RCMP was out of touch. The October Crisis reinforced this view and led to the government placing pressure on the RCMP to act; hence the 'dirty tricks' era of the 1970s and the eventual stripping of the RCMP of its primary intelligence role in the 1980s with the creation of the Canadian Security Intelligence Service.[53]

The Mounted Police's surveillance of religious organizations and individuals like Lotta Hitschmanova did not in itself cause the downfall of the Security Service. Such targeting against those who sought change through peaceful means, however, demonstrates once again that in the Cold War no one was safe from the scrutiny of the state. These examples also pose serious questions to those Cold War revisionists who seek to excuse the abuses of civil liberties and the wasting of resources by emphasizing the necessity of countering espionage activities. Ultimately, the Mounted Police reflected the inherent insecurity of the state toward its own citizens and, indeed, a lack of faith in the sustainability of the political and economic system. In that basic motivation for the state's domestic surveillance operations in the Cold War there is little to differentiate the activities that occurred in Canada from those that took place in the German Democratic Republic: in each case the object was to defend a status quo that was not capable of defending itself.

Notes

1 Clyde Sanger, *Lotta – and the Unitarian Service Committee Story* (Toronto: Stoddart, 1986). The extent of the RCMP's investigation of Hitschmanova is unknown. She died at the beginning of August 1990, meaning that under the Access to Information Act her file can be applied for in that same month in 2010.

2 Leo Panitch, 'The Role and Nature of the Canadian State,' in Panitch, ed., *The Canadian State: Political Economy and Political Power* (Toronto: U of Toronto P, 1977), 3–27; Allan Greer and Ian Radforth, eds., *Colonial Leviathan: State Formation in Mid-Nineteenth-Century Canada* (Toronto: U of Toronto P, 1992); John Torpey, *The Invention of the Passport: Surveillance, Citizenship and the State* (New York: Cambridge UP, 2000), 4–20.

3 Gregory S. Kealey, 'Spymasters, Spies, and Their Subjects: The RCMP and

Canadian State Repression, 1914–1939,' in Gary Kinsman, Dieter Buse, and Mercedes Steedman, eds., *Whose National Security? Canadian State Surveillance and the Creation of Enemies* (Toronto: Between the Lines, 2000), 18–33; Athan Theoharis, *Spying on Americans: Political Surveillance from Hoover to the Huston Plan* (Philadelphia: Temple UP, 1978); Richard Gid Powers, *Secrecy and Power: The Life of J. Edgar Hoover* (London: Hutchinson, 1987); Richard Thurlow, *The Secret State: British Internal Security in the Twentieth Century* (Oxford: Blackwell, 1994); Bernard Porter, *Plots and Paranoia: A History of Political Espionage in Britain, 1790–1988* (London: Routledge, 1992); Christopher Andrew, *Her Majesty's Secret Service: The Making of the British Intelligence Community* (New York: Viking, 1986).

4 Theoharis, *Spying on Americans*; Frank J. Donner, *The Age of Surveillance: The Aims and Methods of America's Political Intelligence System* (New York: Knopf, 1980); Ward Churchill and Jim Vander Wall, *The COINTELPRO Papers: Documents from the FBI's Secret Wars against Dissent in the United States* (Boston: South End, 1990); Frank Donner, *Protectors of Privilege: Red Squads and Police Repression in Urban America* (Los Angeles: U of California P, 1991).

5 Peter Worthington, 'Traitors in our midst,' *Ottawa Sun*, 30 Sept. 1999; Stewart Bell, 'KGB Plans to sabotage Canada revealed,' *National Post*, 14 Sept. 1999; 'Mystery KGB agent in the Civil Service "is still alive,"' *The Times*, 30 Sept. 1999.

6 Timothy Garton Ash, *The File* (New York: Random House, 1997), 229–48. Ash's query is also discussed in Larry Hannant, 'What's in My File?,' in Kinsman et al., eds., *Whose National Security?*, 219–21.

7 Royal Commission of Inquiry Concerning Certain Activities of the Royal Canadian Mounted Police (hereafter McDonald Commission), *Second Report: Freedom and Security under the Law, Volume 1* (Ottawa: Supply and Services Canada, 1981), 518. Special thanks to Reg Whitaker for supplying me with this reference.

8 Christopher Andrew and Vasili Mitrokhin, *The Mitrokhin Archive: The KGB in Europe and the West* (London: Penguin, 1999), 634–61; Jim Bronskill, 'Priests spied in Canada for KGB, book reveals,' *Vancouver Sun*, 6 Oct. 1999.

9 In the 1980s, for example, using its powers to counter terrorism, the FBI investigated the Committee in Solidarity with the People of El Salvador, a peaceful group opposed to the Reagan administration's activities in Central America. Tony G. Poveda, 'Controversies and Issues,' in Athan G. Theoharis, ed., *The FBI: A Comprehensive Reference Guide* (New York: Oryx, 2000), 134.

10 John Earl Haynes and Harvey Klehr, *Venona: Decoding Soviet Espionage in America* (New Haven: Yale UP, 1999); Allan Theoharis, *Chasing Spies: How the FBI Failed in Counter-intelligence but Promoted the Politics of McCarthyism in the Cold War Years* (Chicago: Ivan R. Dee Inc., 2002).

11 Elizabeth Grace and Colin Leys, 'The Concept of Subversion and Its Implications,' in C.E.S. Franks, ed., *Dissent and the State* (Toronto: Oxford UP, 1989), 62.

12 Grace and Leys, 'The Concept of Subversion,' 62–85; Reg Whitaker, 'Cold War Alchemy: How America, Britain and Canada Transformed Espionage into Subversion,' in David Stafford and Rhodri Jeffreys-Jones, eds., *American-British-Canadian Intelligence Relations, 1939–2000* (London: Frank Cass, 2000), 177–210. See also Whitaker and Marcuse, *CWC*, 183–4.

13 Donner, *Protectors of Privilege*, 76; see also Theoharis, *Chasing Spies*.

14 Steve Hewitt, '"Information Believed True": RCMP Security Intelligence Activities on Canadian University Campuses and the Controversy Surrounding Them, 1961–1971,' *Canadian Historical Review* 81.2 (June 2000): 196–9.

15 Dean Beeby, 'RCMP had plan to round up "subversives," documents show,' *National Post* 24 Jan. 2000.

16 Canadian Security Intelligence Service (CSIS), Royal Canadian Mounted Police Security Records, access request 117-99-14, Instructions re: Subversive Investigation and Correspondence, RCMP report, 10 Sept. 1952.

17 CSIS, Royal Canadian Mounted Police Security Records, 'Contacts-Police-Canada,' access request 117-98-71, Insp. J.G. Long, in charge of sources, to William Kelly, Director of Security Intelligence, 28 July 1967.

18 Interview with Donald J. Inch, former member of the RCMP Security Service, 1 March 1998.

19 Donner, *Protectors of Privilege*, 72.

20 Whitaker and Marcuse, *CWC* 359; Whitaker, 'Left-Wing Dissent and the State: Canada in the Cold War Era,' in C.E.S. Franks, ed., *Dissent and the State* (Toronto: Oxford UP, 1989), 193.

21 CSIS, RCMP Records related to J.S. Woodsworth, document no. 23, access request 88–A-60, Records of the Royal Canadian Mounted Police, Record Group (RG) 18, Report of Cpl. W.J. Barker, 17 May 1920; Richard Allen, *The Social Passion: Religion and Social Reform in Canada, 1914–28* (Toronto: U of Toronto P, 1971), 170–3; 'Bulletin No. 45 for 14 October 1920,' in Gregory S. Kealey and Reg Whitaker, eds., *R.C.M.P. Security Bulletins: The Early Years, 1919–1929* (St John's: Canadian Committee on Labour History, 1994), 217.

22 A.E. Smith, *All My Life: An Autobiography* (Toronto: Progress Books, 1949); Tom Mitchell, 'From the Social Gospel to "the Plain Bread of Leninism":

A.E. Smith's Journey to the Left in the Epoch of Reaction after World War 1,' *Labour / Le Travail* 33 (1994): 125–51.

23 National Archives of Canada (NA), Records of the Royal Canadian Mounted Police, Record Group (RG) 18, vol. 1933, file G-57-9-1, 'K' Division Confidential Monthly Report for November 1919. For a study of state persecution of Jehovah's Witnesses in Canada see William Kaplan, *State and Salvation: The Jehovah's Witnesses and Their Fight for Civil Rights* (Toronto: U Toronto P, 1989).

24 S.T. Wood, 'Tools for Treachery,' *R.C.M.P. Quarterly* 8.4 (1941): 394. The KGB took an even more serious approach to the Jehovah's Witnesses and their message that the end of the world was near; see Andrew and Mitrokhin, *The Mitrokhin Archive*, 658–60.

25 NA, RG 146, vol. 3339, access request AH-2000-00116, Major Eric Acland, Military Intelligence, to the Commissioner, 21 January 1942; ibid., Report of Cst. [deleted: name], 21 April 1942; ibid., Insp. C. Batch to Lt.-Col. W.W. Murray, General Staff Officer, Military Intelligence, 9 April 1942.

26 NA, RG 146, vol. 2883, file AH-2000-00118, Communist Infiltration of the Unitarian Church of Canada, 31 January 1966.

27 NA, RG 146, vol. 2883, file AH-2000-00118, Communist Infiltration of the Unitarian Church of Canada, 31 January 1966; ibid., vol. 2852, access request AH-2000-00147, Unitarian Men's Club–Ottawa, pt. 1, Report of Insp. F.A. Syms, 15 February 1937.

28 NA, RG 146, vol. 75, file 96-A-00045, pt. 70, Unitarian Men's Club, 14 December 1960.

29 NA, RG 146, vol. 2852, access request AH-2000-00147, Report of [deleted: name], 25 November 1959.

30 Ibid., Transit Slip, 5 March 1961; ibid., Report of [deleted: name]; ibid., Report of [deleted: name] 9 February 1960; ibid., Report of [deleted: name], 9 March 1960; NA, RG 146, vol. 2852, access request AH-2000-00147, pt. 2, Report of [deleted: name], 18 April 1962.

31 NA, RG 146, vol. 2852, access request AH-2000-00147, pt. 2, Report of [deleted: name], 18 April 1962.

32 J. Edgar Hoover, *Masters of Deceit: The Story of Communism in America and How to Fight It* (New York: Holt, 1958), 107; Elaine Tyler May, *Homeward Bound: American Families in the Cold War Era* (New York: Basic Books, 1988), 94. For an evaluation of the connections between the state's construction of subversion and 'illicit' sexuality, see Kinsman's chapter in the present volume.

33 NA, RG 146, vol. 2882, access request AH-2000-00118, Department of National Defence to Lotta Hitschmanova, 30 December 1953; ibid.,

Unitarian Services Committee, 27 November 1948; ibid., Unitarian Services Committee, 18 December 1949; Sanger, *Lotta*, 61–2

34 NA, RG 146, vol. 2982, access request AH-2000-00118, Report of [deleted: name], 15 February 1950.

35 NA, RG 146, vol. 2883, access request AH-2000-00118, C/Supt. G. Begalki, Officer i/c "D" Ops. to [an External Affairs employee], 4 March 1976; ibid., Unitarian Service Committee, 30 May 1977.

36 NA, RG 146, vol. 3003, access request AH-2000-00116, Transit Slip, 17 November 1977.

37 CSIS, access request 117-99-14, [deleted: name] for Director, Security and Intelligence, to Divisions, 1 November 1967.

38 NA, RG 146, vol. 4241, access request AH-2000-00202, pt. 1, Communist Activities, Marxist Theories, 29 June 1948.

39 NA, RG 146, vol. 4241, access request AH-2000-00202, Report of [deleted: name], 5 December 1961; ibid., 18 November 1964, 17 November 1964.

40 Ibid., pt. 2, Memorandum to Insp. Parent, Transit Slip, 16 February 1965.

41 Ibid., Memorandum for File, 13 May 1965 and 10 February 1965.

42 NA, RG 146, vol. 2942, access request AH-2000-00203, United Church Committee on Education; NA, RG 146, vol. 2941, access requested AH-2000-00117, pt. 2, DSI to Officer i/c SIB, 'E' Division, 28 October 1968; ibid., J.M. Fraser to Blair Seaborn, 11 September 1968; NA, RG 146, vol. 2941, access request AH-2000-00117, pt. 1, Report of Cst. [deleted: name], 10 September 1968; ibid., Report of [deleted: name], 7 May 1968; ibid., K.B. Williamson, Academic Relations Section to Blair Seaborn, cc. Gotlieb among others, 1 May 1968; ibid., Transit Slip, 24 April 1968; ibid., External Affairs to RCMP, 19 June 1952.

43 NA, vol. 2942, file AH2000-00148, Report of Cpl. [deleted: name], 17 November 1970.

44 McGeorge Bundy, *Danger and Survival: Choices about the Bomb in the First Fifty Years* (New York: Random House, 1988), 334–42; Lawrence S. Wittner, *Resisting the Bomb, 1954–1970: A History of the World Nuclear Disarmament Movement, Volume 2* (Stanford: Stanford UP, 1997), 87.

45 NA, RG 146, file 97-A-00172, New Left Committee–Canada, Commissioner C.W. Harvison to Minister of Justice E.D. Fulton, 24 February 1961; NA, RG 146, vol. 4270, file AH-1999–00248, Memorandum from Insp. R.A.S. McNeil, 20 October 1948. For more on Hewlett Johnson's visit to Canada and the Canadian Peace Congress see Stephen Endicott, *James G. Endicott: Rebel out of China* (Toronto: U of Toronto P, 1980), 261–77.

46 Wittner, *Resisting the Bomb*, 203.

47 NA, RG 146, vol. 2942, access request AH-2000-00146, pt. 7, Report of

[deleted: name], Re: Christian Peace Conference International, 22 November 1973; ibid., Re: Vancouver Peace Action League, 13 July 1970; ibid., Report of Cst. [deleted: name], Protests and Demonstrations against U.S. Action in Vietnam–British Columbia, 3 June 1970.

48 NA, RG 146, vol. 74, file 96-A-00045, pt. 63, Major T.P. Haney to RCMP, 31 May 1977; NA, RG 146, vol. 74, file 96-A-00045, pt. 63, University of Waterloo, Project Ploughshares, 28 July 1977. NA, RG 146, vol. 74, file 96-A-00045, pt. 63, University of Waterloo, Project Ploughshares, 22 June 1977; NA, RG 146, vol. 74, file 96-A-00045, pt. 63, 'D' Ops Ottawa to Kitchener, 2 June 1977. NA, RG 146, vol. 74, file 96-A-00045, pt. 63, J.H. Brookmyre, RCMP Security Service, to Major T.P. Haney, Police and Security Liaison, Section, Department of National Defence, Re: Project Ploughshares, 18 August 1977.

49 NA, vol. 2883, access request AH-2000-00148, Report of Cst. [deleted: name], 2 October 1963.

50 NA, RG 146, vol. 2942, access request AH-2000-00146, pt. 7, Report of [deleted: name], 14 September 1982. For more on the Canadian peace movement and state security in the Reagan era see James T. Stark, *Cold War Blues: The Operation Dismantle Story* (Hull, Quebec: Voyageur, 1991).

51 Richard V. Ericson and Kevin D. Haggerty, *Policing the Risk Society* (Toronto: U of Toronto P, 1997), 295.

52 CSIS, access request 117-99-14, Report from NCO, i/c Sault Ste Marie SIS, 19 September 1961.

53 Despite notions to the contrary, the RCMP did not lose its intelligence role in 1984. It retained responsibility for the security of visiting dignitaries, hence its front-and-centre activities during the Asia Pacific Economic Co-operation Conference at the University of British Columbia in 1997. For more on the RCMP Security Service's successor, the National Security Investigations Section, see Steve Hewitt 'Watching the Watchers,' *This Magazine* 34.1 (July/August 2000): 25.

Part II: Hate

3

Freedom Lovers, Sex Deviates, and Damaged Women: Iron Curtain Refugee Discourses in Cold War Canada

FRANCA IACOVETTA

She says sometimes men are following her and she evades them every time. It is difficult to say if it is wishful thinking on her part or not. Seems to have some tendency of a persecution complex, which may be one of the main reasons of termination of her job.

Caseworker, commenting on an East European refugee woman, International Institute of Metropolitan Toronto, 1960s[1]

No longer the exclusive terrain of political historians of diplomacy and foreign policy, the Cold War, especially its domestic side, has become the subject of a rapidly proliferating literature in women's, gender, sexual, and social history.[2] In Canada, as in the United States, studies of the alarmist discourses about dysfunctional families and the moral regulation of delinquent boys and girls; of the repression of homosexuals in the government and the growing popularity of psychiatric definitions of sexual perversion; of the vilification of working mothers as home wreckers or neglectful mothers producing misfit children; and of the red-baiting of housewives' consumer groups and other female activists have demonstrated the myriad ways that the state, courts, schools, and professional and popular experts sought to undermine and eradicate alleged 'deviants' or 'threats' to the body politic, many of whom they described with metaphors of dirt, disease, and contamination.[3] As histories of sexuality have documented, postwar sexual and moral panics were fed not only by experts, police, parents, and other lobby and 'vigilante' groups, but also by sensationalist coverage in the mainstream media of sex crimes and other 'epidemics' that were represented so as to suggest an increase in 'criminal sexual psychopaths.' These 'psychopaths' were assumed to be homosexual, even though the majority of violent sexual offenders were heterosexuals known to their victims.[4] The connections suggested here are significant; moral panic around homosexuality in the early 1950s in Canada led to new, restrictive legislation that not only further criminalized homosexuality but also made it one of the grounds for rejecting immigrant applications.[5]

A concomitant of the notion of moral panic was that of domestic containment, a corollary to the U.S. (and NATO) foreign policy strategy of 'containing' communist threats. As Geoffrey Smith puts it, 'the containment of sexuality to the marriage bed [and to the missionary position, with the men on top], the sanctification of heterosexual monogamy and the outlawry of other forms of sexuality – and, as if to accent the rigid distinction between communist enslavement and the Free World – the maintenance of strict barriers between masculinity and femininity' were part of the arsenal with which mainstream (North) America sought to impose and bolster 'the archetypal white, middle-class family [values] of the 1950s.'[6] Efforts to contain perceived threats from within, whether from reds and pinkos, foreign female spies, treasonous lesbians, or defective refugee men, were linked to social and political developments that profoundly affected North American postwar society through, among other things, a resurgence of conservative family ideology and the undermining of individual freedoms through the assertion of 'democratic' rights. At the same time, it is crucial to be aware of the resistance to such efforts at containment in order to arrive at a nuanced understanding of the Cold War period.[7]

The confluence of the diplomatic history of the postwar period with the radical histories of political, social, and sexual outlaws is producing a growing literature that is rich in the possibilities that it presents for the recovery of alternative and oppositional lives.[8] The application of terms and paradigms from the foreign and military policy of the period, such as the metaphors of contamination discussed above, has led scholars to examine the deep anxieties of the period as they manifested themselves in the national 'insecurity' state,[9] documenting, for example, the RCMP's use of the 'fruit machine'[10] as a form of surveillance that promised, but failed, to ferret out homosexuals from government posts by quantifying reactions to magazine pictures. Such attempts to define nonconformists through moral or political censure were strategies of containment which greatly exceeded U.S. military strategies that sought to halt the spread of the Soviet-Marxist 'disease'; these attempts were also a means through which the body politic in Canada could be made to conform to bourgeois values of obedience, conformity (including sexual and familial), and capitalism.

Only recently have Canadian and U.S. historians begun to explore systematically how and to what degree Cold War anxieties and containment techniques[11] affected the responses of host societies to the European refugees and immigrants who settled in North America (and elsewhere), and particularly, but not exclusively, the anti-communist, East European refugees. Some recent feminist scholarship has considered the ways in which portrayals of postwar refugees and immigrants in terms of pathologies of moral, mental, and sexual diseases brought about by communist totalitarianism also fuelled the moral anxieties of these years, providing additional bases for the 'othering' so characteristic of the Canadian (and American) state during this period. This pathological imperative allowed terms such as 'DP degenerate' to be added to the roster of terms designating 'contaminated' individuals, and, as the opening quotation indicates, prompted social workers trained outside psychiatry to label evidently troubled women from communist regimes as psychological victims of the Iron Curtain, while crudely dismissing these women's sexual fears as a mix of paranoia and desire.[12]

In this recent work on Cold War pathologies, however, relatively little attention has been directed toward studies of the transgressions of moral and social norms made by recently arrived immigrant and refugee women and men. Did Canadian commentators and experts define immigrants and refugees as sexual or moral 'problems' in ways that were similar to or that differed from the ways in which they labelled their Canadian subjects? When and in what ways were East Europeans cast as romantic subjects? What was the role of gender in these characterizations? Given the enormous impact of postwar immigration on Canada – one far greater than that on the United States – these questions require particular scrutiny as we develop analyses of immigration and its relationship to moral and sexual aspects of nation building and citizenship that are more rigorously attuned to gender issues.[13]

In raising these issues, I am not suggesting that there was a moral panic that developed exclusively around postwar European newcomers to Canada. Europeans were not usually constructed as the sole or even primary source of 'problem parents' or 'sex deviates'; rather, they were usually seen as contributing to already declining middle-class

North American standards in parenting, family life, and sexual and moral norms. Nevertheless, these immigrants were often scapegoated in the media and were the targets of bigots. In studying these anxieties historically, it is possible to illustrate how concerns about sexuality, sexual morality, moral regulation, and mental health could be central to the relations between newcomers and gatekeepers, and within refugee reception work.

Love, Fear, and Cold War Romance in the Media

An emphasis on the anxieties and challenges of early postwar Canada, and on the complex lives and negotiations of European newcomers who entered Canada during this period, should not lead us to conclude that there was no room for love, romance, or even giddy excitement. Journalists of the mainstream press clearly enjoyed representing the dramatic narratives of dangerous escapes from communist or devastated Europe as romantic tales of courage and redemption, and played up the value of these tales as political and moral lessons about the evils and deprivations of life under communism, thereby highlighting the superiority of Western capitalist democracies.[14]

Early Cold War escape narratives appeared in mass circulation vehicles such as *Maclean's* and *Reader's Digest*. Their romantic leading figures were most often men, cast as handsome masterminds of risky escapes. Often, however, women, lovers, or couples were profiled as attractive duos who had braved danger in their thirst for freedom. Photographs of happy, smiling women and men often accompanied these stories, especially in newspapers, as in the late 1940s, when Canadian media covered the arrival of displaced persons from Baltic States who refused repatriation to their Soviet-controlled homelands. Among the earliest arrivals were about fifteen hundred anti-Soviet Estonians from Sweden who arrived on boats and were thus, to use Reg Whitaker's term, Canada's 'first boat people.'[15] Generally meeting with a warm welcome from compatriots, co-religionists, and pro-immigration Canadians, the refugees garnered much public attention. One such boatload carried twenty-three Estonians who were characteristically described on the front page of the *Toronto Star* as 'freedom lovers.' As in similar stories, the *Star's* coverage featured photos of smiling men and women who, as individuals or couples, had braved the ocean for the chance of a new life in North America. For example, one photo, captioned 'Happy

Voyagers,' pictured an attractive wife and husband, Mr and Mrs Ernat Lohmus, who, the reporter wrote, could easily have been mistaken as an 'ordinary' Canadian couple – at least until they were heard speaking Estonian. Most of the attention in this article, however, went to boat owner Ludwig Tosine, the attractive 'Blond Seaman' who had 'led his countrymen and women to Canada via Sweden, Belgium, England, and [the] U.S.' on a '5,800 mile journey' that included a 'remarkable' three-month voyage over the rough Atlantic seas in his own 43-foot ketch. The accompanying photo of Tosine featured a suave-looking man, dressed in a shirt and tie, his hat cocked rakishly, accentuating his movie-star looks. It did not appear important to the reporters to ask if he, too, were a DP, and, if so, how he came to own a yacht. Nor was Tosine asked if he had profited financially from this trip. These ambiguities further added to Tosine's allure as a somewhat mysterious individual who was wealthy enough to own a yacht yet cared passionately enough about democracy and the plight of his fellow nationals that he undertook, virtually singlehandedly, to bring them to North America.[16]

Women likewise emerged as romantic Cold War heroines, especially when they were young and attractive. One such woman was Irene Konkova, a twenty-three-year-old doctoral student from Charles University in Prague, whom Canadian journalists patronizingly described as a 'pretty little Czech' girl who 'outwitted Soviet police' and then 'waded mountain snows' for three weeks to reach the West, and, finally, a new life in Winnipeg. A large photo accompanied the story.[17] Imprisoned in February 1949 while a graduate student 'for not conforming to Communist dictates,' Konkova escaped jail a few weeks later with the help of 'friends' (who may have been connected with an illegal church group), and, after a brief visit with her parents, fled through the snow to West Germany. A terrifying moment came early on, she told reporters, when police surrounded the mountain inn where she first took refuge. She had 'sat paralyzed' on her bed while the police searched the rooms, and when they 'pounded' on her door she 'forgot to breathe' for minutes. The police arrested everyone and took them away. 'The only reason I got out alive,' she explained, 'was because the police were too lazy to smash the door of my bedroom down.' After they left, she jumped out the second-storey window and continued her journey. In West Germany, Konkova was offered a job in the U.S. zone as a physical education director with the YW/YMCA. Through that job she met Mollie Christie, a veteran Toronto social worker then posted overseas, who contacted Canadian authorities about Konkova's possible admission to the country. As a result, Konkova was offered a position with the YWCA in Winnipeg.

Interviewed there, Konkova told reporters that she feared that Communist authorities in Prague were persecuting her parents, with whom she had lost contact. Such fears were realistic and well-founded; millions of men and women were victimized or eliminated under Stalinist totalitarianism through the forced labour camp system of the 1920s, the disappearances and party purges of the 1930s Great Terror, the wartime labour armies, and the postwar imprisonment or execution of repatriated nationals as well as 'political' and 'criminal' offenders, who were sent to labour camps, special settlements, and colonies (for certain groups such as scientists), or the Gulag. The ruthlessness with which Stalinism imprisoned or eliminated real and imagined enemies, at times wiping out entire families, haunted many a political defector from postwar communist Europe.[18]

Canadian journalists (like reception and citizenship workers) readily devoted attention to the fears of the East Europeans who had risked much for democracy; in this instance, however, Konkova's interviewers chose another common approach and stressed her story's happy ending, noting, for example, the enormous gratitude she felt towards Canada for giving her a new home in a freedom-loving nation and the excitement with which she was 'looking foward to the Canadian way of life.' When asked what most impressed her about the country she noted (as did many refugees) the abundance of food, as well as 'the lovely looking Canadian girls [with] their smart clothes and immaculate appearance.' While this latter observation was not especially common among refugees asked about their first impressions of Canada, it did fit well with Konkova's self-image and her bourgeois background. In the *Toronto Star* interview, the front-page photo showed her wearing considerable make-up, as well as a fashionable hairdo and scarf; this photo took up more space than the article itself.

In some respects, Konkova's image offered Canadians an attractive contrast to the conventional image of the frumpy, dowdy, mannish women behind the Iron Curtain. As Robert Griswold has recently argued, U.S. commentary on the Soviet woman provided a foil against which Americans 'cast their own ideas about womanhood.' Thus the representation of the Soviet woman's 'cosmetological primitiveness' (i.e., poor make-up skills), flabby bodies, and lack of allure served to confirm 'the superiority of American women, their embodied femininity, and the American free enterprise system.' It was the failure of the Soviet economic system that prevented 'real Soviet women,' as opposed to 'brainwashed Marxist ideologues,' from becoming 'more feminine, more elegant, more attractive' through its inability to produce the necessary goods and services, such as bras and girdles, cosmetics, and decent hair salons, while at the same time subjecting these 'real' women to filthy grunt jobs that wreaked havoc on their bodies and to an ideology that denounced feminine beauty as bourgeois frivolity.[19] Canadian commentators drew similar conclusions; in each case, the presence of East bloc women who could maintain their beauty in a regime that supposedly sought to denaturalize, defeminize, desexualize, and thus uglify women, was cause for celebration. Thus, 'pretty' Konkova could be welcomed as fitting material for North American womanhood. This was not to forget, however, that Konkova had found 'a hole in the old Iron Curtain' and had 'escaped through it after matching wits with the Soviet secret police' and completing a 'perilous flight through Austria.'

In a manner that echoed pulp fiction stories of 'love under fire,' other media stories of Iron Curtain escapes featured young and attractive lovers or newlyweds whose stories combined the elements of romance, political intrigue, sexual adventure, and danger. Under the headline 'Chose to Flee from Red Poland rather than Perform before Stalin,' Ottawa *Citizen* reporter Pat Best told of how the 'slim, blue eyed beauty,' twenty-seven-year old Polish actress Lydia Prochinicka, and her theatre-producer partner Leonidas Dudarew-Ossetynski, escaped communist Europe and eventually found a glamorous life in American theatre. The *Citizen* interviewed the actors while their troupe was on a Canadian tour performing comedic and dramatic works celebrating Poland's pre-Soviet past. The story was accompanied by a large photo of a smiling Prochinicka in a sleeveless dress, engaged in a romantic stage embrace with her on- and off-stage lover, who was dressed in a medal-adorned military uniform. While the photo suited the tone of Best's article, it also served the role of 'star-gazing' and thus risked trivializing the couple's complex and courageous story of escape.

Lydia had begun her acting career in the underground theatre during the Nazi occupation of Poland, performing in cellars and bombed-out buildings. Following her country's liberation by the Russians, she had joined the Polish national theatre and earned 'recognition as Poland's best actress,' and her status as the 'beauteous' star of the Polish theatre brought with it an invitation in 1947 to appear in a command performance before Marshall Stalin. 'I hated Stalin,' she told Best, 'but it was difficult to refuse such an invitation. It was go to Moscow or escape – I chose to escape.' As Best wrote, Lydia fled 'the Communist clutch' by way of France, Belgium, and then Chile, the United States, and, briefly, Canada. Leonidas, an officer of the Polish cavalry, had been imprisoned in a German concentration camp in Morocco until freed by U.S. forces in 1942. Having served with U.S. forces in North Africa, he emigrated after the war to Hollywood, where he set up a theatre group that Lydia joined. Currently, they were touring North America in their 'theatrical caravan – a station wagon laden with costumes and props' – and performing work that 'combines a serious interpretation of the current international crisis with a timely sense of humour.'

The accompanying photo of the couple's posed embrace, captioned 'Love and Paris,' relates to a scene from one of the plays they were performing at the University of Ottawa as a benefit for the Polish Boy Scouts of Canada. Romance is mingled with patriotism in the couple's eagerness to meet with compatriots in Canada who had similarly suffered under communism. Referring to 'the successful uprising of the past few weeks' in Poland to protest against Russian domination, Leonidas also expressed the hope that 'our appearance here will instil in Polish Canadians some of the fervour being shown by these people of the homeland now striving for independence of their country.'[20] Ironically, the beneficiary of the couple's fundraising performance – the Polish Boy Scouts of Canada – had raised the ire of Canadian immigration authorities and Boy Scout leaders who suspected the group of being a Polish nationalist front for recruiting youngsters into their political campaign against Soviet-style Communism. For this reason, the group was not considered to be entirely legitimate as a volunteer youth organization, and had been refused entry into the umbrella organization of Canadian Boy Scouts.[21]

In another Cold War romance, a young Czech couple became known among Canadian and U.S. reporters, tourists, and newspaper readers as the 'Niagara Falls Lovers.' Their frustrating tale of separation – she in the United States and he in Canada – offered an engrossing tale of love under fire. So great was the interest in their story that large crowds assembled at Niagara Falls to witness the couple's reunion along the forty-ninth parallel on a Canadian pleasure craft, the *Maid of the Mist*, as it plied back and forth on the Niagara River.

The story about the couple broke in early October 1949, five months after twenty-four-year-old 'Kitty' Kleiner, a Czechoslovakian nurse now based in the United States, and her fiancé, twenty-five-year-old 'Denny' Chrastanku, a DP recently arrived in Canada, had begun meeting illegally at the border. The newspapers reported on the many delighted spectators who crowded the Canadian dock where the ferry picked up passengers in order to catch a glimpse of the Czech lovers. They had come in response to the rumour that U.S. immigration officials had finally agreed to grant the couple's request for 'a brief land tryst.'[22] Having 'bypassed the stern immigration men' on the previous day 'by meeting aboard the little craft that plies beneath the roaring falls,' the couple went out again that morning for 'another get-together.' Alas, wrote one reporter, the *Maid of the Mist* was 'not the world's best place for long parted lovers. It's like a public show and, besides, they have to spend their time on a spray-swept deck, raincoated and hatted, and try to talk over the roar of Niagara.'

These sentiments, however, did not prevent this Canadian journalist (and others) from prying into the lives of the refugee lovers, who were given (or adopted) the anglicized names 'Kitty' and 'Denny.' 'As honeymoon couples huddled along the railing of the ship's deck gazing at the wonders of the Horseshoe Falls,' the reporter wrote, 'an understanding crew' let the lovers make several trips for one fifty-cent fare, during which they were mostly 'oblivious to everything but each other.' Earlier that morning, reporters had descended on the couple with flashing cameras, joining Denny at breakfast and accompanying him to the planned rendezvous. When asked about an engagement ring, Kitty, 'in perfect English,' responded: 'I don't like rings so Dennis gave me a gold-and-pearl brooch.' In response to a question asking if they would honeymoon in Niagara Falls, she replied: 'I have been on this boat many hours. We've seen a lot of water go over the Falls. I think maybe we'll honeymoon somewhere else.' And when asked about their proposed reunion on the Rainbow bridge, a laughing Kitty joked, 'I always say never cross your bridges till you come to them.'[23]

Despite this jocular tone, the couple's predicament was genuine. They had fallen in love in early 1946 while students at Prague University, shortly before Kitty, an economics major, won a scholarship allowing her to study in the United States. Denny, a medical student, remained behind, and for two years they had written 'constantly.' By 1948, Denny was unable to bear their separation; he fled his homeland in the night with only his briefcase, crossing the heavily guarded border and eventually arriving in Germany.[24] On the mistaken assumption that admission to Canada would give him easy access to the United States, Denny had decided to apply for Canadian entry, which was easier to obtain. He entered Canada on a farm labour contract, only to learn that he could not move freely outside Canadian borders until he became a citizen. For five years he had 'battered vainly at the rigid barriers of immigration' without securing permission to visit Kitty in the United States. Kitty, too, had 'found herself meshed in red tape' in the United States, where she had enrolled at the University of North Carolina.'[25] By June 1948, Kitty was determined to meet Denny on the Rainbow Bridge in Niagara Falls and took a job at a New Jersey hospital so that she would be closer to the border. But, as one reporter put it, 'immigration laws afford no concessions for love'; had Kitty entered Canada, she would not have been permitted to return to the United States, since she was not yet a U.S. citizen.

The couple's predicament revealed some of the arbitrariness of post-war refugee and immigration admissions. Denny had been denied entry into the United States because the military prohibited admission to the country of DPs who had entered Germany after 1948. As a result, Denny and his brother John, also a medical student, an escapee, and a farm work recruit, had ended up in Toronto briefly before being placed on farms in the Holland Marsh. Their story thus conformed to the familiar Cold War plot whereby the educated and cultured East European professional, intellectual, or artist was forced by war and communism into a less appealing life. As the media accounts related, the brothers were also 'keen students of music' (John played 'piano exceptionally well'), and their DP camp was filled with 'university men' who had been able to outwit the communist authorities.

Canadian authorities were so impressed by Denny and Kitty's story – embellished by newspaper reports cast in the form of a Harlequin romance – that they had stretched the law to facilitate their reunion on the *Maid of the Mist*. While the government authorities stated 'with unusual wistfulness' that 'there's just nothing Canada can do for lovers,' they nevertheless said they would permit Denny to visit the United States and Kitty to enter Canada (though she risked being refused re-entry to the United States). They also suggested that Denny seek employment with an international agency, such as the United Nations, which might allow him to cross borders more easily, and that Kitty appeal directly to President Truman, or at least apply for admission to Canada.[26] Public interest was engaged less by these stories of officialdom, however, than by accounts of the couple's activities on the boat, what a local journalist called 'their trysting place – 1,000 feet of this romantic river.' But despite the predictable innuendos, the most that reporters could say with any confidence was that 'they sit and hold hands and talk' while 'the little pleasure-boat ... plies up and down the Niagara River.' In response to the media frenzy the couple was diplomatic but also expressed their frustration over the lack of privacy.[27] U.S. officials had responded by allowing them time alone in the U.S. immigration office.

Like most romances, this one had a happy ending,[28] which readers learned about a year later. As the *Toronto Telegram*'s Dorothy Haworth put it, 'Maid of Mist Lovers Conquer Border Ban, Reunited in Toronto.' The article and photo marked the occasion of Kitty's arrival on Canadian soil at Toronto's Union Station, where the 'tall, dark and blue-eyed' Denny greeted his 'pretty girl friend with a big hug and a bouquet of carnations.' The flowers, Howarth continued, 'were no brighter than Kitty's blue suit and red beret,' adding that 'Kitty's eyes are blue too, and her lashes, eyebrows and hair are jet black.' The couple planned to marry at Christmas time provided that Denny, who was still a farm worker, could get a job in Toronto and apply again to the School of Medicine at the University of Toronto. (He was refused admission the first time because of quotas on DP applicants to the professional faculties.) Kitty had gained admission to the university's School of Social Work (having become interested in the profession while working in New Jersey), receiving assistance from its director, H.M. Cassidy, as well as from the university's President, Sidney Smith, and from Toronto MP for St Paul, C.H. Rooney. It was Kitty who gave the story a fitting Canadian conclusion, even if some readers might not have fully grasped the element of fear that it contained: 'It is wonderful to be here ... And not only because of Dennis. Without my visa into Canada I might have been sent back behind the Iron Curtain, because my U.S. student's visa had expired.'[29]

From 'Public' Heroes to 'Private' Derelicts

While romantic stories of men and women such as the Niagara Falls couple attracted popular support, the sexual immorality of other 'freedom fighters' or 'freedom lovers' gave Canadian officials and reception workers cause for frustration, embarrassment, and, at times, denunciation. Such transgressions were not usually broadcast publicly; instead, they were recorded and discussed in confidential files of international relief bodies, RCMP investigations, social agencies, and legal and extralegal institutional regimes, including psychiatric clinics and mental hospitals. One case that did acquire public notoriety, however, involved three young men, 'freedom fighters' who had escaped Hungary following the failed uprising of 1956. In June 1959, the youths were convicted of 'indecently assaulting' an 'attractive young' female compatriot. The unidentified complainant, who rented a flat in the same rooming house as that occupied by the youths, was attacked when she went to one of their rooms to pick up a letter from her family in Hungary. While waiting for the letter, the door 'suddenly opened' and 'five naked men entered, one with a gun,' and she was gang-raped at gunpoint. Judge Harry Donley delivered a suspended sentence on the case arising, telling the defendants, however, that 'I am placing you on probation for two years so that you can learn to live by the laws of this country.'[30]

A more complicated case underscoring the role that sexual morality (and regulation) could play in reception work concerns a couple who were part of a group of women and men from communist Czechoslovakia who had come to Canada via a daring escape on a 'freedom train' that had taken them to a West German border town. Following speedy negotiations between the International Rescue Committee in Europe and Canadian government officials, Canada agreed to provide a haven for the 'freedom lovers' who had risked their lives for an opportunity to live in a democratic country. However, not all of the 'freedom train' refugees matched the highly romantic media portraits that depicted them as defying 'red slavery,' outwitting corrupt and incompetent communist thugs, and stoically enduring long treks across frontier regions in order to find success in a liberal capitalist democracy. In this case, most of the 114 train passengers had been completely unaware of the escape until it happened; it had been the idea of three men, one of whom held a pistol to the conductor's head as the train sped past the startled border guards. As Western journalists reported, most of the passengers had chosen to return home, largely out of the well-founded fear that the Soviets would retaliate against their families should they remain in the West.

Of the circa twenty-eight refugees who did request asylum, twenty gained admission to Canada, including a recently married couple, Vladimir, a former government clerk, and his younger wife, Natasha. They had been on the train heading for a holiday destination when the hijacking occurred. Initially hailed as a charming couple in love with freedom and each other, they quickly earned the disapproval and ire of the international and Canadian officials involved in the rescue operation, who came to see the duo as troublesome, then sexually deviant, and eventually as mentally ill, making them less than ideal prospects as future Canadian citizens. Ironically, just as Canadian newspapers were publicly welcoming the freedom train refugees, Canadian immigration and labour officials had begun deportation proceedings.[31] As well, Toronto social workers and medical doctors expressed deep frustration with the couple's sexually promiscuous and antisocial behaviour, their inability or unwillingness to hold down jobs, and their apparent psychiatric troubles.

The couple's behaviour before entering Canada had already attracted attention. The first reports came from International Refugee Commission (IRC) officials in Munich, who briefed Canadian officials in the Departments of Labour and Immigration, as well as social workers in Toronto (the refugees' destination), on the whereabouts of the freedom train refugees. 'We have two lovers' in the group, writes IRC Munich staff to Toronto colleagues in late September, 1951, who 'love each other [,] he as if, in her [,] he had, at last, discovered woman,' adding bemusedly that, while they are 'jokes' to the others in the group, 'they are no jokes' but rather 'innocents.' This observation referred to various incidents in which the lovemaking of the couple had disrupted schedules; officials noted, in particular, Natasha's sexual boasting. One such incident occurred at Valka in the early morning, when refugees had gathered at a designated place prior to continuing their journey. Natasha announced to them all that, because Vladimir 'had made love to her till five a.m.,' they had decided that 'instead of sinking into love's deep sleep they must get up and walk back and forth in the cool morning air until time for their rendezvous with us.' Another such incident soon followed, an International Refugee Organization (IRO) officer remarking 'We lost them again in Nuremberg'; the couple had snuck off on their own. Another refugee eventually discovered them on a street corner, where they were behaving oddly, prompting an IRO officer to quip, 'they are no "darlings" as they are called in Czechish.'[32] Later in the trip, the couple became the object of a practical joke. The young men in the group told 'our Romeo that he would have to shave off that Clark Gabel [sic] moustache he wore because in Canada it was not permitted.' When Vladimir related this news to his wife, she was dismayed, asking the group, 'Couldn't something be done? When he kisses me I feel his moustache,' asking 'must I lose this because of Canada?'

Then disturbing news began to surface about 'serious trouble' on the boat taking the refugees to Canada. The couple was reported to have

engaged in fights and recriminations, shouting obscenities at each other,
exchanging insults and accusations, and annoying the other refugees
and the crew. During one such fight, the husband accused his wife of
being a prostitute and she denounced him as a former mental patient.
The outbursts continued until the ship docked at Halifax, and continued on the train to Toronto, where the other refugees urged the local
IRO staff to keep the couple away from publicity, 'as they were a
disgrace.' Several months after their celebrated arrival, officials noted
that the couple were the only ones in the group who had not yet
'adjusted' well to life in Canada. The husband was unemployed because, as he argued, he could not handle the physically demanding
manual labour that officials kept assigning to him. Furthermore, he was
worried about not being able to afford proper medical attention for his
wife, who suffered from an unidentified serious and recurring illness.
The confidential case records note further instances of the couple's
sexual impropriety in hostels and welfare hotels; evaluations that they
were 'unemployable'; renewed allegations of syphilis, betrayal, wife
abuse (the wife filing at least two family court charges against her
husband); professional diagnoses of mental instability; and threats of
deportation. Evidence such as this, and from similarly complicated
cases, reveals some of the common threads that emerge in studies of
marginal people, including sexual and moral 'transgressors,' whose
lives were far more troubled than can be captured by dichotomies of
'state vs victim' or 'expert vs client.'[33]

The recovery of at least part of this couple's story, however incom-
plete or skewed by the record keepers, is possible because they became
immersed in an immense web of social welfare services, at times initiating these encounters and at other times having them imposed. In particular the couple's refusal to accept without question job placements
and other requirements led Canadian authorities to brand them a 'very
tough problem.' The couple 'flatly refused' to be placed temporarily in
the government's immigration hostel in Ajax, Ontario, because each
feared the other would be 'unfaithful to their marriage vows at the
hostel.' They became clients of a social agency, the New Canadians
Service Association, whose mandate was to assist East European refugees.[34] It was this agency that branded the couple 'unemployables,'
while another social worker admitted her disgust with them in a refer-
ral letter, insisting that they could not be rehabilitated. Another caseworker with the Department of Labour's Special Service Branch declared
that 'these people' had became a 'terrible problem,' not only because

they showed no interest in 'working and maintaining themselves,' but because 'Madame spends money like crazy on lipstick and chewing gum,' while her husband had 'spread the story far and wide' that she had syphilis. Officials discussed the need for psychiatric evaluations of the couple and debated whether to begin deportation proceedings, based not only on the couple's refusal of employment but on their sexual mores as well. Officials were especially concerned that Vladimir had beaten Natasha, though the reports never portrayed her as an innocent victim.

After a year's absence, Vladimir returned to the NCSA, now the International Institute of Metropolitan Toronto, and told the caseworker (herself East European), that 'he felt very lonesome, as his wife had friends, made love to other men etc.' The caseworker was suspicious, however, having heard the allegations of wife abuse; she noted that Vladimir's behaviour resembled paranoia, feelings of persecution, and other signs of mental illness. (This, it should be noted, was an assessment that trained and untrained Canadian observers frequently made of communist refugees, and of refugees from totalitarian regimes more generally.)[35] In a two-hour 'conversation' with Vladimir, who was 'weeping and then laughing alternatively [sic],' the caseworker learned that 'he ... has a complex of people laughing at him – he is afraid to get on streetcars or walk home from work.' Despite having asked him 'what exactly he wanted' from her, she could not get a 'definite answer' until he finally revealed he had been at family court where he had denied his wife's accusations of marital abuse and told 'everyone who would listen' that she was a foul-mouthed liar. The court officials did not convict him for assault, in large part, it appears, because Natasha made for a less than convincing victim. Instead, the court referred him to a Czech social club in Toronto for help with 'socializing,' and it was the club that had referred him to the IIMT. When the IIMT caseworker contacted a Czech social worker associated with the club and the Canadian Czech Association, her response was blunt: report him to the Department of Immigration and Citizenship for deportation as 'a disgrace to everyone.' Instead, the caseworker suggested having a psychiatric evaluation done, which appeared to be the consensus of the agencies involved in the case. Indeed, the IRO officials said they were hesitant to initiate formal deportation proceedings until the couple had had the opportunity to speak in their own language to a medical expert, and had ordered them to undergo an evaluation by a 'Czech'[36] doctor, who determined that they were both 'mentally unbalanced.' He also expressed surprise that they had ever been 'allowed' into Canada. In making this comment, the doctor flagged a sensitive issue that many Canadians did find troubling: the possibility that, by waiving medical screening tests for certain anti-communist refugees fleeing Soviet-bloc countries, the government could grant admission to emotionally troubled, mentally ill or sexually dysfunctional Europeans. In the case of the Czech lovers, several observers found the situation all the more galling because they had been merely happenstance refugees who, as one IRO worker predicted, would likely never be 'self-supporting.'

At this point, the IRC began the formal application for deportation, but almost a year later, the couple was still in Canada. An astonished IRC worker reported that the couple 'seem to have found their bearings.' 'To our considerable surprise,' the report read, Vladimir had found work (a factory job) and was supporting his wife. They were enjoying 'the conveniences of hotel life,' staying at the welfare hotel in Toronto where the IRC had put them up. The extent to which the threat of deportation had influenced this behaviour is debatable, though there is little doubt that it had an effect. What also bears examination is the basis on which officials now declared that the couple was adjusting to Canadian society, namely that of the hegemonic family ideology comprised of the contradictory elements of a companionate and egalitarian relationship together with patriarchal privilege. This ideology was fully capable of asserting family unification, or reunification, over the needs of an abused wife.[37] Though officials were aware of the couple's marital conflicts and Natasha's charges of abuse, they nonetheless chose to applaud the couple's 'progress' and to cease all deportation proceedings, based, it would appear, partly on the periodic reports of the hotel manager where the couple lived. As the officials noted, 'although [the manager] is called in to umpire their marital spats, he seems to have no difficulty in collecting their rents.' Clearly, the threat that the couple might become public charges was greater to the postwar nation than the occasional 'marital spat.'

This reading is confirmed by one remaining item of information in the couple's file, which, like many such files, ends abruptly. The final entry on the husband's IIMT case file, dated at the end of the 1950s, several years after the file was opened, notes that he had spent a good portion of the intervening years in a provincial mental hospital. There is no further information on the wife. Combined with the other items in their file, this meant that the couple could have easily been deported for a number of reasons under Canadian immigration laws.[38] However, it appears that the husband escaped deportation because he became the family breadwinner. This suggests that deportation did not always play a definitive role in containing, or removing, newcomers deemed to be sexual, moral, or mental threats to the remaking of the postwar nation, reminding us that the practical effects of state policies and laws cannot necessarily be predicted in advance. As Mariana Valverde observes, the outcomes 'vary a great deal depending on who is using the tactic for what purpose.'[39] The apparent trade-off that officials were prepared to make, tolerating the occasional 'marital spat' – however violent it might be – in exchange for an employed patriarch who could support his wife, can be seen as one of the ways in which 1950s family ideology could play itself out in local settings and on the bodies – literally – of refugee women. While none of the caseworkers explicitly suggested that Natasha's behaviour required a physical response, there was tacit acceptance of this possibility in the context of resolving what was clearly the more important issue of Vladimir's predicament.

Sex and Security: Dangerous Women – or Damaged?

Although the discussion of the Czech freedom-train lovers treated them as a couple, it also highlighted some important gender differences that emerged both in public and confidential discourses concerning refugees and immigrants suspected of having psychological or emotional problems congruent with then current themes of sexual deviance. The first of these differences is the relative silence of public sources on issues of sexuality with reference to women. As feminist scholarship has demonstrated, historians interested in discourses of female sexuality need to turn to private sources or confidential records, such as family court-ordered client assessments and social agency case files.[40] A second difference is that public discourses were inflected along gender lines. When public attention was focused on newcomer men in connection with marital and/or sexual issues, it usually dealt with troubling themes, including, most dramatically, profiles of violent men.[41] In contrast, the public record, particularly that of the mainstream media, on newcomer women and marital, domestic, and sexuality issues, was more likely to highlight women as victims (abused wives, poor widows, rape victims, etc.). Suicides and suicide attempts could receive front-page coverage, at least in Toronto dailies such as the *Star* which, on 2 May 1949 ran a typical headline, 'Hysterical D.P. Girl on Forty-Foot Perch Rescued by Firemen.' The ensuing story covered the suicide attempt in the heart of Toronto's business centre of a 22-year-old Jewish survivor.[42]

Public sympathy could be paid to immigrant and refugee men who suffered from severe depression or other forms of psychological stress seen to have its origin in the devastation and loss caused by the war, or who were suffering from what scholars have called the 'crisis of masculinity'[43] engendered by their failure to adequately fill the role of family breadwinner. The group of men who gained the greatest amount of public and professional sympathy in these years, however, were the professional East European refugees – doctors, academics, architects, artists, musicians – who had become stateless refugees performing menial jobs, and in some cases, dependent on their wives' wages.[44] There was also public sympathy for single European men, immigrant or refugee, who found themselves isolated and alone, and shunned by the women they approached, including Canadian women whom they encountered at dances and other social programs organized by reception activists and social agencies such as the International Institute. That some experts considered these men more likely than others to develop sexual hang-ups and possibly lash out violently against women made all the more urgent the pleas that Canadians extend a friendly hand to the newcomers. Also recipients of considerable public sympathy were men who found their lives damaged by sudden death, or who themselves turned to suicide as a way out of personal anguish.[45]

Public coverage of women as victims of patriarchal European men should not elide the fact that many such women endured and remade their lives. The media of these years did cover defiant women. And related sources, such as the advice columns published in daily newspapers, revealed angry and mistreated women who were perfectly willing to make their complaints public, as well as some who fought back against abusive partners through the legal system. One case covered by the media involved two young German immigrant women who laid a charge of theft and assault causing bodily harm against Metro Toronto police detectives who, along with the former lover of one of the women, had entered their apartment without a search warrant. The women had returned to their apartment to find the men removing a TV set that the boyfriend had given them. Following the men's refusal to leave, the women lunged at them and, according to courtroom testimony, 'in [the] scuffle that ensued the pair [of women] charged that they were roughly handled by the detectives ... [and] also given blows and kicks by a third man [the ex-boyfriend].' During their day in court, the women complained about having been locked up in a 'filthy and smelly' jail for the night, and explained that the boyfriend had been dropped because he had been abusive, both physically and verbally, to his girlfriend. The women added that this experience had shattered their image of Canada, where such things were not supposed to happen.[46]

The stories arising from secret or confidential contexts offer some of the most compelling, if also troubling, narratives of female sexuality and sexual discourses in the Cold War.[47] One of the cases to emerge from RCMP files investigating the real or suspected sexual and illegal activities of women from Soviet bloc countries occurred in the 1950s, and involved an Estonian DP, Tiina, whom Immigration Branch officials suspected of being a femme fatale who had convinced a compatriot living in England, and employed as a merchant sailor, to jump ship and enter Canada illegally, so as to join her.[48] As with other cases of suspected illegalities around immigration, the RCMP investigation of Tiina occurred at the request of the Chief of Operations in the Immigration Branch, and, as with most of the cases in my sample, they were headed by the same Special Investigator, L.V. Turner. Turner had previously investigated Tiina on suspicion of sheltering illegally a foreign seaman deserter, an Estonian named Leopold who had resettled in England. Several pieces of evidence had triggered the investigation: the master of Leopold's ship reported him missing to the Montreal Port Authorities when the sailor did not return to work after a short stay there. Later a letter was discovered in Leopold's possession from a Mrs Tiina T. of Toronto, urging Leopold to jump ship and join her. The letter also stated that an Estonian minister in Toronto who had helped other compatriots to desert ship and disappear into Canada – and had even christened their children some years later – would extend the same help to Leopold.

As the following excerpts suggest, Tiina's letter was extremely suggestive on several levels; written to 'Dear Leo,' the letter was part of an ongoing correspondence between the couple. Tiina sounds both self-deprecating and anxious, willing to break the law to bring her lover into Canada. Evidently, Leopold had been considering a plan whereby he simply ask his captain for permission to go ashore, head to the local immigration office in Montreal, tell them he wished refugee status, and, with the help of an Estonian pastor in Montreal, simply wait until the pastor could free him. Tiina countered emphatically that she had learned from her Toronto pastor that without proof of marriage to a Canadian or landed immigrant, Leopold would be sent back immediately. She also tried to convince Leopold not to trust the Montreal pastor, telling him that she had once been in the same refugee camp with that pastor and 'I had heard only bad talk about him, he is selfish, takes bribes ... makes a lot of words.' Moreover, she 'had the feeling' that he might be 'pink or red,' and told the following story: 'In the [refugee] camp, he wouldn't come to bury someone without receiving coffee etc. For a good pay he was willing to do anything. If someone would now give him a bribe, wouldn't he also now be willing to do anything? Do you know it for sure that he has freed people? Maybe it is only a rumour?' It was thus Tiina's suggestion that they follow the advice of her Toronto pastor, whom she described as a 'wonderful' man who 'has helped all the Estonians who have knocked at his door,' adding that while she was 'not going very much to church,' he had nonetheless treated her 'as if he was my own father, as well as everybody else['s].' She also used the pastor to justify the illegalities in which she was involving her lover, saying that the minister had told her that while he agreed with God's laws, he felt differently about man-made laws that created false 'border lines' and kept loved ones apart. He claimed that he had already helped at least ten seamen 'who disappeared by skipping the ship to reach the shore, and later on married, bought houses, and had their children.' It was the only way, Tiina insisted; it would entail no trouble with police, and then they could 'live a whole life in peace.'

Not surprisingly, Turner and the RCMP and Immigration officers began their investigation with the Toronto pastor, but soon concluded that he had not been involved. The focus of the investigation then shifted to Tiina, who revealed in a lengthy interrogation that she had lied about the Toronto pastor in order to encourage Leopold to join her. But this lie hardly proved that she was a femme fatale; in fact, she was a lonely, divorced, refugee woman who was trying to rekindle a childhood friendship.[49] Other women suspected of sexual indiscretions and illegalities, including prostitution, emerge in the RCMP investigations conducted for the Immigration department, and, like the case described in detail here, they are less about sexual 'deviance' than about the effects separation, first by war and then by immigration, had on individuals. Cold War fears, the desire of impoverished peoples to emigrate, and difficulties of repatriation to Soviet-controlled homelands all played their role in the uncertain period following the war. These cases offer a necessary backdrop for our attempts to understand the myriad ways in which refugees, immigrants, and their hosts loved, hated, and feared in early Cold War Canada.

Notes

1 Archives of Ontario (AO), International Institute of Metropolitan Toronto Confidential Case Files. To insure anonymity, I identify this case as belonging to a database of 1,105 IIMT case files organized according to my own system for the period 1952–65. See also note 31.

2 Among the pertinent literature are the following: Reg Whitaker and Gary Marcuse, *Cold War Canada: The Making of a National Insecurity State, 1945–1957* (Toronto: U of Toronto P, 1994); Gary Kinsman, *The Regulation of Desire: Homo and Hetero Sexualities* (Montreal: Black Rose, 1996; first published in 1987 as *The Regulation of Desire: Sexuality in Canada*), chs. 6–8; Mary Louise Adams, *The Trouble with Normal: Postwar Youth and the Making of Heterosexuality* (Toronto: U of Toronto P, 1998); Mona Gleason, *Normalizing the Ideal: Psychology, Schooling and the Family in Postwar Canada* (Toronto: U of Toronto P, 2000); Gary Kinsman and Patrizia Gentile (with Heidi McDonell and Mary Mahood-Greer), '"In the Interests of the State": The Anti-Gay, Anti-Lesbian National Security Campaign in Canada,' preliminary research report (Laurentian University, April 1998); Kinsman et al., eds., *Whose National Security? Canadian State Surveillance and the Creation of Enemies* (Toronto: Between the Lines, 2000); Deborah Van Seters, 'The Munsinger Affair: Images of Espionage and Security in 1960s Canada,' *Intelligence and National Security* 13.2 (1998): 71–84; Valerie Korinek, *Roughing It in Suburbia: Reading* Chatelaine *in the Fifties and Sixties* (Toronto: U of Toronto P, 2000). On the United States, see, for example, Jennifer Terry, *An American Obsession: Science, Medicine and Homosexuality in Modern Society* (Chicago: U of Chicago P, 1999), especially its discussion of 'treasonous' lesbianism; Elaine Tyler May, *Homeward Bound: American Families in the Cold War Era* (New York: Basic Books, 1988); Joanne Meyerowitz, ed., *Not June Cleaver: Women and Gender in Postwar America, 1945–1960* (Philadelphia: Temple UP, 1994).

3 The disease metaphor was closely associated with U.S. policy-makers such as George Kennan and FBI Director J. Edgar Hoover and entered into popular culture. Some of the works treating this discourse include Geoffrey Smith, 'National Security and Personal Isolation: Sex, Gender, and Disease in the Cold War United States,' *International History Review* 14.2 (1992): 307–35; Kinsman and Gentile, '"In the Interests of the State"'; Louis Hyman, 'Dirty Communists,' unpublished manuscript presented to Toronto Labour Studies Group, Spring 2000; Elaine Schrecker, *Many Are the Crimes: McCarthyism in America* (Boston: Little, Brown, 1998); Paul A. Chilton, *Security Metaphors: Cold War Discourse from 'Containment' to 'Common*

European Home' (New York: Peter Lang, 1996). I am especially grateful
to Geoffrey Smith for sharing his published and unpublished research
with me.

4 Scholars of sexuality, sex crimes, and juvenile delinquency who argue that
   the early Cold War decades witnessed a moral panic draw on a number of
   key works. Stanley Cohen, in *Folk Devils and Moral Panics: The Creation of
   the Mods and Rockers* (London: MacGibbon and Kee, 1972), defines moral
   panic as 'a condition, episode, person or group of persons' who 'become
   defined as a threat to societal values and interests; its nature is presented
   in a stylized and stereotyped fashion by the mass media; the moral barri-
   cades are manned by editors, bishops, and politicians, and other right-
   thinking people; socially accredited experts pronounce their diagnoses
   and solutions; ways of coping are evolved, or (more often) resorted to; the
   condition then disappears, submerges or deteriorates' (9). At times, the
   panic 'passes over and is forgotten' whereas at other times 'it has more
   serious and long-lasting repercussions, and might produce ... changes ... in
   legal and social policy or even in the way the society conceives itself' (9).
   Policing the Crisis: Mugging, the State, and Law and Order, ed. Stuart Hall et
   al. (London: Macmillan, 1978), argues that when official reaction to certain
   persons or events is out of proportion to the actual threat posed we are
   witnessing a moral panic. Jeffrey Weeks, in *Sex, Politics and Society: The
   Regulation of Sexuality since 1800* (London: Longman, 1981), identifies
   certain historical moments when social anxieties (often involving a sexual
   element) are displaced onto 'folk devils' who are then blamed for moral
   and social decay generally. The crucial role of 'media excess' in such
   panics is studied by Simon Watney in *Policing Desire: Pornography, AIDS,
   and the Media* (Minneapolis: U of Minnesota P, 1989). See also Jacques
   Donzelot, *The Policing of Families,* trans. Robert Hurley (New York: Pantheon, 1979). Judith Walkowitz provides a nineteenth-century example of
   moral panic in *City of Dreadful Delight: Narratives of Sexual Danger in Late-
   Victorian London* (Chicago: U of Chicago P, 1992). As Kinsman cautions in
   The Regulation of Desire: Homo and Hetero Sexualities, it is important to
   avoid using moral panic as 'an explanation of a social process.' Instead,
   the term should be employed to point 'towards an investigation of social
   relations,' such as those among the media, the police, the courts, citizens'
   groups, professional experts, and state agencies, which 'combine in different ways in different "panics."'

5 Kinsman, *Regulation of Desire: Homo and Hetero Sexualities,* ch. 8 and passim.

6 Smith, 'National Security and Personal Isolation,' *International History
   Review* 14.2 (1992): 307–35.

7 See, in this regard, Gary Kinsman's chapter in the present volume.

8 In addition to the material cited in note 2, see Regina Kunzel, *Fallen Women, Problem Girls: Unmarried Mothers and the Professionalization of Social Work, 1890–1945* (New Haven: Yale UP, 1993), and her 'Pulp Fictions and Problem Girls: Reading and Rewriting Single Pregnancy in the Postwar United States,' *American Historical Review* 100.5 (1995): 1465–88; Becki L. Ross, 'Destaining the Delinquent Body: Regulatory Practices at Toronto's Street Haven, 1965–69,' *Journal of the History of Sexuality* 7.4 (1997): 561–95; Wini Breines, *Young, White and Miserable: Growing Up Female in the Fifties* (Boston: Beacon Books, 1992); Mary Louise Adams, *The Trouble with Normal: Postwar Youth and the Making of Heterosexuality* (Toronto: U of Toronto P, 1998); the essays by Kinsman and Iacovetta in Kinsman et al., eds., *Whose National Security?*; and the essays in the present volume by Cavell, Kinsman, Adams, Korinek, Waugh, and Martin.

9 On the term 'national insecurity state' see H.W. Brands, 'The Age of Vulnerability: Eisenhower and the National Insecurity State,' *American Historical Review* 94.4 (1989): 963–89, and Smith, 'National Security and Personal Isolation,' *International History Review* 14.2 (1992): 307–35. For the Canadian context see Wesley Wark, 'Security Intelligence in Canada, 1864–1945: The History of the National Insecurity State,' in Keith Neilson and B.J.C. McKercher eds., *Go Spy the Land: Military Intelligence in History* (Westport, CT: 1992); Louis Hyman, 'Dirty Communists'; Whitaker and Marcuse, *CWC*; and the essays in Kinsman et al., eds., *Whose National Security?*

10 See Gary Kinsman, '"Character Weaknesses" and "Fruit Machines": Towards an Analysis of the Anti-Homosexual Security Campaign in the Canadian Civil Service,' *Labour / Le Travail* 35 (1995): 133–61; David Kimmel and Daniel J. Robinson, 'The Queer Career of Homosexual Security Vetting in Cold War Canada,' *Canadian Historical Review* 75.3 (1994): 319–45. For the flipside to such concerns see Patrizia Gentile, '"Government Girls" and "Ottawa Men": Cold War Management of Gender Relations in the Civil Service,' in Kinsman et al., eds., *Whose National Security?*, 131–42.

11 I borrow the term 'technique' from Foucault. See, for example, his essay 'Technologies of the Self,' in *Technologies of the Self: A Seminar with Michel Foucault*, ed. Luther H. Martin, Huck Gutman, and Patrick Hutton (Amherst: U of Massachusetts P, 1988), 16–49.

12 My forthcoming book, provisionally titled *Making New Citizens in Cold War Canada*, devotes considerable space to the complex of 'rehabilitating' supposedly 'damaged' newcomer women.

13 For some preliminary efforts to address these and related questions see

Iacovetta, 'The Sexual Politics of Moral Citizenship and Containing Dangerous Foreign Men in Cold War Canada, 1950s-1960s,' *Histoire Sociale / Social History* 33.66 (2000): 361–89; Elise Chenier, 'Seeing Red: Immigrant Women and Sexual Danger in Toronto's Postwar Daily Newspapers,' in *Atlantis* (Special Issue: 'Whose Canada Is It?,' ed. Iacovetta and Tania Das Gupta) 24.2 (2000): 51–60. For an earlier period, see Mariana Valverde, *The Age of Light, Soap, and Water: Moral Reform in English Canada* (Toronto: U of Toronto P, 1993). For a contemporary angle, see Fred Bosworth's 'What's Behind the Immigration Wrangle?' in *Maclean's* 68 (14 May 1955). Bromley L. Armstrong recalls that immigration agents at Malton Airport, Toronto, gave medical tests to arriving Caribbean women and grilled them about their sex lives; see Armstrong and Sheldon Taylor, *Bromley: Tireless Champion for Just Causes* (Pickering, ON.: Vitabu Publications, 2000): 163–4. For more recent attacks against Caribbean women as promiscuous single mothers and Somalian refugee women as welfare cheats, see Cynthia Wright, 'Nowhere at Home: Gender, Race and the Making of Anti-Immigrant Discourse in Canada,' *Atlantis* 24.2 (2000): 38–48.

14 In examining the form, content, and style of the mainstream media's coverage of Cold War escape narratives, I do not wish to replicate their flippant tone or indulge in postmodernly ironic readings of these texts, which would do a disservice to the people whose lives were damaged, endangered, or eliminated by Stalin's ruthless policies. However, given current debates over materialist versus postmodern approaches to the writing of history, especially in the context of gendered processes and features (debates which resurfaced at the initial reception of the present book in manuscript form), it is important here that I rehearse the central historiographical issues. As I have argued in 'Gossip, Contest and Power in the Making of Suburban Bad Girls: Toronto, 1945–60,' *Canadian Historical Review* 80.4 (1999): 585–625, Canadian feminist scholars of differing political and intellectual paradigms have developed gendered approaches that cannot be collapsed into a single, postmodern pigeonhole. Thus, to critique all work that examines gendered processes as 'postmodern' denies the theoretical nuances that differentiate approaches within the broader category of feminist analysis, within which I include my own socialist-feminist work. It is also necessary to note that a postmodern sensibility is evident in work that has not been written from a feminist position. For a sampling of this debate as it has occurred in Canada, see Bryan Palmer, 'Historiographical Hassles: Class and Gender, Evidence and Interpretation,' *Histoire Sociale / Social History* 33.65 (2000): 105–44, and his 'Class and the Writing of History: Beyond B.C.,' *B.C. Studies* 111 (1996): 76–84; Joan

Sangster, 'Women and Work: Assessing Canadian Women's History at the Millennium,' *Atlantis* 25.1 (2000): 51–62, and her 'Feminism and the Making of Working Class History: Exploring the Past, Present and Future,' *Labour / Le Travail* 46 (2000): 127–65; Lynne Marks, 'Heroes and Hallelujahs: Labour History and the Social History of Religion: A Response to Bryan Palmer,' *Histoire Sociale / Social History* 33.65 (2000): 169–86; and Mariana Valverde, 'Some Remarks on the Rise and Fall of Discourse Theory,' *Histoire Sociale / Social History* 33.65 (2000): 59–77. On postmodernity and materiality in the broader cultural sphere in Canada, see Richard Cavell, 'Material *Querelle*: The Case of Frye and McLuhan,' *Essays on Canadian Writing* 68 (2000): 238–61.

15 Reg Whitaker, *Double Standard: The Secret History of Canadian Immigration* (Toronto: Lester and Orpen Dennys, 1987), 78–9. As Whitaker notes, about 25,000 Estonians had gone to Sweden during the war, and their homeland, occupied by Soviet troops, had been formally 'incorporated' into the USSR in 1945. Viewing the Estonians as their citizens, the Soviets demanded their repatriation, but thousands of Estonians refused to go. Some of them, fearing Soviet advances into Scandinavia, risked crossing the Atlantic in small, overcrowded boats. Canadian immigration officials fretted about the lack of proper procedures for handling these refugees (though they quickly developed some), and feared a mass influx of them into the country. The crisis proved to be short-lived, however, because, as Whitaker argues, Estonians were well-treated in Sweden and because fears of Soviet advances into Scandinavia declined.

16 *Toronto Star*, 17 January 1948. The group eventually settled in Kitchener, Ontario, among Lutheran co-religionists.

17 'Outwitted Soviet Police, Waded Mountain Snows, Czech Girl in Winnipeg,' *Toronto Star* 23 September 1950. This story appeared on the front page and had a large photo of Konkova wearing make-up and a fashionable scarf.

18 The estimates of Stalin's victims vary considerably; for example, famine victims in the 1930s are estimated to have been from 3 to 7 million. With reference to the Gulag, Galina Mikhailovna Ivanova estimates that its population (in the time frame under scrutiny here) had reached 2.8 million by the summer of 1950. Drawing on recently opened Soviet archives, which suggest that the camp populations grew even larger after the war, Galina suggests that, from the 1930s to the 1950s, circa 20 million Soviet citizens moved through the camps of the Gulag. About one-third of the inmates were political prisoners and 10 to 15 per cent criminal recidivists, while millions of others were subjected to forced labour and other punish-

ments. She is reluctant to provide a figure for deaths in the camps and colonies except for the war years, when she argues that the evidence indicates that more than 2 million people perished in the camps during the 1941–4 period. During the same period, about 1 million prisoners were released to fight on the front, while another 5 million were conscripted into the wartime industrial labour camps. See Ivanova, *Labour Camp Socialism: The Gulag in the Soviet Totalitarian System*, ed. Donald J. Raleigh, trans. Carol Flath (Armonk, NY: M.E. Sharpe, 2000). See also J. Arch Getty, Gabor T. Rittersporn, and Viktory N. Zemskov, 'Victims of the Soviet Penal System in the Pre-War Years: A First Approach on the Basis of Archival Evidence,' *American Historical Review* 98.4 (1993): 1017–50. I am grateful to my University of Toronto colleague Lynne Viola, a Soviet historian, who generously fielded my questions and directed me to several sources, including those cited above, which can be read against Alexander Solzhenitsyn's *The Gulag Archipelago, 1918–1956*, trans. Thomas P. Whitney (London: Collins / Fontana, 1973). See also Helene Celmins, *Women in Soviet Prisons* (New York: Paragon, 1985); part 3 of this book is relevant to East European immigration and the making of Cold War culture. For specific examples of how the topic was discussed within the Canadian context, see the publications and speeches of the Latvian Information Centre (Toronto), the Imperial Order Daughters of the Empire, and La Ligue Anti-Communiste Canadienne, all in the National Archives of Canada. For example, the NA RG 26 vol. 12 file on the Ligue includes publications titled 'Communist Tactics' and 'Alert to Organizations – Some Meetings of International Front Organizations – A New Communist Front Organization.' See as well discussions of speeches by Canadian Citizenship Branch officials such as Dr Vladimir Kaye, its Chief Liaison Officer, in Iacovetta, 'Making Model Citizens,' in Kinsman et al., *Whose National Security?* 154–67.

19 Robert L. Griswold, '"Russian Blonde in Space": Americans View the Soviet Woman in the Early Cold War' (unpublished ms). My thanks to the author for allowing me to quote from his paper; I provide a detailed discussion of the Canadian production of this discourse in my forthcoming book.

20 Pat Best, 'Chose to Flee from Red Poland Rather Than Perform before Stalin,' *Ottawa Citizen*, 14 September 1957.

21 A related irony is suggested by a former Catholic boy scout who recalled that in the 1950s his group met in the local Catholic church in Rochester, New York, where they regularly prayed for the destruction of communism. My thanks to a colleague at the University of Manitoba for sharing

this anecdote during the discussion following my lecture 'Containing Threats to Democracy: Decency, Sexuality, Morality and the Gender Politics of Citizenship in Post-War Canada' (University College Lecture Series; 26 October 2000).

22 'Report U.S. Officials Relenting to Let Lovers on Boat Meet Briefly Ashore,' Special to *Star*, p. 1; Robert Taylor, 'Canada Can Do Nothing to Unite Niagara Lovers,' p.1; 'Spend Yule by Fire, Is Hope of Lovers on Maid of Mist,' Special to *Star*, p. 1, *Toronto Star*, 1 October 1949. On tales of romance in connection with the history of Niagara Falls see Karen Dubinsky's excellent *The Second Greatest Disappointment: Honeymooning at Niagara Falls* (Toronto: U of Toronto P, 2000).

23 These details are reported in 'Spend Yule by Fire'; 'Report U.S. Relenting'; and Taylor, 'Canada Can Do Nothing.'

24 These details surface in later reports; see Dorothy Howarth, 'Maid of Mist Lovers Conquer Border Ban,' *Toronto Telegram*, 22 September 1950, front page, and also her 'Lovers Conquer Barrier,' same page.

25 At this time, she was described as a nursing student; later, when the couple was reunited in Canada, she was described as having been an economics major at Prague and having earned her masters degree in economics at UNC.

26 'Report U.S. Relenting'; Taylor, 'Canada Can Do Nothing.'

27 Denny remarked: 'We're rubbing elbows with three dozen others – many of them happy honeymooners,' and Kitty added, 'If only we were allowed to be together, to walk in the lovely parks, to be alone instead of being on this little deck.' Quoted in 'Spend Yule by Fire.'

28 The happy ending of this romance was heightened, perhaps, by the stories being reported alongside it about East bloc tensions, especially between Stalin and Tito. See *Toronto Star*, 1 October 1949.

29 Dorothy Howarth, 'Maid of Mist Lovers Conquer Border Ban, Reunited in Toronto,' *Toronto Telegram*, 22 September 1950, front page; and 'Lovers Conquer Barrier' (with photo of couple), p. 2. At the time of the reunion, Dennis had applied for Canadian citizenship and had his temporary papers; he had completed his one-year labour contract with the Canadian government.

30 *Toronto Star*, 22 June 1959; the case is also recorded in International Institute of Metropolitan Toronto (IIMT) case files.

31 The newspaper clippings and private correspondence between officials with the international refugee groups and Canadian social workers relevant to this case are contained in AO, IIMT Confidential Case Files. To protect identities I have not divulged full or real names of clients; I

have also omitted or slightly modified biographical details. For example, here I use the generic term 'clerk' to give a general indication of the man's occupation. The case is taken from my database of 1,105 IIMT confidential case files. To ensure anonymity, I do not provide precise citation of individual files. In addition to the database, which contains information on each client (age, nationality, gender, date of arrival, etc.), overall case-file statistics (by nationality, years in Canada, gender, etc.), and other features (the caseload of specific case workers, information on domestic violence, unemployment, etc.), there are detailed notes on a sampling of 315 files, of which this case is one. I am deeply indebted to Stephen Heathorn for creating the IIMT database, and to Jane Thompson for her assistance.

32 The letter relative to this point reads: '[the man] was (hear this: it's true) holding his hands out in front of him and around them was [wound] wool [yarn], and she was winding up what the Germans call a dumpling, but we call a ball. Do you like that?' IIMT, S248.

33 On this point, the relevant literature is extensive; see, for example, Linda Gordon, *Heroes of Their Own Lives: The Politics and History of Family Violence, Boston 1880–1960* (New York: Viking, 1988); Franca Iacovetta and Mariana Valverde, eds., *Gender Conflicts: New Essays in Women's History* (Toronto: U of Toronto P, 1992); Mary E. Odem, *Delinquent Daughters: Protecting and Policing Adolescent Female Sexuality in the United States, 1885–1920* (Chapel Hill: U North Carolina P, 1995); Molly Ladd-Taylor and Lauri Umanski, eds., *'Bad' Mothers: The Politics of Blame in Twentieth Century America* (New York: New York UP, 1998); Kunzel, *Fallen Women, Problem Girls*; Iacovetta and Wendy Mitchinson, eds., *On the Case: Explorations in Social History* (Toronto: U of Toronto P, 1998); Robert A. Campbell, *Sit Down and Drink Your Beer* (Toronto: U of Toronto P, 2002); and Ladd-Taylor's paper 'Sterilizing the Feeble-Minded in Inter-War Minnesota,' presented to the American Studies Conference, Montreal, 1999.

34 In 1956, the mandate of the New Canadians Service Association expanded to include all non-English speaking newcomers, and the name was changed to the International Institute of Metropolitan Toronto, partly to reflect the organization's new affiliation with the U.S.-based international institutes. The IIMT became the sole Canadian member of the U.S. institutes, whose origins went back to the early YWCA movement. See the finding aid of the IIMT, AO.

35 These assessments of mental illness are more fully discussed in my forthcoming book.

36 It is unclear if this doctor was a refugee or a Canadian.

37 A preliminary exploration of this theme can be found in my 'Making New Canadians,' in Iacovetta and Valverde, *Gender Conflicts*.
38 Grounds for deportation were many (becoming a public charge; mental illness, criminal records, and so on), and the relevant clauses gave enormous discretionary powers to immigration officials; for example, the term 'unsuitability' could be used to reject prospective immigrants on racial, sexual, moral, political, and even 'climate' (i.e., racialist) grounds. The Canadian government argued that they showed leniency in deportation cases, which is partly true, but the threat of deportation nevertheless instilled fear in many newcomers.
39 Mariana Valverde, 'Symbolic Indians: Domestic Violence and the Ontario Liquor Board's "Indian List," 1950–1990,' paper presented to the Berkshire Conference on the History of Women, University of Connecticut, June 2002. For further illustrations see Valverde, ed., *Radically Rethinking Regulation: Workshop Report* (Toronto: Centre of Criminology, U of Toronto, 1994), and Iacovetta and Mitchinson, eds., *On the Case.*
40 See Linda Gordon's influential *Heroes of Their Own Lives*, and Iacovetta and Mitchinson, eds., *On the Case.*
41 For a detailed discussion see Iacovetta, 'Sexual Politics of Moral Citizenship.' Examples of the *Toronto Star*'s coverage of stories about European-born men accused of violence, including murder, against women and/or children, include 'Hunt All Night in Vain for Shotgun Terrorist, May Call Army to Aid,' 17 September 1949 (Italian man who allegedly beat his wife and daughter and held police at bay in Alliston, Ontario); 'Fires 100 Shots at Police, Flees Tear-Gas Filled Shack with Bride,' 7 January 1956 (Russian railway worker and alleged wife-abuser in northern Ontario); 'Immigrant Hangs Jan. 25 for Strangling of Wife,' 6 November 1954 (Italian man in St Cath-arines, Ontario, who killed his newly arrived wife, whom he suspected of adultery); 'Son Taken from School, Slain, Guard House of Mother,' 18 Oc-tober 1958 (Hungarian stepfather's alleged murder of an eight-year-old boy in Simcoe, Ontario). With the invaluable assistance of Cheryl Smith, I have compiled a sample of hundreds of articles and columns on newcomers and related issues (such as family, women, sexuality, youth, Cold War) in the *Star* and its supplements for the period 1945–65.
42 See Chenier, 'Seeing Red'; Iacovetta, 'Sexual Politics of Moral Citizenship'; and, for a contemporary account, Sidney Katz, 'How Mental Health Is Attacking Our Immigrants' *Maclean's* (4 January 1958). Public discourse, however, could also impose a form of censorship. The 'D.P. Strangler Case' concerned the murder in Toronto of two refugee women, a Ukrainian and a Russian, in 1954; it spawned several Cold War conspiracy plots, fuelled

postwar anxieties about the supposed rise in the number of 'criminal sexual psychopaths,' and produced acute embarrassment within ethnic communities, especially among East European men, who offered their help in trying to solve the case. Yet, once the police determined the identity of the strangler – a former mental patient of East European origin diagnosed as unfit to stand trial – both they and the Liberal government divulged nothing to the public, in the interest of preventing the further spread of fear about dangerous foreign men.

43 See the introduction to this volume and the chapter by Waugh.

44 For numerous contemporary examples see the files of the New Canadians Service Association, precursor to the IIMT, which had been created to help precisely these professional refugees. AO, IIMT.

45 Note, for example, the considerable media coverage and fundraising devoted to Trillo, the Italian immigrant father whose wife had committed suicide while in a holding cell on minor shoplifting charges. See Iacovetta, *Such Hardworking People: Italian Immigrants in Postwar Toronto* (Toronto: U of Toronto P, 1992).

46 'Battle Over TV Set,' the *Toronto Star* 11 April 1959. The article is accompanied by a photo showing two attractive women; above it the caption reads 'Josephine Siek and Rena Brewers Say They Were Man-Handled'; below it the caption states 'Women Charge Police Had No Entry Warrant.'

47 Tiina's case presages, in its sexual politics, Canada's most famous sex and security scandal of the period – the Gerda Munsinger case of the 1960s. The scandal was triggered by the public revelation that two federal cabinet ministers may have had sexual relations with Munsinger, a German-born immigrant who worked as a nightclub hostess and might have been a call-girl and Soviet spy. In a recent feminist analysis, Deborah Van Seters argues that the trial and the public opinion surveyed during its course indicate that there were at least three distinct positions held on the case: that of the politicians 'caught in the act,' who sought to portray Munsinger as a cultured and refined lady who had never been more than an engaging social acquaintance; that of the RCMP, determined to see communists and dangerous infiltrators under every bed, and who insisted Munsinger was a spy; and that of public opinion, which found the trial distasteful, rejected the RCMP's conspiracy theories, and generally wished to protect the private lives of leading political figures. See Deborah Van Seters, 'The Munsinger Affair: Images of Espionage and Security in 1960s Canada,' *Intelligence and National Security* 13.2 (1998): 71–84. For more conventional accounts see J.L. Granatstein, *Canada 1957–1967: The Years of Uncertainty and Innovation* (Toronto: McClelland and Stewart, 1986), and his book,

co-authored with David Stafford, *Spy Wars: Espionage and Canada from Gouzenko to Glasnost* (Toronto: Key Porter, 1990). My forthcoming book examines other possible female spies, as well as the two women convicted in Canada's infamous spy trials, Emma Woiken and Kathleen Willsher.

48 This was by no means a unique case; discussions and investigations of foreign sailors jumping ship on the promise of marriage to young immigrant women came up frequently in the Operations Division of the Immigration Branch. The Italians, for instance, were suspected of having played this illegal game on more than one occasion, running an apparent scam in which women agreed to be claimed as fiancées and to sign their names to fake marriage certificates. See NA, DCI, RG26, vol. 85, file 1-37-8, pt. 1 (Ottawa, 23 November 1953).

49 NA, DIC, RG 26, vol. 85, file 1-37-8, pt. 1, 'Report of Investigation, Administrative Branch of DIC, Re: Alleged Sheltering of Seamen Deserters – Toronto, Ontario.' SI Reporting officer Turner, investigation at Toronto on 10 and 11 November 1953, assisted by Constable A. Skagfeld, RCMP 'O' Division, Toronto. The file contains Tiina's letter.

4

The Canadian Cold War on Queers: Sexual Regulation and Resistance

GARY KINSMAN

We even knew occasionally that there was somebody in some police force or some investigator who would be sitting in a bar ... And you would see someone with a ... newspaper held right up and if you ... looked real closely you could find him holding behind the newspaper a camera and these people were photographing everyone in the bar. (12 May 1994)[1]

David is speaking in an interview about his experiences of police surveillance in the basement tavern at the Lord Elgin Hotel around 1964, which was by then one of the major gathering places for gay men in Ottawa. This surveillance was one way that the RCMP collected information on homosexuals during the Cold War against 'queers.' What is most remarkable, however, is how David described the response of the men in the bar to this surveillance:

We always knew that when you saw someone with a newspaper held up in front of their face ... that somebody would take out something like a wallet and do this sort of thing [like snapping a photo] and then of course everyone would then point over to the person you see and of course I'm sure that the person hiding behind the newspaper knew that he had been found out. But that was the thing. You would take out a wallet or a package of matches or something like that ... it was always sort of a joke. You would see somebody ... and you would catch everyone's eye and you would always go like this [snapping a photo]. And everyone knew watch out for this guy. (12 May 1994)

Rather than diving under the tables, these men acted to turn the tables on the undercover agents.

David is among more than thirty-five gay men and lesbians whom Patrizia Gentile and I have interviewed about their experiences with the national security regime.[2] David's involvement in the security campaigns began when a friend gave the RCMP his name during a park sweep of one of the cruising (or meeting) areas for men interested in sex with men in Ottawa. The RCMP had jurisdiction over the parks in the capital, and these sweeps were fairly common. According to David, the RCMP was far more interested in getting the names of homosexuals than in arresting people for 'criminal' activities, and would threaten to lay 'criminal' charges against the men they rounded up unless they gave the names of other homosexuals. (At this time all homosexual acts were criminalized in Canada; a partial decriminalization took place only in 1969.) David was interrogated and followed by the RCMP and his home was searched, but he refused to cooperate. He was one of the more than 9,000 'suspected,' 'alleged,' and 'confirmed' homosexuals that the RCMP investigated in the 1960s.[3]

David's account indicates the extent of national security surveillance in the 1960s, as well as the awareness concerning this security campaign in the gay networks in which he participated. The resistance of gay men to this police surveillance has been confirmed in a number of our other research interviews, as well as in RCMP documents themselves that I discuss later in this chapter.[4] These men were thus not simply victims of the national security war against queers; they also tried to identify and isolate the spies. They exerted their own agency[5] and resistance in a creative fashion within major social constraints. The social and historical conditions that made such resistance possible emerge from David's story, which provides us with a sense of the social standpoints taken up by gay men and lesbians who were directly affected by the security campaigns. A major advantage of this standpoint is that it allows us to pursue Cold War issues from a position outside the confines of national security discourse and ideology. This standpoint is crucial to our investigation because 'national security' is an ideological practice or code that occludes the social practices that actually bring it into being.[6] This stance allows us to disrupt and decentre the master-narrative of heterosexual Cold War Canadian history by placing the social experiences and resistances of 'queers' at the centre of our analysis.[7] I use 'queer'[8] to reclaim a term of abuse and stigmatization in order to turn it back against our oppressors. I also use it as a term that is broader than 'lesbian and gay' in that it can include experiences of non-normalized consensual sexual and gendered practices that would not usually be included under 'lesbian and gay.' Finally, the term 'queer' helps to construct a place from which to challenge heterosexual hegemony and the dichotomous notion of gender that is hegemonic in society.[9]

Queer History: Sociology from Below

There are three main theories/methods[10] that inspire this investigation. The first is a history/sociology from below that derives from the work of E.P. Thompson,[11] an approach that rewrites history from the standpoints of the exploited and oppressed, releasing the knowledges based on their lived experiences which are suppressed within ruling histories. I combine this approach with the work of Marxist-feminist Dorothy Smith, who has developed sociologies for women and the oppressed which attempt to produce social knowledge for the benefit of the oppressed rather than to govern and rule them,[12] an approach that has been productively extended into sociologies for gay men and lesbians.[13] In particular I draw upon Smith's notion of institutional ethnography,[14] which I apply in a historical context.[15] The focus is on *how* cultures work, on *how* social organization operates, and on developing rich descriptions of cultural and social organization.[16] Such institutional ethnographies critique ruling relations in our society by critically interrogating the social organization of institutional relations.

In this chapter I critically interrogate the social organization of the national security regime and the Cold War against queers by starting from the standpoint of the oppressed, in this case those directly affected by the national security campaigns. It is vital to this approach that one hold to this standpoint when interrogating security texts and operatives, since the goal of institutional ethnography is to analyse 'national security' itself as an ideological code. This analysis is partly based on a broader notion of work and activity derived from feminist domestic labour debates[17] and attempts to make visible the concerted activity going on to produce *and* resist institutional relations. This allows us to grasp the work of security operatives not recorded in the official texts released through the Access of Information Act[18] and to recognize the possibility of resistance by gays and lesbians to these national security campaigns. Finally, institutional ethnography allows for the integration of local institutional analyses with the broader social relations to which they belong. Such an analysis connects the national security campaigns to broader social relations; these campaigns include the criminalization and stigmatization of homosexuality in Canadian social relations and in the international security alliances with the United States and NATO that the Canadian state had entered into.[19]

I also draw upon the work of Michel Foucault on disciplinary power, social surveillance, and power/knowledge relations,[20] while avoiding the problems of discourse determinism that are often present in his work.[21] There are clear connections between the operations of the national security state and the disciplinary power strategies of surveillance, examination, and normalization. Foucault has also been a major influence on the development of 'queer theory,' a discourse based on literary analysis that is culturally derived and puts in question the binary opposition of homo- and heterosexualities.[22] Queer theory is limited, however, in that it tends to contest heterosexual hegemony only in literary, discursive, and cultural terms. The social world, however, cannot simply be read as a cultural or literary text. The 'theory' of language used in queer theory – drawn from postmodernism and poststructuralism[23] – has a non-social aspect to it in not clearly describing how language and discourse are social practices.[24] This can lead queer theory towards a form of reductionism, such that the complexities of social processes are restricted to the discursive domain alone. One of my objectives, thus, is to ground the insights of queer theory socially, historically, and materially.[25]

Developing this historical materialism for queers,[26] which is at the same time a queering of historical materialism, requires shattering the 'natural' and ahistorical appearances of heterosexual hegemony and the present gender system; disclosing the oppressions lying beneath the 'natural' appearance of these hegemonic practices; and excavating the socially and historically produced character of sexualities and genders. This points us towards the possibilities of overturning heterosexual hegemony and transforming erotic and gender relations, and relations of state, class, gender, and race. Marx's work and method still have a lot to tell us about the dynamics of capitalist social relations and how these shape the lives of queers and others, thus sharpening our focus on class relations and struggles, including those within queer communities.

Finally, I draw on dialectical theories of mediation that allow for the combination in social analysis of the mutually constructed character of social relations while also preserving the moments of autonomy of each specific form of social oppression and exclusion.[27] We are never just queer (or heterosexual, for that matter); we also live in the context of class, gender, race, ability, age, and other social relations. The Cold War against queers cannot be grasped by focusing only on its anti-queer dimensions; analysis also requires the determination of how its classist, anti-socialist, and anti-immigrant aspects shaped and constructed its anti-queer dimensions.[28] At the same time, not to see the autonomy of the anti-queer dimensions of the Cold War is to subordinate this aspect of the Cold War to narrow notions of its class or anti-communist character, an attitude which has been standard in the histories of the Cold War up to now.[29]

Towards the Genealogy of 'Commie Pinko Fag'

'Commie pinko fag' used to be scrawled on my locker and used as a greeting in the halls when I was a student at Victoria Park Secondary School in Don Mills in the early 1970s. I was a member of the Young Socialists and later of the Revolutionary Marxist Group so the 'commie' part made some sense to me. I never understood where 'pinko' came from. The sole basis for the 'fag' part seemed to be my refusal to laugh at the anti-gay jokes that were all pervasive at my school. A 'cutting out' operation,[30] much as George Smith describes,[31] was mobilized against me, as I was socially cut out of 'normal' heterosexual interaction. During these years I was beginning to explore my sexuality and starting to come out to myself and to others as gay, and eventually I did become an anti-Stalinist 'commie fag.' My interest in the national security campaigns against queers flows from this association between commies and fags that has been integral to my experience. This association was forged in major part during the years of the national security campaigns against gay men and lesbians and also through the alliances between some queer activists and sections of the left.[32]

In this chapter I want to *remember* the deep roots of heterosexism in Canadian state and social formation and to interrogate the anti-queer history which continues to shape our present. As David McNally points out, drawing on cultural critic and theorist Walter Benjamin's Marxist and Freudian work, 'Rather than something laid down once and for all the past is a site of struggle in the present.'[33] Capitalism and oppression rule through what I call the social organization of forgetting, which seeks to annihilate our social and historical memories. This is also how strategies of 'respectability' and 'responsibility' gain hegemony in queer communities. We have been forced to forget where we have come from; our histories have never been recorded and passed down; and we are denied the social and historical literacies that allow us to remember and relive our pasts and therefore grasp our present. Thus, telling stories of the sort with which I began is an act of rebellion.

In my work I focus on the development of human, social capacities for agency,[34] creativity, and resistance, which can be missed if we simply rely on the official stories and texts of the national security campaign. Relying on the official texts, and even critical readings of them, can leave us trapped in the discursive processes of reification[35] – or "thingification" – whereby social practices and relations between people get transformed into relationships between things, variables, or concepts, as they are in official discourse and often in official histories. Reifying approaches prevent us from remembering the struggles and compromises of the past that shape our present. As Adorno and others have stressed, 'all reification is a form of forgetting,'[36] a forgetting of the human, social practices involved in creating our past, present, and possible futures. The national security texts were an active part of constructing queers as a national security threat. Using institutional ethnography I read these texts for the social organization they reveal but I start outside this official discourse in the first-hand accounts of queers.[37]

Queering the Cold War

The hegemonic view of the Cold War that I am contesting here is that it represented a conflict between the American and Soviet empires.[38] The present chapter thus follows from *Whose National Security?*, which argues a rethinking of the bases for the national security program and for expanding the analysis of the Cold War to include relations of ethnicity, immigration, race, gender, and sexuality.[39] The Cold War was not only about defending Western capitalism and the expanding U.S. empire against the bureaucratic class societies that emerged in the USSR and elsewhere.[40] It was also very much a neo-colonialist war against Third World liberation movements. It was thus not only a Cold War but also sometimes a very hot war. This imperialist war had a clear racial character which contributed to the construction of the hegemony of a white,[41] middle-class way of life. It was also a war against transformative working-class movements and movements of the oppressed, including anti-Stalinist working-class political movements. Similarly, it was very much a Cold War to reassert gender and sexual 'normality' after the social disruptions of the Second World War mobilizations.[42] The focus on queers was thus not simply about homophobia;[43] the anti-queer aspect of the Cold War was central to its deeply rooted social character.[44] Indeed, by the late 1960s and 1970s these anti-queer mobilizations were attempting to contain the broader political sphere of gender and sexual struggles.

A key objective of these Cold War mobilizations has been the making of the 'normal,' as Mary Louise Adams[45] has argued. Moral regulation[46] was always a key feature of these mobilizations. This 'making normal' was always constructed against 'others,' 'dangers,' and 'risks' outside the fabric of 'the nation.' But this is a relational social process. The other side of these mobilizations is that the Cold War fought for heterosexual hegemony, producing heterosexuality in the national interest as 'loyal' and 'safe,' such that heterosexuality becomes the 'national' sexuality.

The Cold War in its various phases was mobilized against forms of political, social, sexual, and cultural 'subversion.' As Elizabeth Grace and Colin Leys argue in relation to state definitions of subversion:

Many writers on subversion have complained that the term refers to a 'grey area' and is difficult to define. Our view is that it has always referred to a fairly clear reality: legal activities and ideas directed against the existing social, economic and political [and, I would add, sexual and gender] order ... Any radical activity or idea with the potential to enlist significant popular support may be labeled 'subversive' ... [Subversion] is invoked ... to *create* a 'grey area' of activities that *are* lawful, but will be denied protection from state surveillance or harassment by being *declared* illegitimate, on the grounds that they *potentially* have unlawful consequences. In capitalist societies the targets of this delegitimation have been overwhelmingly on the left.[47]

Subversion that is given the form of a 'national security risk' is an administrative collecting category[48] into which various social and political practices and movements can be placed so that they can be read as lying outside the 'normal' and 'national' social fabric. These conceptualizations can be expanded or contracted depending on the social and political context. Some groups get excluded from their rights and become targets of surveillance in a 'cutting-out operation'[49] of the sort I described above that separates them from 'the nation.' Once successfully claimed as a 'subversive' or a 'national security risk' these groups can then be denied their human and citizenship rights. At various points in Canadian history, communists, socialists, peace activists, trade unionists, Red power and Black power activists, Quebec sovereignists, immigrants, high school students, and queers have been designated as 'subversive.'[50]

We need constantly to ask which nation and whose security is being defended through these national security practices. It is important not to take constructions of the nation and national security for granted. The image of Canada as unitary is based on the suppression of all the national, linguistic, class, sexual, cultural, and other social differences that constitute the Canadian social formation. At the same time, some of these social differences get 'othered' as 'different' and as 'deviant.' National security rests on the interests of 'the nation,' defined in the Canadian context by capitalist, racist, heterosexist, and patriarchal relations. But notions of the nation and national security can easily draw people in by appearing to be consensual. These constructs can thus be very useful for the making of ruling-class hegemonies, obscuring who is being actively excluded through these 'cutting-out' mobilizations and also who is being actively placed at the centre of the social fabric through these mobilizations.[51] As Harold (one of the gay men purged from the Canadian Navy whom I spoke to in 1994) wrote in the early 1960s, 'security is a sacred cow of a word in the name of which highly dictatorial and sweeping actions are possible for which no explanation can be forced.'[52] Initially, queers were seen as 'fellow travellers' of communists because of our violation of political, class, social, and sexual boundaries. R.C. Waldeck, in 'The International Homosexual Conspiracy,' published in *Human Events* in 1960, gives us a taste of this right-wing discourse:

Homosexual officials are a peril for us in the present struggle between West and East: members of one conspiracy are prone to join another ... [M]any homosexuals from being enemies of society in general become enemies of capitalism in particular. Without being necessarily Marxist they serve the ends of the Communist International in the name of their rebellion against the prejudices, standards, ideals of the "bourgeois" world. Another reason for the homosexual-Communist alliance is the instability and passion for intrigue for intrigue's sake, which is inherent in the homosexual personality. A third reason is the social promiscuity within the homosexual minority and the fusion of its effects between upperclass and proletarian corruption.

There are some interesting dialogical connections[53] between this right-wing discourse and the discourse of the Canadian Security Panel, the interdepartmental committee set up to coordinate the national security campaigns within the Canadian state. In a 1959 memorandum they wrote:

> The nature of homosexuality appears to adapt itself to this kind of exploitation. By exercising fairly simple precautions, homosexuals are usually able to keep their habits hidden from those who are not specifically seeking them out. Further, homosexuals often appear to believe that the accepted ethical code which governs normal human relationships does not apply to them. Their propensity is often accompanied by other specific weaknesses such as excessive drinking with its resultant instabilities, a defiant attitude towards the rest of society, and a concurrent urge to seek out the company of persons with similar characteristics, often in disreputable table bars, night clubs or restaurants ... The case of the homosexual is particularly difficult for a number of reasons. From the small amount of information we have been able to obtain about homosexual behaviour generally, certain characteristics appear to stand out – instability, willing self-deceit, defiance toward society, a tendency to surround oneself with persons of similar propensities, regardless of other considerations – none of which inspire [sic] the confidence one would hope to have in persons required to fill positions of trust and responsibility.[54]

While this discourse has shifted from its more overtly right-wing form, it still carries with it the notion that homosexuals are deviant towards 'society.'

Gender and Heterosexuality

The campaigns against queers were also integrally tied up with practices of gender regulation and the redrawing of the boundaries of heterosexual 'normality' following the Second World War. For example, gender regulations were imposed on women as they entered into the public service and the military. These included dress codes and beauty contests, in the attempt to secure the performance of heterosexual femininity in the civil service.[55] Sue tells us about these practices and also about resistance to them in the militia and at military camp in the late 1950s:

We would be out with sergeants, staff sergeants, corporals, privates, lieu-
tenants ... no rank was untouched ... So we would be running all over
camp. And the deal was you weren't allowed to leave the premises, so of
course, we wanted wine, women, and song. So in order to get wine,
women and song you had to leave the base. So you had to go out. But you
weren't allowed to wear butchy clothing. You had to wear a *dress* [her
emphasis]. So what we used to do was pull our pant legs up and hide
them with our skirt. And you'd go out and through the gates in your skirt
right, lookin' all femmy and lovely. Well this one night we came home and
we got a little too drunk. Well trust me that the pants were down. And we,
we were up on charges the next day for being in some place we weren't
supposed to be, improper attire, all kinds of things. So we learned that we
shouldn't drink too much. [23 February 1996]

There was also a redrawing of the boundaries around heterosexual and
queer sex during these years. While in previous periods, emerging
heterosexual identifications could have included some same-gender
erotic sexual play or experimentation, this now became suspect. There
was an uneven shift away from gender inversion as the queer problem
– the effeminate man or butch woman – towards same-gender eroticism in general. In the military this meant that not only were the
effeminate fairy[56] or the butch woman seen as a problem, but so too
was the 'normal' masculine man who might engage in same-gender
sex occasionally, or the 'feminine' normal woman who might occasionally engage in same-gender eroticism. Now all these individuals
were supposedly vulnerable to blackmail and compromise by 'evil'
Soviet agents.[57] There were important connections between this shift
and the reconceptualization of homosexuality as a 'sexual orientation'
based on sexual-object choice.[58]

Moral Failings and Blackmail Fears

The major focus of the national security campaigns was thus on those
individuals having a moral or 'character' weakness, rather than on
'ideological' or political subversives. These 'weaknesses' were defined
as an inability to perform oneself as 'normal.' Because queers were
defined as being outside 'normality,' they were seen as having something to hide and therefore as subject to blackmail. The security regime's
texts display an interesting grasp of the relations of living in the closet

or living a double life,[59] but they nowhere note their own active partici-
pation in the construction of these relations.

The 'invisibility' of homosexuals during the Cold War was not a
'natural' aspect of their sexuality but instead was deeply rooted in the
social relations produced by heterosexual hegemony. The national security campaigns of the postwar period played a central role in organizing the social relations of the closet; there is considerable evidence that
there was far more openness to queer erotic and gender practices earlier
in the twentieth century. This conclusion is arrived at by moving beyond the mainstream – and often gay – social mythology of monolithic
oppression. In our research, for example, we have found that there was
more openness to queer practices in Victoria, BC, prior to the military
and RCMP investigations of the murder by Leo Mantha of his es-
tranged boyfriend, and also in Ottawa before the major campaigns
against homosexuals began in the late 1950s.[60] It was in this context that
fears over blackmail were constructed and mobilized. While the RCMP
defined gay men and lesbians as the blackmail threat, from the point of
view of those gays and lesbians who were interrogated it was the
RCMP who were the blackmailers. In interview after interview we have
heard that the RCMP asked for the names or identities of other homosexuals, trying to pressure homosexuals to inform on other homosexuals.[61] For instance, Hank stated that he was 'only ever blackmailed by
the RCMP' (20 February 1995), and Harold wrote about the RCMP
'applying a form of blackmail very difficult to resist.'[62] The RCMP also
counterposed people's loyalty to their gay/lesbian friends with their
loyalty to the state. For instance, during one interrogation, Harold was
asked 'Which is the greater treason, treason to your country or treason
to your friends?'[63]

The anti-queer campaigns affected thousands of people from the
1950s to the 1990s. A 1960 RCMP document reveals that the security
investigations intruded into many departments and especially into
External Affairs and the Navy. The RCMP report discovered 76 'suspected' and 123 'confirmed' homosexuals in the Navy, and it appears
(in a document with numerous deletions) that they found 17 'alleged,'
33 'suspected,' and 9 'confirmed' homosexuals in External Affairs in the
same period, with totals of 139 'suspected,' 168 'alleged,' and 156 'confirmed' overall in the report.[64] The RCMP interrogations attempted to
move those investigated from the 'suspected' or 'alleged' categories
into the 'confirmed' category so that action could be taken against the
individual;[65] to do so they relied on other homosexuals to confirm that

these individuals were indeed gay. Fred, who worked in the character weakness subdivision of the Directorate of Security and Intelligence (Ottawa) of the RCMP in 1967–9 described his work as hanging around with gay men, trying to make friends with them, and converting them into informants. He would ask the gay men he knew about any gay parties they had been at and whether there had been any public servants present at these events. If a public servant had been present, Fred would then try to have this person photographed in order to see if the gay informant could identify this person as homosexual so that they could be moved into the 'confirmed' category. Fred reported (21 October 1994) no similar dealings with lesbians, who tended to be more apprehensive; the RCMP only had male officers at this point. Once an individual was placed in the 'confirmed' category they could be purged from their position in the public service or the military, or demoted and transferred to lower-level positions where they would have no access to security information. This process of identification and confirmation was dependent on there being 'cooperative' and 'reliable' homosexual informants; ironically, reliance on gay informants became the weak link in the process.

The Fruit Machine

In response to costly RCMP field investigations of public servants, and perhaps in response to the non-cooperation of previously 'cooperative' homosexual informants, there was an attempt to develop an 'objective' scientific means of determining sexual orientation based on the research of 'experts' in the psychological and psychiatric disciplines. This program was part of the expanding social and state administration of the 1950s and 1960s;[66] the Security Panel, the RCMP, the military, and National Health and Welfare were engaged in this research for more than four years.[67] Professor Wake of Carleton University's Psychology Department was actively involved in the development of this detection technology, illustrating the linkage between the academy and Cold War research. At the centre of his research was the pupillary response test, which showed images of naked men and women to research subjects and photographed the level of dilation of their pupils to determine their 'involuntary' response. The research also drew on masculinity/ femininity scales as a general marker of homosexuality, although Wake did not subscribe to theories of homosexuality as gender inversion. It also combined use of a word association test with the Palmer sweat test to examine anxious responses to 'homosexual' words such as 'queen,' 'circus,' 'gay,' 'bell,' 'whole,' 'blind,' 'camp,' 'coo,' 'cruise,' 'drag,' 'dike' (i.e., 'dyke'), 'fish,' 'flute,' 'fruit,' 'mother,' 'punk,' 'queer,' 'rim,' 'sex,' 'swing,' 'trade,' 'velvet,' 'wolf,' 'blackmail,' 'prowl,' 'bar,' 'house,' 'club,' 'restaurant,' 'tea room,' and 'top men.'[68] There was resistance to this project from members of the RCMP who feared that even though they were supposed to be the 'normal' control group for the study, they might be exposed as 'fruits.'[69] The research was eventually abandoned, its technology deemed a failure.[70]

Queer Resistance

As David's story has already demonstrated, there were possibilities for non-cooperation and resistance to the Cold War against queers. Sue, for example, describes resistance to military policies in the 1950s:

> And the deal was you were supposed to go out with men. So what we did was at military camp we went out with men in the early part of the evening, and then because we were very virtuous young women we said 'OK, we have to go home early.' And the military being very accommodating said, 'This is where the women sleep, this is where the men sleep.' We said 'Fine, that's cool, we'll go back with the women.' Back we go with the women ... What we used to do, we dykes, we would want to go out and party. And we would take our bunk beds and we would fill them with pillows. And then we would ask the heterosexual women, and we would say to them 'We really want to meet Charlie.' We would lie to them and they would cover cause they thought we were goin' out to meet men. We were goin' out to meet women. But we had it set up at the back of the barracks, and took over this room. We barricaded it from one side and then we had, had women on the other side guarding it, cause that's where we were with Charlie. But they never saw Charlie! So here we had all these straight women, guarding us and guarding our beds and making sure that the [authorities] never knew we were out. And we weren't supposed to be. (23 February 1996)

In 1962–3 the RCMP reported that their security campaign 'was hindered by the lack of cooperation on the part of homosexuals approached as sources. Persons of this type, who had hitherto been our most consistent and productive informers, have exhibited an increasing reluctance to identify their homosexual friends and associates.'[71] This report is corroborated by Michael, who was employed as a civilian employee of the armed forces. Interrogated by the RCMP in the 1960s, he stated that the advice in the gay networks he was familiar with was to say nothing to the RCMP about people's names or identities and 'if anybody did give anything they were ostracized.' Michael also reported a conversation in the interrogation room with an RCMP officer:

'Is it true that you are a homosexual?' [the official asked]. And I said 'yes!' And he looked at me and I said, 'Is it true that you ride side-saddle?' and he laughed and that almost ended the interview. I mean, my intent was there, don't bother me any more, because I began to get the impression that it was a witch-hunt. It was a real witch-hunt. (15 July 1994)

This response and the response in the bar reported by David suggest that these men were using humour and camp[72] as a survival strategy. As David expressed it, 'I think that the way people coped with the whole situation of surveillance and harassment and so on was basically to make the best of it. And turn it as much as possible into a humorous situation' (12 May 1994).

These narratives of resistance begin to flesh out the social organization of the 'non-cooperation' the RCMP reports mention. Gays and lesbians had a sense of themselves and the networks they participated in that allowed them to engage in these collective and individual acts of defiance. Participants in these networks had an awareness of what the RCMP was up to but also had an awareness of a collective community response. The social basis for these forms of non-cooperation and resistance was in the development of gay networks and social space formed on the basis of eroticism, friendship, and love, and the concomitant development of queer solidarity and 'talk.'[73] The national security campaigns of the late 1950s and 1960s are thus not only about oppression and exclusion but are also about resistance and non-cooperation in difficult circumstances.

Spying on Queer Organizations

The Cold War against queers did not end, as some have imagined, in the late 1960s or early 1970s,[74] but continued into the 1970s and 1980s though a policy of spying on the new gay liberation and lesbian feminist organizations as they emerged. These organizations challenged the national security policies of the Canadian state and thus came under

RCMP surveillance. These groups were seen as subversive in their challenge to state policies, including those on national security questions, but they were also seen to be subversive because of the involvement of many of these early groups with Trotskyist organizations, the League for Socialist Action, and the Young Socialists. In this national security discourse, 'Trotskyist' was mobilized in the same way that 'communist' had been in other contexts. The RCMP also developed new classifications for 'gay political activist' and 'radical lesbian' as part of their attempt to survey, analyse, and thus contain these activists.[75]

When gay and lesbian activists gathered for the first time in a protest rally on Parliament Hill in August 1971, the RCMP were there conducting surveillance, as they were at the 1975 founding conference of the National Gay Rights Coalition conference in Ottawa. In their analysis of the activities of the Gay Alliance Towards Equality (GATE) in Vancouver in 1973 they even expressed the fear that 'unless another stronger group takes the initiative – a liberal grouping – leadership and direction of what could be a real force in the gay community and in the community as a whole could fall into the hands of GATE.'[76] RCMP surveillance of the feminist movement likewise led them to discover 'radical lesbians,' such as the lesbian group 'Wages Due,' who were part of the Toronto 'Wages for Housework' campaign. The RCMP report points out that the 'T.W.H.C.'s membership has been described by [blanked out] as being 'Born Losers' who in appearance and attitude are both lower working class and welfare cases and involved in living alternative life-styles [blanked out].' The next comment emphasizes the physical appearance of these women: 'This is especially true of the radical lesbians in W.D., who take a perverse pride in de-feminizing themselves by cultivating the dirty and unkempt appearance.'[77] Here the anti-working class and anti-poor perspective is combined with a particular gender standpoint defending hegemonic discourses of femininity.[78] The lesbians in 'Wages Due' are defined as taking a perverse pride in 'de-feminizing' themselves because they construct and perform their femininity differently and engage in specifically lesbian cultural practices of gender performance.[79]

The RCMP had great difficulty handling the new gay and lesbian feminist activists in the 1970s. These activists were no longer hiding their sexualities nor were they trapped within the relations of the closet or living a double life. Instead, by being out and building political movements they began to undermine the social relations of the closet and to undermine the notion of 'character weakness' based on the need to maintain the secrecy and invisibility of queers. These new movements and the emergence of broader gay and lesbian communities gradually undermined the main features of the Cold War against queers.

The Continuing Cold Wars

The Cold War against queers continued at a high level of intensity within the military and the RCMP itself until at least the late 1980s and early 1990s, when official policies excluding gay men and lesbians were changed owing to lesbian and gay activism and legal challenges.[80] The Canadian Security and Intelligence Service (CSIS), which took over national security work from the RCMP following the revelations of RCMP 'dirty tricks' against the sovereignty and left movements in Quebec, can still to this day deny security clearances to gay men and lesbians who are not 'out' on the grounds that, since they have 'something to hide,' they could be 'blackmailable.'[81] The same Cold War logic is thus still in place, although now only for queers who are not 'out.' In the public service it is still possible for lesbian and gay employees to be 'outed' against their wishes to family, friends, co-workers, and neighbours as part of security clearance checks and investigations. One woman I talked to was forced to leave her public service position in the early 1990s for fear of the consequences of her partner being 'outed' during her security check.[82]

New targets for national security campaigns since the 1990s include Arab and Muslim Canadians during and since the Gulf War,[83] and again with the current 'war on terrorism' and the global justice movement against capitalist globalization.[84] Defending the new international trade and investment alliances the Canadian state is entering into has now become part of defending national security. During the protests against the Asia Pacific Economic Cooperation (APEC) at the University of British Columbia in 1997, demonstrators were pepper-sprayed and arrested because the Canadian state had built an alliance with other governments, including the Suharto regime in Indonesia, that had to be defended against demonstrators in Canada.[85] And recently we have seen major police and national security mobilizations against those protesting the Summit of the Americas and the Free Trade Area of the Americas (FTAA) in Quebec City.[86] CSIS and much of the mainstream media focused on 'anarchists' as the problem in these protests, and this focus has some similarities to the use of 'communist' at the

height of the 1950s/1960s Cold War. What this suggests is that a political Cold War in a broad sense continues against threats to capitalist
social relations even though the USSR no longer exists.

A major and central part of the Canadian Cold War was the campaign
against queers. Heterosexual hegemony has been key to the making of
the Canadian state and its social formations, and sexual, gender, and
moral regulation was at the heart of the social organization of the Cold
War. The Cold War against queers had a detrimental impact on the lives
of thousands of people and played a crucial part in constructing the
'normality' of heterosexuality that we continue to confront today. But
there is also a history of resistance to this Cold War which provides an
important resource for our continuing struggles.

Notes

1 The dates when interviews took place are indicated in parentheses at the
   end of the interview extracts. To protect confidentiality, all names given for
   people I have interviewed are pseudonyms.
2 I thank Patrizia Gentile for her part in the research that this chapter is
   based on. See Gary Kinsman and Patrizia Gentile, with Heidi McDonell
   and Mary Mahood-Greer, '"In the Interests of the State": The Anti-Gay,
   Anti-Lesbian National Security Campaigns in Canada,' research report,
   Laurentian University, 1998; and Kinsman and Gentile, *The Canadian War
   on 'Queers': National Security as Sexual Regulation* (Vancouver: U British
   Columbia P: forthcoming).
3 RCMP, *Directorate of Security and Intelligence: Annual Report* 1967–1968.
4 For more on this see Kinsman and Gentile, *The Canadian War on 'Queers'*
   (forthcoming).
5 On the importance of an active sense of agency in developing liberationist
   social theory, see the work of Himani Bannerji, especially 'But Who Speaks
   for Us?' in *Thinking Through: Essays on Feminism, Marxism and Anti-Racism*
   (Toronto: Women's Press, 1995).
6 'Ideology refers to all forms of knowledge that are divorced from their
   conditions of production (their grounds),' writes Roslyn Wallach Bologh in
   Dialectical Phenomenology: Marx's Method (Boston: Northeastern UP, 1979),
   19. On ideology see also the work of Dorothy Smith, including *The Everyday World as Problematic: A Feminist Sociology* (Toronto: U of Toronto P,
   1987); *The Conceptual Practices of Power: A Feminist Sociology of Knowledge*
   (Toronto: U of Toronto P, 1990); and *Texts, Facts, and Femininity: Exploring*

the Relations of Ruling (London: Routledge, 1990); and the work of Himani Bannerji, including *Thinking Through* (1995), and her articles on the ideological construction of India: 'Beyond the Ruling Category to What Actually Happens: Notes on James Mill's Historiography in *The History of British India*,' in Marie Campbell and Ann Manicom, eds., *Knowledge, Experience, and Ruling Relations: Studies in the Social Organization of Knowledge* (Toronto: U of Toronto P, 1995), 49–64; and 'Writing "India," Doing Ideology,' *Left History* 2.2 (1994): 5–17. On ideological codes see Dorothy Smith, 'The Standard North American Family: SNAF as an Ideological Code,' and '"Politically Correct": An Organizer of Public Discourse,' in Dorothy Smith, *Writing the Social: Critique, Theory and Investigations* (Toronto: U of Toronto P, 1999), 157–94. I find the notion (developed in this last text) of an ideological code which 'coordinates multiple sites within the intersecting relations of public text-mediated discourses' useful in the analysis of national security issues. At the same time, I have difficulty with Smith's suggestion that ideological codes are analogous to 'genetic codes' (159) since this suggests that these are automatic and cannot be disrupted or subverted. I want to hold on to the possibilities for disruption and subversion and to avoid the reification of human, social practices.

7 Kinsman and Gentile (1998) have been criticized for producing 'revisionist' history. While I reject this way of framing struggles over history, I do intend this to be a work of transformative historical sociology – a work that transforms and redefines what Canadian history and sociology is all about. This is not simply about adding the campaign against 'queers' to the established history of Cold War Canada but about 'queering' and transforming our overall analysis of the Cold War in the Canadian context.

8 On the use of 'queer' in this context see Annamarie Jagose, *Queer Theory: An Introduction* (New York: New York UP, 1996), 72–126.

9 On heterosexual hegemony see Gary Kinsman, *The Regulation of Desire: Homo and Hetero Sexualities* (Montreal: Black Rose, 1996). On the dichotomous notion of gender see Suzanne Kessler and Wendy McKenna, *Gender: An Ethnomethodological Approach* (Chicago: U Chicago P, 1978) and Kessler's *Lessons from the Intersexed* (New Brunswick, NJ: Rutgers UP, 1998). For the concept of hegemony see Antonio Gramsci, *Selections from the Prison Notebooks* (New York: International Publishers, 1971).

10 I am blurring the distinction here between theories and methods in order to foreground the interrelationships of these terms as part of my practice of adopting theories and methods that are epistemologically and ontologically committed to active agency and anti-reification. Given that the social/historical world is produced through the practices of people work-

ing within social constraints it can likewise be transformed through these social practices. Similarly, the social world can only be known through active engagement with it and not by standing outside it and developing some sort of 'objective,' top-down analysis. For a critique of mainstream sociological theory see Dorothy Smith, *Writing the Social*.

11 While E.P. Thompson's *The Making of the English Working Class* (New York: Vintage, 1966) did not adequately take up relations of gender, race, or sexuality, or their mediated construction in and through class relations, Thompson's approach has been extended by others into these areas. See also Ellen Meiksins Wood, *Democracy Against Capitalism* (Cambridge: Cambridge UP, 1995), 13, 49, 107.

12 Campbell and Manicom, eds., *Knowledge, Experience and Ruling Relations.*

13 See George Smith, 'Policing the Gay Community: An Inquiry into Textually-Mediated Social Relations,' *International Journal of the Sociology of Law* 16 (1988): 163–83, and 'Political Activist as Ethnographer,' *Social Problems* 37 (1990): 401–21; Madiha Didi Khayatt, *Lesbian Teachers, An Invisible Presence* (Albany: State University of New York P, 1992), and 'Compulsory Heterosexuality: Schools and Lesbian Students,' in Campbell and Manicom, eds., 149–63; and Gary Kinsman, 'The Textual Practices of Sexual Rule: Sexual Policing and Gay Men,' in Campbell and Manicom, eds., 80–95.

14 Dorothy Smith, *The Everyday World as Problematic*, 147–207; Marjorie L. Devault, 'Institutional Ethnography: A Strategy for Feminist Inquiry,' in *Liberating Method: Feminism and Social Research* (Philadelphia: Temple UP, 1999), 46–54; Marie Campbell and Frances Gregor, *Mapping Social Relations, A Primer in Institutional Ethnography* (Aurora, ON: Garamond, 2002).

15 Gary Kinsman, 'The Textual Practices of Sexual Rule,' in Campbell and Manicom, eds, 80–95.

16 Dorothy Smith, 'On Sociological Description,' *Texts, Facts, and Femininity* (1990): 86–119.

17 Dorothy Smith, *The Everyday World as Problematic*, 161–75.

18 Kerry Badgley, 'Researchers and Canada's Public Archives: Gaining Access to the Security Collections,' in Kinsman et al., eds, *Whose National Security?* 223–8; Heidi McDonell, 'The Experiences of a Researcher in the Maze,' in Kinsman et al., eds, 229–32.

19 For further elaboration on this use of institutional ethnography see Kinsman and Gentile, *In the Interests of the State*, 52–71.

20 Michel Foucault, *Discipline and Punish, the Birth of the Prison* (New York: Vintage, 1979); *The History of Sexuality, Volume 1: An Introduction* (New York: Vintage, 1980); *Power/Knowledge*, ed. C. Gordon (New York: Pantheon,1980).

21 Bob Fine, 'Power without People: Michel Foucault,' in *Democracy and the Rule of Law: Liberal Ideals and Marxist Critiques* (London: Pluto P, 1984) 189–202.

22 Eve Kosofsky Sedgwick, *The Epistemology of the Closet* (Berkeley: U of California P, 1990); Steven Seidman, ed., *Queer Theory/Sociology* (Oxford: Blackwell, 1996); Judith Butler, *Gender Trouble: Feminism and the Subversion of Identity* (New York: Routledge, 1990); Michael Warner, ed., *Fear of a Queer Planet* (Minneapolis: U of Minnesota P, 1993); Rosemary Hennessy, 'Queer Theory, Left Politics,' *Rethinking Marxism* 7.3 (1994), 85–111; Rosemary Hennessy, *Profit and Pleasure, Sexual Identities in Late Capitalism* (New York: Routledge, 2000); Ki Namaste, '"Tragic Misreadings": Queer Theory's Erasure of Transgender Subjectivity,' *Queer Studies: A Lesbian, Gay, Bisexual and Transgender Anthology* (New York: New York UP, 1996) 183–203; Viviane K. Namaste, *Invisible Lives* (Chicago: U of Chicago P, 2001).

23 Poststructuralism can be seen as a broad theoretical approach which resists forms of analysis whereby the social is constituted and determined exclusively through pre-existing social structures. Rather than focusing on unitary structures, poststructuralists focus on fragmentation and difference. 'Postmodernism' combines a number of shared themes: on the social and political terrain, there is an assumption that we are moving beyond 'modernity' and the classic analysis of capitalism; there is also an emphasis on psychoanalytical and literary deconstructive theory. In general, subject positions are seen as being constituted through discourse.

24 Dorothy Smith, *Writing the Social* (1999); David McNally, 'Language, History and Class Struggle,' in Ellen Meiksins Wood and John Bellamy Foster, eds., *In Defence of History: Marxism and the Postmodern Agenda* (New York: Monthly Review, 1997), 26–42; David McNally, *Bodies of Meaning, Studies on Language, Labor, and Liberation* (Albany, New York: State University of New York P, 2001).

25 I use 'materialist' in a broad sense to include human sensuous practices, following from Marx's 'Theses on Feuerbach,' where a new social and historical notion of materialism can be seen as a synthesis of vulgar 'materialism' and the active side of 'idealism.' See in this regard Derek Sayer, ed., *Readings from Karl Marx* (London: Routledge, 1989), 7–10, and Bannerji, *Thinking Through*. I do not read Marxism or historical materialism as a form of political economy; on this approach to Marx see Dorothy Smith, 'Feminist Reflections on Political Economy,' in Smith, *Writing the Social*, 29–44, and H. Cleaver, *Reading Capital Politically* (London: Anti/thesis P, 2000), 31–77.

26 Some of the resources for this view of Marxism and historical materialism are Derek Sayer, *Marx's Method* (Atlantic Highlands, NJ: Humanities P

1983), and his *The Violence of Abstraction* (Oxford and New York: Basil Blackwell, 1987); Roslyn Wallach Bologh, *Dialectical Phenomenology* (Boston: Portledge & Kegan Paul, 1979); I.I. Rubin, for his emphasis on social forms and social relations, in *Essays on Marx's Theory of Value* (Montreal: Black Rose, 1982); Frigga Haug, *Beyond Female Masochism: Memory-Work and Politics* (London: Verso, 1992); Cleaver, *Reading Capital Politically*; and the work of Himani Bannerji and Dorothy Smith.

27 Bannerji, *Thinking Through*.

28 The lack of mediational analysis is one of the limitations of the pathbreaking article by David Kimmel and Daniel J. Robinson, 'The Queer Career of Homosexual Security Vetting in Cold War Canada,' *Canadian Historical Review* 73:3 (1994): 319–45.

29 Kinsman et al., eds, *Whose National Security?* 2–5.

30 Dorothy Smith, *Texts, Facts, and Femininity*, 30–43.

31 George Smith, 'The Ideology of "Fag": The School Experience of Gay Students,' *Sociological Quarterly* 39.2 (1998): 309–35.

32 In the United States, leftist and ex–Communist Party members were centrally involved in the early 1950s in the formation of the Mattachine Society, the first attempt at a homophile organization. See John D'Emilio, *Sexual Politics, Sexual Communities* (Chicago: U of Chicago P, 1983) 57–74. At the height of the Cold War frenzy, communists and ex-communists leaders were turfed out of such groups by their more conservative members (75–91). Left-wing activists were also centrally involved in the formation of gay liberation fronts after the Stonewall riots in New York City in 1969.

33 McNally, *Bodies of Meaning*, 191.

34 On the development of human capacities see Sam Gindin, 'Socialism with Sober Senses, Developing Workers' Capacities,' in Leo Panitch and Colin Leys, eds, *The Communist Manifesto Now* (New York: Socialist Register, 1998), 75–101. See also Philip Corrigan, *Social Forms / Human Capacities* (London: Routledge, 1990).

35 On reification see Georg Lukács, *History and Class Consciousness* (London: Merlin, 1968). On how reification takes place in the writing of sociology, and within sociological theory, see Dorothy Smith, *Writing the Social*, 45–69.

36 McNally, *Bodies of Meaning*, 195.

37 On the postmodernist bias against 'experience' as 'contaminated' by discourse see Campbell and Manicom, eds, *Knowledge, Experience, Ruling Relations*, 7–10; Rosemary Hennessy, *Profit and Pleasure, Sexual Identities in Late Capitalism* (New York: Routledge, 2000), 17–22; and Ellen Meiksins Wood, *Democracy against Capitalism* (Cambridge: Cambridge UP, 1995),

96–7. However, while accounts of social experience are not an absolute truth and are always shaped by forms of social discourse, they can exist in rupture with official accounts and discourse, as in David's story.

38 This is the underlying assumption in Reg Whitaker and Gary Marcuse, *Cold War Canada: The Making of a National Insecurity State* (Toronto: U of Toronto P, 1993).

39 Kinsman et al., eds, *Whose National Security?*, 2–5, 278–85.

40 Numerous theories of the social formation of the USSR have been put forward. The view I find most persuasive argues that after the initial revolutionary period, the new bureaucratic ruling class mobilized Marxism-Leninism as an ideology to obscure the oppression and the exploitation of the workers and peasants. On this and other approaches see Mose Mochover and John Fantham, *The Century of the Unexpected: A New Analysis of Soviet Type Societies* (London: Big Flame, 1979).

41 See Ruth Frankenburg, *White Women, Race Matters: The Social Construction of Whiteness* (Minneapolis: U of Minnesota P, 1993); David Roedigger, *The Wages of Whiteness: Race and the Making of the American Working Class* (London: Verso, 1993).

42 Allan Berube, *Coming Out under Fire: The History of Gay Men and Women in World War Two* (New York: Free Press, 1990); Gary Kinsman, *The Regulation of Desire*, 148–57.

43 On the limitations of conceptualizing homophobia as a strictly individual phenomenon, and of analysing heterosexist practices solely in terms of psychological phobia, thus obscuring how homophobia is shaped through broader social relations, see Kinsman, *The Regulation of Desire*, 33.

44 Kimmel and Robinson's 'The Queer Career' neglects this aspect of the national security texts.

45 Mary Louise Adams, *The Trouble with Normal: Postwar Youth and the Making of Heterosexuality* (Toronto: U of Toronto P, 1997).

46 See Philip Corrigan, 'On Moral Regulation,' *Sociological Review* 29 (1981): 313–16, and Kinsman, 'National Security as Moral Regulation: Making the Normal and the Deviant in the Security Campaigns against Gay Men and Lesbians,' in Deborah Brock, ed., *Making Normal: Social Regulation in Canada* (Toronto: Thomson / Nelson, 2003), 121–45.

47 Elizabeth Grace and Colin Leys, 'The Concept of Subversion and Its Implications,' in C.E.S. Franks, ed., *Dissent and the State*, 62–3.

48 Corrigan, *On Moral Regulation*.

49 Dorothy Smith, *Texts, Facts, Femininity*, 30–43.

50 See Kinsman et al., eds., *Whose National Security?*

51 Kinsman et al., eds., *Whose National Security?*, 2–5, 278–85. These Cold War

mobilizations against queers also had major and lasting impacts on the left
which affected not only those who identified with the USSR who already
had overt positions against queers but also those who had broken with
Stalinism. See Laura Engelstein, 'Soviet Policy toward Male Homosexuality: Its Origin and Historical Roots,' in Gert Hekma, Harry Oosterhuis, and
James Steakley, eds., *Gay Men and the Sexual History of the Political Left*
(New York: Harrington Park/Haworth, 1995) 155–78. In the United States,
during the Cold War, the Trotskyist Socialist Workers Party came to view
lesbian and gay members of the organization as 'security risks' to the
party and prohibited lesbians and gays from membership in the SWP. See
Kinsman, 'From Anti-queer to Queers as "Peripheral": The Socialist
Workers' Party, Gay Liberation and North American Trotskyism, 1960–
1980' (unpublished manuscript, 2000); David Thorstad, ed., *Gay Liberation
and Socialism: Documents from the Discussions on Gay Liberation inside the
Socialist Workers Party (1970–1973)*; and Steve Forgione and Kurt T. Hill,
eds., *No Apologies: The Unauthorized Publication of Internal Discussion
Documents of the Socialist Workers Party (SWP) Concerning Lesbian/Gay Male
Liberation* (New York: Lesbian/Gay Rights Monitoring Group, 1980). The
Cold War mobilizations against queers helped to produce the heterosexism
on the left that the gay and lesbian liberation movements confronted in the
late 1960s and 1970s.

52 Harold, 'A Case Study with Observations' (1960–1; unpublished ms), 17.
53 Dialogism and its variants are central terms used by Russian literary
theorist M.M. Bakhtin to get at how 'Everything means, is understood, as
part of a greater whole – there is constant interaction between meanings,
all of which have the potential of conditioning others.' See M.M. Bakhtin,
The Dialogic Imagination: Four Essays (Austin: U of Texas P, 1981) 426–7. In
this case we can see how the earlier, more explicitly right-wing, discourse
came to condition and live on within national security discourse.
54 D.F. Wall, 'Security Cases Involving Character Weaknesses, with Special
Reference to the Problem of Homosexuality,' Memorandum to the Security
Panel, 12 May 1959, 12–13.
55 See Patrizia Gentile, 'Searching for "Miss Civil Service" and "Mr. Civil
Service": Gender Anxiety, Beauty Contests and Fruit Machines in the
Canadian Civil Service, 1950–1973,' MA thesis, Carleton University,
Ottawa, 1996, and '"Government Girls" and "Ottawa Men": Cold War
Management of Gender Relations in the Civil Service,' in Kinsman et al.,
eds., *Whose National Security?*, 131–41.
56 George Chauncey, 'Christian Brotherhood or Sexual Perversion? Homo-
sexual Identities and the Construction of Sexual Boundaries in the World

War One Era,' in M. Duberman, K. Vicinus, and Chauncey, eds., *Hidden from History: Reclaiming the Gay and Lesbian Past* (New York: Meridian, 1989), 294–317; and Chauncey, *Gay New York* (New York: Basic Books, 1994), 47–63.

57 Kinsman and Gentile, '"In the Interests of the State,"' 46–9.

58 Kinsman, *The Regulation of Desire*, 200.

59 On the limited but significant distinction between the closet and living a double life see Chauncey, *Gay New York*, 375 n.9.

60 Kinsman, *The Regulation of Desire*, 173; Kinsman and Gentile, '"In the Interests of the State,"' 38–49; Kinsman and Gentile, *The Canadian War on 'Queers': National Security as Sexual Regulation* (forthcoming).

61 Kinsman and Gentile, '"In the Interests of the State,"' 98–106.

62 Harold, 'A Case Study with Observations' (1960–1).

63 Ibid.

64 J.M. Bella, 'Appendix "A": Homosexuality within the Federal Government Service – Statistics,' in Director of Security and Intelligence, *Homosexuality within the Federal Government Service*, 29 April 1960.

65 Kinsman, 'Constructing Gay Men and Lesbians as National Security Risks, 1950–1970,' in Kinsman et al., eds., *Whose National Security?*, 145–7.

66 Ellen Herman, 'The Career of Cold War Psychology,' *Radical History Review* (Special issue: 'The Cold War and Expert Knowledge') (1995): 52–85; Nikolas Rose, *The Psychological Complex: Psychology, Politics and Society in England, 1869–1939* (London: Routledge and Kegan Paul, 1985).

67 Kinsman and Gentile, '"In the Interests of the State,"' 106–16.

68 Ibid.

69 John Sawatsky, *Men in the Shadows: The RCMP Security Service* (Toronto: Totem Books, 1983), 133.

70 Kinsman and Gentile, '"In the Interests of the State,"' 106–16.

71 Directorate of Security and Intelligence, RCMP (1962–3), 19.

72 Camp sensibility and humour is a cultural form produced by gay men to manage and negotiate the contradictions between our particular experiences of the world as gays and the institutionalized heterosexuality that hegemonizes social relations. A crucial part of this cultural formation is to denaturalize normality and heterosexuality by making fun of it. On this see Kinsman, *The Regulation of Desire*, 226–7.

73 Kinsman and Gentile, '"In the Interests of the State,"' 118–29; Kinsman, 'Constructing Gay Men and Lesbians as National Security Risks, 1950–1970,' in Kinsman et al., eds., *Whose National Security?*, 149–51.

74 Kimmel and Robinson, 'The Queer Career.'

75 Kinsman and Gentile, *The Canadian War on 'Queers'* (forthcoming).

76 RCMP, 'Assessment of the Gay Alliance towards Equality' (Vancouver 1973); released under the Access to Information Act.

77 RCMP, 'Report on the Toronto Wages for Housework Committee (TWHC) and Unaligned Marxist and Pressure Groups' (Toronto 1976); released under the Access to Information Act.

78 Dorothy Smith, 'Femininity as Discourse,' in *Texts, Facts and Femininity*, 159–208.

79 On performances of lesbianism in relation to gender see Becki Ross, *The House That Jill Built: A Lesbian Nation in Formation* (Toronto: U of Toronto P, 1995), and her 'Destaining the Delinquent Body: Moral Regulatory Practices at Street Haven, 1965–1969,' *Journal of the History of Sexuality* 7.4 (1997): 561–95; Joan Nestle, 'Butch-Femme Relationships: Sexual Courage in the 1950s,' in Nestle, *A Restricted Country* (Ithaca: Firebrand, 1987), 100–9; Elizabeth Lapovsky Kennedy and Madeline D. Davis, *Boots of Leather, Slippers of Gold: The Making of a Lesbian Community* (New York: Routledge, 1993); and *Forbidden Love*, Aerlyn Weissman and Lynne Fernie, directors, National Film Board of Canada, 1993.

80 Kinsman, *The Regulation of Desire*, 359–60.

81 Brian K. Smith, CBC Radio News, 14 April 1998; Jeff Sallot, 'The spy masters' talent hunt goes public,' *Globe and Mail*, 22 June, 1999, A1, A14.

82 Kinsman and Gentile, *In the Interests of the State*, 143.

83 Zuhair Kashmeri, *The Gulf Within: Canadian Arabs, Racism and the Gulf War* (Toronto: James Lorimer, 1991).

84 Naomi Klein, *No Logo: Taking Aim at the Brand Name Bullies* (Toronto: Knopf, 2000); David McNally, *Another World Is Possible: Globalization and Anti-capitalism* (Winnipeg, Arbieter Ring Publishing, 2002).

85 Karen Pearlston, 'APEC Days at UBC: Student Protests and National Security in an Era of Trade Liberalization,' in Kinsman et al., eds., *Whose National Security?*, 267–77; W. Wesley Pue, *Pepper in Our Eyes: The APEC Affair* (Vancouver: U of British Columbia P, 2000).

86 McNally, *Another World Is Possible*.

Part III: Love

5

Margin Notes:
Reading Lesbianism as Obscenity in a
Cold War Courtroom

MARY LOUISE ADAMS

In March 1952, the National News Company, an Ottawa periodical distributor, was charged, under Section 207 of the Criminal Code, with eleven counts of distributing obscene materials. Seven 'girlie' magazines and four novels were named in the charges. The magazines included titles like *Peep Show, Eyefull, Titter,* and *Wink.* The novels were examples of inexpensive drugstore pulp: *Women's Barracks, Journeyman, Tragic Ground,* and *Diamond Lil.* All eleven publications were eventually found to be obscene and National News was fined a total of eleven hundred dollars.[1] An appeal of the decision was rejected.

The trial against National News was 'believed to be the first of its kind in Canada' and was 'regarded by legal experts as a "test."'[2] Three years earlier, amendments to the Criminal Code had greatly increased the power of the courts to crack down on wholesalers and distributors of so-called obscene materials. No longer permitted to defend themselves with claims of ignorance about the content of the materials they carried, distributors were forced to take on the responsibility of policing their own stock.[3] In successfully convicting National News, the Crown demonstrated the willingness of the government to fight obscenity and what one social commentator called 'the pornographic flood' in drugstores and on newsstands.[4]

For the present-day historian of sexuality, the National News case takes on importance not so much because it marks a legal innovation but because one may learn a great deal from the trial about how obscenity was defined then, and about the sexual discourses that made this definition possible. In this chapter, I am concerned with the charges against *Women's Barracks*, a novel included in the action specifically because of its lesbian content. While the seven magazines were barely mentioned in the courtroom, and while discussion of the other three novels occupied a single day, the discussion of *Women's Barracks* took up two days of the trial.[5] The trial thus stands as a unique and relatively lengthy consideration of female homosexuality, a topic that, in the 1940s and 1950s, rarely made it into public discourse. After the Second World War, newspapers, magazines, and advice books were very concerned about nonconforming sexuality, and frequently discussed sexual perversions and sexual abnormalities; however, specific mentions of homosexuality are more difficult to find. Rarer still are acknowledgments that some homosexual 'perverts' were actually women. Given this, the *Barracks* transcript is an important document that can tell us much about Cold War discourses about lesbianism and homosexuality. It also points to the ways such discourses were constructed in a vast postwar landscape of moral and sexual regulation.

The Context: Domesticity, Deviance, and the Cold War

According to historian Doug Owram, the physical and emotional disruptions caused by the Second World War, and the significant social changes it motivated, oriented Canadians towards home, family, and stability to a degree that is unparalleled in other historical periods. Owram argues that 'the attachment to home and family was a primary value of the age and therefore may be crucial to understanding the economy, gender relations, politics and other facets of the post-war years.'[6]

During the Great Depression of the 1930s, fears about security and the future had been attributed to material deprivation and the social disruptions that followed from it. But after the Second World War, discourses about an uncertain future existed in spite of considerable improvement in material circumstances across North America. While 25 per cent of the Canadian population continued to live in poverty into the 1960s, this figure was down substantially from the 50 per cent that had been the average in the interwar years.[7] During the postwar period, the United States and Canada had the first and second highest standards of living in the world. Total industrial output rose by 50 per cent in the 1950s. Canadian manufacturing wages doubled between 1945 and 1956, while prices rose only slightly. Unemployment remained between 2.8 and 5.9 per cent, depending on the region, until the mid-

1950s.[8] In contrast, the 1933 national unemployment rate had been 20 per cent.[9] Between 1948 and 1961, home ownership jumped from just over 30 per cent to 60 per cent. Clearly, many Canadians were better off than they had been. Still, public speakers and journalists referred to a kind of collective distrust of the future. This complicated social anxiety is a hallmark of the Cold War, a time when Canadians were nervous about the world beyond their borders, about the unknown, and about the 'other.'

In the face of rapid social and economic changes, Canadians were encouraged to devote themselves to building solid, stable families, which at that time meant patriarchal, nuclear families constructed around heterosexual married couples.[10] As an institution, the family was promoted in magazines, school board curricula, and instructional films as the first line of defence against the perceived insecurity of the Cold War years. Family life would protect Canada against the threat of outside turmoil.

While Canada was not a big player in the East/West conflict, the country was most definitely a participant. And, as Elaine May has shown in her book *Homeward Bound*, international affairs, in those years of prosperity, were central to family discourse and contributed to the need North Americans expressed for control on a personal level. According to May, the postwar family was located firmly 'within the larger political culture, not outside it,'[11] although contemporary representations of the family usually portrayed the opposite. In the Canadian context, the relationship between 'the family' and the political realm still needs to be subjected to investigation, especially given the rise of the welfare state and the specifics of the Cold War experience in Canada.[12] Cold War rhetoric and the activities that followed from it were not the same in Canada as they were in the United States. However, few Canadians could have escaped the U.S. Cold War hype that infused the popular culture of the era – from the predominantly American films and television shows that came across the border, to the magazines that, by 1954, occupied 80 per cent of Canadian newsstand space.[13]

In Canada, the East/West conflict that eventually came to be known as the Cold War started in 1945 when Igor Gouzenko, a cypher clerk in the Soviet embassy in Ottawa, defected and claimed that the Soviets had been running a spy ring in Canada. Investigations into his allegations focused national attention on the need for internal defences against communism. According to Len Scher, an unsuccessful search for spy

rings gave way to efforts to track 'domestic dissidents.'[14] Between
October 1950 and June 1951, the RCMP dealt with 54,000 requests to
screen both civil servants and private sector workers.[15] Those who were
most likely to be put under surveillance included labour organizers,
members of communist and socialist organizations, peace activists, and
homosexuals. Deviance from any number of mainstream norms, writes
Philip Girard, 'represented an independence of mind that could no
longer be tolerated' during the Cold War. In such a climate, 'the unknown' – homosexuals for instance – 'represented a triune denial of
God, family and (implicitly or potentially) country at a time when
departing from any one of these norms was immediately suspect.'[16]
Deviance also undermined the homogenization that was seen to be
central to Canada's strength as a nation. The conformity that is so often
identified as a primary aspect of postwar social life wasn't simply a
characteristic of increased consumerism and/or the centralization of
popular culture and entertainment industries. It was also produced by
an approach to citizenship that demanded a willingness to participate
in social consensus, to adopt a shared set of behavioural standards and
mores.

In 1946, the interdepartmental Security Panel (National Defence, External Affairs, and the RCMP) was established to check on federal civil
servants who had been identified by the RCMP as security risks. In the
first three months of the panel's operation, the RCMP offered panel
officials 5466 names. Checks on these individuals resulted in 213 'adverse reports,' but only 27 of the people in question were determined to
be bona fide security risks – that is, possible spies. The remainder had
been included on the original list because of 'moral' failings or 'character' weaknesses, a category that included homosexuals and parents of
illegitimate children, among others.[17] To security officials, these character weaknesses suggested an inability to do the right thing, a tendency
to compromise, an impairment of moral fibre. These were the character-
istics of someone who might be influenced by communists or, worse,
who might *be* a communist. 'Normal' sexual and moral development
signalled maturity and an ability to assume responsibility. By contrast,
those who transgressed sexual and moral norms were assumed to be
trapped in adolescence and thus immature. How, then, could they be
counted on to stand on guard for their country?

In the 1950s, the RCMP developed a special unit to root out homosexuals from the civil service. In 1952, Canadian immigration laws were
quietly changed to prevent homosexuals from entering the country.

The fact that homosexuals and other moral deviants were identified as particularly dangerous by the guardians of national security suggests the importance of normative sexuality on the social and political landscape of postwar Canada. The vilification of sexual deviants did much to shore up the primary position of the heterosexual nuclear family as the only legitimate site of sexual expression. However, the links made between sexuality and national security also suggest the way that sexuality functioned as a site for the displacement of general social and political anxieties. In official discourses, homosexuality was constructed not simply as the tragic fate of particular individuals but as a force so menacing that it had the potential to undermine the strength of the nation. In the context of the Cold War, communists, spies, and those with mysterious, questionable sex habits or morals were almost equal threats to the sanctity of the Dominion.

Indecency as a National Threat

With sexual discourses playing a central role in the definition of the nation's future, it is not surprising that many Canadians grew to be concerned over representations of sexuality in so-called indecent or lewd publications. In 1952, the Canadian Senate established a special committee to investigate 'salacious and indecent literature.' Initiator J.J. Hayes Doone, a senator from New Brunswick, had appealed to his colleagues 'on behalf of the children' to look into the proliferation of 'offensive publications.' Such materials, he said, provoked juvenile delinquency, were 'dangerous to the permanence of family life,' and were 'evidence of a breakdown in our social machinery.'[18] Apparently, Hayes Doone's views were shared by many. The committee met over two parliamentary sessions, it heard twenty-five witnesses and received hundreds of briefs, letters, and petitions. The committee's 1953 report stated that 'in the world-wide struggle between the forces of darkness and evil and those of good, the freedom-loving, democratic countries have need of all the strength in their moral fibre to combat the evil threat, and anything that undermines the morals of our citizens and particularly the young is a direct un-Canadian threat.'[19]

The Senate Special Committee on Salacious and Indecent Literature was the most institutionalized manifestation of a postwar preoccupation with and disapproval of obscenity. Its efforts were mirrored by church groups, Parent Teacher Associations, and labour unions, at town and city council meetings, and on the editorial pages of newspapers.[20]

'Concerned citizens' claimed that trashy books and magazines were powerful enough not just to threaten but to cancel the efforts of church, school, and home to educate young people about proper forms of sex and family living. Members of the Canadian Committee for the International Conference in Defence of Children worried that indecent literature might turn young people from the goals adults had set for them: 'high ideals, noble emotions and constructive action directed to the general good.'[21] Pulp literature was seen as subversive competition for the approved forms of sex education that promoted the normalization of sexual and moral standards. The outcome of this contest could affect 'the whole moral tone of the nation' and the future of its citizens.[22]

In the 1930s and 1940s, producers of mass market literature had experienced a tremendous boom. New genres, and new approaches to marketing and distribution, were combined with improvements in printing techniques to make the publication of comics, cheap magazines, and pocketbooks increasingly profitable.[23] In Canada, the pulp trade had been curtailed temporarily by wartime restrictions on both the use of paper and the importation of publications from the United States. But, after the war, Canadian newsstands felt the full impact of this growing sector of the publishing industry.

Alongside the boom in pulp novels and comic books, 'sexy magazines' were becoming increasingly visible. In a 1952 *Reader's Digest* article, Margaret Culkin Banning describes a sample of the genre: 'In one magazine published recently there were 58 photographs of girls in varying states of undress: some wore only G-strings and brassieres; others were naked except for muffs of fur and feathers. One girl was posed removing her bra; another had a man's picture painted high up on her thigh. The girls were photographed from the back, from the front, upside down. Captions read: "Hot from toes to Bikini," "A yum-yum platinum blonde," "A blue-eyed beauty who likes tall rugged guys."'[24] According to Banning, 'obscene' magazines were not, in and of themselves, new; what was new was their accessibility. In the years before the Second World War, they could be found in (male) adult environments like 'barbershops, saloons and army posts.' By the 1950s, however, 'sexy magazines' were being sold, along with other kinds of material perceived to be indecent, right at the corner drugstore, on the same shelves as family magazines and 'useful books.'[25] It was in 1953 that 'sexy magazines' made their biggest move toward legitimacy with the launch of the 'tasteful' and expensively produced *Playboy*.[26]

Anxiety about the availability and variety of indecent material merged with anxiety about its content in calls for government control of the new media. Concerned citizens, as individuals and as members of a wide spectrum of organizations, condemned the 'licentiousness of magazines,'[27] the 'flood of objectionable literature,'[28] 'pornography for profit,'[29] and, among other things, the transformation of Canada into 'an open end[ed] sewer' for filth from the United States.[30] For the most part, these objections were articulated through a discourse of concern for youth, who, it was assumed, had relatively unlimited access to inexpensive printed materials over which their parents and teachers had little control. As a Toronto man protested in a letter to the (nonexistent) Ontario Government Censorship Bureau (for which the Attorney General's office responded), 'These books, many of them filthy in the extreme, have alluring colour covers, and any adolescent can buy publications for 25 [cents], that his parents would be shocked to read.'[31]

This fear that mass media were dividing parent from child was not unique to postwar North America.[32] It had followed the emergence of novels in the nineteenth century and of silent films in the 1910s and 1920s. It would re-emerge over the popularization of television in the late 1950s and the 1960s. We can see it today in discussions about the Internet. Writing about the British campaign of the mid-1950s against horror comics, Martin Barker says that 'each rising mass medium in turn has been targeted in the name of revered values.'[33] But, he adds, the source of parental and social concern is less a factor of the medium to which they object than of the values they assume to be threatened. Where turn-of-the-century working-class parents worried that commercial entertainments, like cheap movies, undermined traditional gender roles and put their daughters in too close proximity with boys,[34] middle-class parents of the 1950s worried about standards of sexual behaviour and whether the pulps led their children towards deviance. In both cases, the medium was an easier target of popular protest than the general social context which spawned it.

In Canada, in the late 1940s and the 1950s, debates about the moral effects of mass market publications crystallized concerns about the nature of youth, their relationship to sexuality, and the place and character of sexuality within Canadian society. Those who argued for censorship of the new media or for control over its distribution almost invariably claimed to be motivated by fears for their children's future moral development and the future of the nation. Teenagers with corrupted morals would be less likely to be influenced by 'concerned adults,' and less likely to meet the normative standards of heterosexual behaviour that were assumed to be critical to social stability.

In the context of Cold War Canada, 'youth' as a category was a primary source of social anxiety about moral decay and changing sexual attitudes. It was precisely these discourses about the 'corruptibility' of youth, and their need for protection from worldly affairs – sex in particular – that provided the impetus for the judgment against *Women's Barracks* and National News. Discursive constructions of youthful innocence were critical to the attempts to marginalize non-normative forms of sexual expression in this case. Indeed, it was notions about youth and teenage sexual development that gave arguments on both sides of the courtroom their moral weight.

The Book

The first published work of a French author named Tereska Torres,[35] *Women's Barracks* follows a group of women in the Free French Army who lived in a London barracks during the Second World War. Torres writes about their work assignments and drills, their hopes for France, and their social and sexual lives. The characters are a mixed lot, mostly young heterosexuals, although there are two 'real' lesbians and an 'older,' forty-year-old, sexually experienced woman who has affairs with both men and women. Some of the straight women have affairs with married men and one of them gets pregnant. The bisexual woman 'seduces' a naive sixteen-year-old girl who instantly falls in love with her. All of the women drink.

In the midst of this activity, the narrator operates as the moral centre of the book. She distances herself from the other women and their sexual and emotional experiments – engaging in none of her own – trying to maintain her ideals about love, fidelity, and marriage. In her forward to the book, Torres identifies herself as the narrator. She says that the stories in the novel are based on her own experiences in London during the war, and, indeed, she repeats many of them in her 1970 autobiography, *The Converts*.[36] A daughter of Polish Jews who had converted to Catholicism, Torres grew up in Paris. But as German armies approached, her family fled to Portugal. Later they moved to England, where, at the age of seventeen, Torres volunteered for service in De Gaulle's Women's Army Corps. In the foreword to *Women's Barracks* she writes, 'Naturally I was not present myself during all of the incidents that I am about to relate. Yet I know that these things happened, and I know well the women to whom they happened. These episodes are important, because they are significant of the pressures and tensions that all of us felt, and that all women must inevitably feel when they are isolated from normal living, caught in the strange turmoil of war.'[37]

The book's preface, written by translator George Cummings, takes a similar position. Cummings, who claims to have met Torres while he was working in the Office of War Information in London, says that the novel is the 'story of women in war.' It is, he claims,

> the story of the effect of living together in military barracks upon a group of young girls, many of them utterly innocent when they entered the service, where they were to encounter jaded women who had lived through every type of experience. I recognized the authenticity of every line. The problems brought forward here are problems that must be recognized wherever women have to live together without normal emotional outlets. What is told here should help to bring understanding of these special problems, for the story of Down Street [where the barracks was located] reminds us that women must be women, even in war.[38]

To the present-day reader, Torres's writing is far from lurid. Nevertheless, *Women's Barracks* was packaged in typical 1950s pulp style and marketed as 'THE FRANK AUTOBIOGRAPHY OF A FRENCH GIRL SOLDIER.' On the cover are five women in various states of dress: one sits in full uniform, smoking a cigarette, gazing at the others; another in pink bra and panties, steps into her skirt; a third, also wearing a pink bra and the cap to her uniform, holds a cigarette between her lips as she zips up her skirt; a fourth sits wrapped in a towel, putting cream on her face; and a fifth, partially obscured by the others and facing away from us, appears to be naked. All of them are young and attractive. As an invitation to titillation, however, the cover promises more than the book delivers.[39]

The Trial

When the book first came to trial in Ottawa, Crown Attorney Raoul Mercier's strategy was simply to prove that the book had been for sale in a particular cigar store, that the book had been distributed by National News, and that copies of the book had been found on the premises of the distribution company. He had no doubt that the judge would find the text itself obscene.

In 1952, the test of obscenity used by Canadian courts was 'whether the tendency of the matter charged as obscene is to deprave and corrupt those whose minds are open to such immoral influence and into whose hands a publication of this sort may fall.'[40] It was a lowest common denominator definition of what was appropriate for Canadian readers, adults and children alike. Known as the Hicklin test, after the British judge who first defined it in 1868, this test assumed the potential of reading material to 'deprave and corrupt.' It also took for granted that there existed persons whose minds were 'open' to influence. In the years after the Second World War, the innocent and impressionable youth of popular discourse easily fit that description. Thus, what was bad for the young could be declared bad in general, and for this reason adolescents and children were routinely invoked by both sides of the *Women's Barracks* obscenity case.

Obscenity legislation fell under Section 207 of the Criminal Code, according to which no one could be charged with obscenity if they could prove that the 'public good' had been served by the publication, image, or act in question. As one of the judges who rejected the appeal of National News wrote, this provision could 'not change something which is obscene into something which is not obscene'; it merely recognized that so-called filth and ugliness sometimes had to be aired publicly in service of its own elimination. This was the basis of the defence strategy pursued by National News's lawyers G.W. Ford and J.M. McLean. As they put it, even if Torres's book was technically obscene, it still might have fulfilled a useful social purpose.[41] While Torres and her translator fancied the book an argument against war – a position most of the defence witnesses apparently agreed with – Ford and Maclean portrayed *Women's Barracks* as a treatise against the dangers of lesbianism. After 'experts' were called to back this claim, the Crown attorney revised his original game plan and called his own experts to prove the first lot wrong.

While lesbianism is clearly not the focus of the novel, it was the cornerstone of courtroom debate. A copy of the novel is presently on file with the court transcripts at the Archives of Ontario. Inside the book's front cover, written in black pen, are the initials 'R.M.,' presumably referring to the Crown attorney on the case, Raoul Mercier. Throughout this copy of the book, the text is underlined and annotated in both pencil and black pen. Fifteen individual pages are marked with tags made out of sticky tape, possibly pages from which Mercier might have wanted to read in the courtroom. On all but two of these pages there is some reference to lesbianism (the other two tags mark a slang reference to prostitution and a scene where a young woman loses her virginity to a man). In the margins is written repeatedly 'lesbianism' and 'sex act.' Other markings say: 'lesbian crave' (p. 56), 'ménage à trois' (p. 87), 'homosexual' (p. 32), 'act of lesbianism' (p. 125), followed, on the same page by 'all previous chapters lead to but this one climax' (p. 46), referring to the single scene of lesbian seduction. An untagged passage after the seduction scene is annotated: 'very little war service, so far, all a preparation for a show of lust and lesbianism.' There are no tags on the parts where heterosexual women find themselves pregnant, or where they discuss their plans to sleep with married men or where they try to commit suicide. What made this book obscene – as Mercier argued clearly throughout the trial – was, quite simply, its discussion of lesbianism.

Here is a sample of some of that discussion, from the text of a heavily underlined passage, where the margin note reads, 'lesbianism':

Like most of the girls in the barracks, I had taken Ann and all Lesbians somehow as freaks, even to be considered amusing. Listening to her in that tragic purgatory [as bombs fell on London], I wanted to weep. Ann had spent her childhood in France, raised by her mother in poverty. She was an illegitimate child. She had shown unusual sexual tendencies when she was still scarcely grown. She had left her mother, and little by little cut herself away from all her early connections as she entered the spheres of her particular passion. She had come to England with a woman. When she had broken with her, Ann had found herself alone and penniless in London. It was just at the time of the defeat of France, and Ann had volunteered for De Gaulle's forces ... Ann could not live without [a] liaison. It wasn't so much a need of love as a need of an affair with all its accompaniment of intrigue, mystery, and the consequent pleasure. By herself, she was not outside the normal; she was only so when she had a partner. And yet this departure was necessary to her, as she had found out when scarcely more than a child. She could not live otherwise. Without a partner she felt as though something were amputated from her.[42]

From this and other passages in the book, it seems that Torres herself was well-versed in mainstream perspectives on female homosexuality: her 'real' lesbians are objects of pity, sad creatures who make the best of their pathetic lot in life. Not surprisingly, they play only supporting roles as the plot of *Women's Barracks* unfolds, a fact that seems to have been lost on Mercier.

Needless to say, none of the 'expert' witnesses called to the stand were experts on lesbianism per se. They were called not to pass judgment on lesbianism but to testify as to the literary and social merits of the novel. But, knowledgeable about lesbianism or not, all took the opportunity to discuss the subject. Witnesses for the defence included John Verner McAree, columnist and literary critic for the *Globe and Mail*; Professor Henry Alexander, head of the Department of English Literature at Queen's University in Kingston; Professor Allan Seiger, Department of English at the University of Michigan, former editor of *Vanity Fair* and published novelist and short story writer; Professor John Bakless, Department of Journalism at the University of New York, and writer of book reviews; and, Robertson Davies, editor of the Peterborough *Examiner*, a writer and literary critic. Witnesses for the Crown included Professor Emmet O'Grady from the English Department at the University of Ottawa; Reverend Terrence Findlay, Rector of St John's Anglican Church in Ottawa and chaplain to the WRENS stationed in Winnipeg during the war; Vincent Kelly, principal of St Patrick's High School in Ottawa; and, Isabelle Finlayson, housewife, mother of two children, member of the Ottawa Public School Board, former president of the Ottawa Council of Women and of the Women's Canadian Club, and former corresponding secretary and vice-president of the National Council of Women.

McAree, O'Grady, and Finlayson all admitted to having no knowledge of lesbianism or lesbians. Bakless claimed he had read 'as little as possible' about lesbianism. He had, however, seen lesbians first-hand while working with U.S. Army Intelligence during the war. Crown Attorney Mercier asked him: 'Did you ever look [for or at lesbians]?' Bakless answered: 'Yes, it was not nice.' Mercier continued: 'Did you see lesbians?' To which Bakless answered: 'I think once by accident' (transcript p. 65). Reverend Findlay was also asked about his wartime experiences with lesbians. He claimed not to have seen any, and certainly not 'in our Canadian WRENS' (transcript p. 370).

Robertson Davies said he'd learned of lesbianism from women friends: 'I have not had experience of life in a women's barracks, but I have had a number of women friends who have been attendants at girls' schools in France, and the incidents which occurred in the book do not appear to me to be exaggerated' (transcript p. 304). He adds: 'From what I have read in books of sexual studies [perhaps referring to the Kinsey report on *Sexual Behaviour in the Human Male* which was released in 1948], sir, it seems to me in any large collection of people, men or women, there will be a certain number of people who would be sexually abnormal' (transcript p. 304).

While the two groups of witnesses were divided over their definitions of obscenity, they spoke as one in their conflation of lesbianism and immorality. In fact, arguments on both sides of the courtroom depended on an understanding of lesbianism as a social 'problem,' a sexual aberration. The basis of defence arguments was that Torres's book was valuable for the service it performed in warning her readers, particularly teenaged girls, of the dangers of lesbianism. As Queen's English professor Henry Alexander said, 'It is difficult to get inside the mind of an author, but as far as I could judge I would think she wants to show what effect this unnatural environment has on the characters of some of the women who are rather unbalanced, and the others who become somewhat unbalanced through the pressure of circumstances' (transcript p. 33). He went on to say that reading the book 'would deter anybody who was inclined in that subject. There is so much degeneration, so much pathos in the atmosphere, so many people end up unhappy, that it would act more of a deterrent than anything else' (transcript p. 35).

Dr John Bakless, from the University of New York, stated that the book presented the lesbian episodes as being 'positively repulsive to any normal male or female' (transcript p. 64). He also said that in 'the context of the book as a whole they clearly point out that the wages of sin is death' (transcript p. 54). But the Crown rejected Bakless's arguments. Mercier asked, '[Wouldn't] a little girl who is not maybe a French woman in the same barracks, but who is in a convent or in a boarding school reaching the puberty age, does not know anything about these things, reads this passage from this book, wouldn't you say they would be willing to indulge in this practice to see if it is as described?' Bakless replied: 'I have read that book through, and I wouldn't want to be near a lesbian. Don't forget what happens.' The Crown Attorney tried again: 'And you do not think they [young girls who have read the book] would be tempted to try lesbianism?' 'No,' Bakless said, 'there is disaster there too plainly, and it is only with sympathy and regret that you can read it' (transcript p. 64).

These comments relate to that part of the narrative involving Ursula, the sixteen-year-old, who sleeps with Claude, the forty-year-old bi-

sexual, and falls in love with her. Claude 'toys' with Ursula emotionally, and in her tormented state, Ursula can muster no feelings for a
Polish male soldier who is interested in her. Later she tries to have sex
with a male sailor from France. But she can't do it and he ends up
treating her like a little sister for the several days they spend together.
After this, Ursula's affections for Claude diminish. She falls in love with
the Polish soldier, they plan to marry, she gets pregnant, he goes off to
the front and is killed. In despair, she kills herself. This is a disaster,
certainly, but the sequence of events is hardly caused by her one night
of lesbian sex.

In spite of all this pathos, Mercier and his collection of expert witnesses continually pointed to the pleasures to be found in the picture
of lesbianism painted by Torres. Indeed, they claimed that Torres's
account was far too attractive an image of something more properly
understood to be dangerous. They referred again and again to the
passage where Ursula finds herself in bed with Claude – the only
explicitly 'lesbian sex' scene in the book (and not surprisingly, the
markings in Mercier's copy of the book become quite frenzied at this
point):

> Ursula felt herself very small, tiny against Claude, and at last she felt
> warm. She placed her cheek on Claude's breast. Her heart beat violently,
> but she didn't feel afraid. She didn't understand what was happening to
> her. Claude was not a man; then what was she doing to her? What strange
> movements! What could they mean? Claude unbuttoned the jacket of her
> pajamas, and enclosed one of Ursula's little breasts in her hand, and then
> gently, very gently, her hand began to caress all of Ursula's body, her
> throat, her shoulders, and her belly. Ursula remembered a novel that she
> had read that said of a woman who was making love, 'Her body vibrated
> like a violin.' Ursula had been highly pleased by this phrase, and now her
> body recalled the expression and it too began to vibrate. She was stretched
> out with her eyes closed, motionless, not daring to make the slightest
> gesture, indeed not knowing what she should do. And Claude kissed her
> gently, and caressed her ... Ursula didn't feel any special pleasure, only an
> immense astonishment. She had loved Claude's mouth, but now she felt
> somewhat scandalized. But little by little, as Claude continued her slow
> caressing, Ursula lost her astonishment. She kept saying to herself, I adore
> her, I adore her. And nothing else counted. All at once, her insignificant
> and monotonous life had become full, rich and marvelous ... Ursula wanted
> only one thing, to keep this refuge forever, this warmth, this security.[43]

What, Mercier wanted to know, would become of a normal teenage girl who read this passage? Adult women, surely, would have had the moral strength to resist the temptations of such a positive image. But teenagers, their moral characters not yet fully developed, would have been less able to distinguish right from wrong in this case. According to Isabelle Finlayson, speaking for the Crown, teens had not had enough experience to 'be expected to form their [moral] standards, therefore, they would take it [the lesbian sexual activity] as a proper conduct, as conduct accepted generally' (transcript p. 380). Finlayson was suggesting that teens had not yet had time to bring their standards in line with socially approved ones. They were still, in a sense, moral works-in-progress who might choose pleasure over indignation and denial.

According to Reverend Terrence Findlay, another Crown witness, the danger of the seduction scene was that a young girl might read such a passage and learn that lesbian sexual activity was possible and that it might be pleasant. Books like *Women's Barracks*, the Reverend said, tended to sway normal girls toward the abnormal, by making the latter seem both attractive and possible. 'I only wish to add,' he said, 'the background of the teenager, her training would, I think, affect the reaction from the reading of that book. The girl who had had no training – as you [defence attorney] suggest it would be a good thing for them to be instructed in the dangers of lesbianism, a girl who had not had training, I think that book would have a tendency to suggest to that girl that here is a way of satisfying sexual desires without the danger of consorting with male companions' (transcript p. 361).

The discussion about the tendency of the book to incite abnormality in 'normal' readers was entered into again and again during courtroom debate. In the years after the Second World War, 'normality' was a critical measure of difference between individuals and between groups of people. As defined by the psychological and psychoanalytic theories that became increasingly popular during the 1950s, normality was seen as the desired result of an individual's emotional and psychic development, a product of social and environmental factors.[44] Such had not been the case at the beginning of the century when normality and abnormality were both seen, primarily, as bodily and not psychic conditions,[45] and, as we know from present-day discourses about sexual orientation, such biological explanations have never been completely overturned. Books and magazines published in the years after the war were littered with discussions of what was normal and what was not, from parenting styles to housekeeping plans. In the late 1950s, June

Callwood wrote an article with psychiatrist Alastair MacLeod for *Chat-elaine* called 'How Do You Know You're Normal?'[46] Teachers at the Toronto Board of Education invoked 'normality' no fewer than four times on the first page of a 1948 brief on sex education.[47] Advice books for teens, as a genre, were, for the most part, lengthy explanations of how to reach normality.[48] And, for teens, especially, it was thought to be a critical issue. They were to be the parents of the future; they were the ones who would carry Canada towards success or failure in the modern world. But in the popular theories of the day, teens were the most vulnerable to corruption, to derailment from the straight path. They were most at risk from the uncertainties of the era, and thus their achievement of normality was in no sense inevitable.

After the Second World War, teens and those who advised them saw adolescence as a time of learning about and being measured by prevailing social standards. As adults-in-process, adolescents were in training for a 'maturity' which was equated with nothing if not normality.[49] And, once having achieved normality, they would be ready to create the strong, heterosexual families that were thought necessary to defend Canadian freedoms – strong families were based on sexually fulfilling marriages for both men and women. In this context, sexual abnormalities were not only a sign of personal failure, they were tears in a protective social fabric.

While the Crown tried to suggest that 'normal' girls could be corrupted by books such as *Women's Barracks*, the defence lawyers argued that, to the contrary, their normality would protect such girls from the book's less savoury passages. Wouldn't the pleasure of the seduction scene be annulled by the scene where Ursula finds herself unable to have sexual relations with the French sailor? For Ford (one of the two defence lawyers), these two scenes were intrinsically linked – lesbian sex led to frigidity with men. (One is puzzled as to how he accounted for Ursula's pregnancy at the book's end.) Wouldn't a 'normal teenage girl' with 'normal sexual reactions' be 'nauseated' by Ursula's 'abnormal relations' – the latter phrase referring both to sex with a woman and an inability to engage in intercourse with a man (transcript p. 365)? Ford asked Professor O'Grady, testifying for the Crown, 'whether or not it is a fact in this novel [that] the effect of lesbianism on Ursula, a victim of it, is painted such as to indicate an abnormal effect on her sexual instincts?' O'Grady agreed. For Ford, the possibility of 'abnormal effects' was enough to keep young girls from lesbian experimentation.

Ford wanted *Women's Barracks* to be taken up as a cautionary tale that might warn young women of the dangers of lesbianism and, in this way, might serve the public good. No one disagreed with him over the need for this, although Crown witnesses rejected Torres's book as appropriate to the task. But, asked Ford, weren't they all better informed on the subject after having read the novel? Isabelle Finlayson, in particular, claimed she had known nothing about lesbianism before she read the book. How then, asked Ford, could she possibly have warned her own daughter of lesbian dangers (transcript 388)? Ford's argument had nothing to do with the book's effects on Finlayson herself; as an adult she was assumed to be beyond its influence, capable of reaching her own conclusions on such a vexing moral issue. Reading the seduction scene, someone like Finlayson, well-schooled in popular discourses about sexual deviance and perversion, would have been able to see past the pleasure to the downfall which would inevitably follow. A teenage girl, on the other hand, needed to have that downfall made explicit. According to Ford, Torres's novel did just that. It provided the dangerous context that schoolgirl gossip and curbside chatter about lesbianism might not.

The Judgment

Judge McDougall did not accept Ford's case. In his judgment he wrote:

> [The book] deals almost entirely with the question of sex relationships and also with the question of lesbianism. A great deal of the language, and particularly the description of two incidents of unnatural relationships between women, is exceedingly frank. The argument advanced before me was that publicity should be given to the question of lesbianism in order that it might act as a deterrent influence and in this respect would be a matter of public good. The dissemination of such information is no doubt a matter that should receive proper attention from a medical and psychological standpoint, but the manner in which the material is presented in this book does not comply with those standards in any manner.[50]

It is impossible to know how the judgment actually affected the circulation of *Women's Barracks* or the many other lesbian and gay pulp novels that were produced in the 1950s and 1960s. The trial itself was not widely publicized and the coverage of it that did exist was not consistent. The two stories that appeared in the Ottawa *Evening Citizen*, for instance, focused only on the other three novels in the trial; no mention was made of *Women's Barracks* or of the lesbian content that led to its being included in the charges against National News.[51] The *Toronto Globe and Mail*, on the other hand, focused exclusively on Torres's book in the two very short articles it published on the trial.[52] If media coverage is any indication, the National News trial was not a major event. This is not to say, however, that it did not have a significant impact on the distribution of pulp novels more generally. In February 1954, just two and a half months after the National News conviction, the Periodical Distributors of Canada submitted a brief to the Attorney General of Ontario with suggestions of how to mitigate the effects of future complaints about so-called obscene materials. The association proposed to employ an officer in Toronto who would investigate complaints and who would be responsible for encouraging publishers to remove such publications from circulation.[53] It seems the suggestion was not taken up by the government as it appeared in another brief, three years later.[54] At that time, Attorney General Kelso Roberts invited the Periodical Distributors to participate in a government committee on obscenity: '[The distributors] are bent on improving the standards and helping to eliminate the bad spots in this problem, progress should result of a worthwhile nature.'[55]

In Ottawa, the non-court-ordered restraint of materials was more than just a proposal. In 1955, a distributor called American News faced eleven charges of 'having in possession for the purpose of distribution obscene written matter relating to some 11 paper covered novels. In addition to these charges there are 7 charges concerning the same books of distributing to certain named retailers.'[56] In a letter to the Attorney General's office, R.K. Laishley, lawyer for American News, details how the charges came about:

> My understanding of how the complaints arose in respect of this Company was due to the publications with which the charges are concerned being brought to the attention of the Local Crown Attorney through information obtained by a group of persons in this City who for some time past have interested themselves in this type of publication and who call themselves The Good Reading Committee. This Committee is headed by Mr. Vincent Kelly [a Crown witness during the National News trial] who was appointed by the Knights of Columbus in this area to report on this type of thing ... For some time this Committee has been reading and vetting books distributed by the National News Company Ltd. in this

City. This arrangement was arrived at some time after the conviction of the National News Company in 1953.[57]

Apparently, American News also had been requested to submit books to the Good Reading Committee after the National News conviction, but American News had declined because the committee was 'unauthorized.' After American News had been charged, their representatives approached the Crown attorney, Raoul Mercier (again), and the Good Reading Committee, saying that they would submit their stock for vetting in exchange for the charges being dropped. While Kelly was pleased with the change of heart, neither he nor Mercier would interfere in a case that would soon be before the courts.

The kind of insidious censorship practised by the Catholic Church-dominated Good Reading Committee is an excellent example of how legislative regulation can have effects that extend far beyond the courtroom. On the surface, the National News trial led to a fine, and, presumably, to nothing more than restrictions on the circulation of four pulp novels and seven 'girlie' magazines. In reality, the trial – which was made possible, in part, by postwar concerns about changing sexual moralities and how those would affect young people – facilitated restrictions on the entire National News stock. It permitted an ad hoc citizens' group, with the backing of the Catholic Church, to impose its values on all those who visited newsstands in the city of Ottawa. When American News refused to cooperate with this unofficial form of censorship, the Good Reading Committee complained to the police, charges were laid, and the courts were relied upon to validate and promote a particular moral vision. In February 1956, American News was convicted and fined five thousand dollars.

What stands out in the discussions during the *Barracks* case is the way that discourses about the vulnerability of young people, about their potential to be sexually corrupted, operated as the catalyst for this whole chain of regulation of so-called indecent material. At no point during the trial was *Women's Barracks* constructed as a danger to grown women. It was, instead, presented as a threat to teenage girls. Discursive constructions of young people as potentially corruptible bolstered the moral regulation of non-dominant representations of sexuality that obscenity legislation achieved. Regulatory efforts undertaken on 'behalf of youth' – for instance, the Senate investigation of obscene literature and the case against *Women's Barracks* – carried a certain moral weight that helped justify their implementation and increased their chances of success. In the *Barracks* case, both sides of the courtroom obviously understood this equation.

In 1953, *Women's Barracks* was the focus of another trial in St Paul, Minnesota, where notions of the corruptibility of young people were *not* part of the definition of obscenity and therefore had no sway over the final judgment. The court concluded that '*Women's Barracks* does not have a substantive tendency to deprave or corrupt by inciting lascivious thoughts or arousing lustful desire in the ordinary reader in this community in these times. It is the finding of the Court that the likelihood of its having such a salacious effect does not outweigh the literary merit it may have in the hands of the average reader.'[58] In Minnesota, the court was concerned not with children, or moral innocents, but with the average, and therefore, adult reader. For such readers, presumably able to make their own moral judgments, there was no reason to regulate representations of nonconforming sexuality, and so the book was not declared to be obscene.

What was at stake in the Canadian furore over obscenity were accepted standards of sexual morality. Indecent material, in its various guises, offered competing ways of making sense of sex, morals, and relationships. Young people – presumed to be moral innocents – and the future they symbolized were seen to be at great threat from the various genres of pulps. Trashy novels and dirty magazines contradicted the many efforts to build 'fine moral citizens' that were popular in postwar Canada, such as sports clubs, teen canteens, and lectures on family life education. The discourses available in material such as *Women's Barracks* threatened the complex of processes that encouraged the normalization of particular forms of sexual expression. Pulps suggested alternative ways of organizing sexuality, ways that might upset the dominance of a family-centred monogamous heterosexuality. Indeed, attentive teenaged readers of *Women's Barracks* might have noticed that it wasn't either of the 'real' lesbians who committed suicide at the end of the book.

Notes

1 *The Queen v. National News Company Limited*, 8 October 1952. Archives of Ontario, RG 4-32, 1953, #830.
2 'Magazine distributor convicted,' *Ottawa Citizen*, 22 November 1952.
3 For a discussion of how the amendment affected the distributors, see 'Brief

Submitted on Behalf of the Periodical Distributors of Canada to Dana Porter, Attorney-General for Ontario,' 9 February 1954. Archives of Ontario, RG 4-32, 1954, #26.

4 F.L.B. Marston of Willowdale, Ontario, in a letter to the editor of the *Globe and Mail*, 9 October 1952.

5 *The Queen v. National News Company Limited.*

6 Doug Owram, 'Home and Family at Mid-Century.' Paper presented at the Canadian Historical Association, Charlottetown, June 1992, p. 1.

7 Alvin Finkel and Margaret Conrad with Veronica Strong-Boag, *History of the Canadian People, 1867–Present* (Toronto, Copp Clark Pitman, 1993), 429–30.

8 R. Douglas Francis, Richard Jones, and Donald B. Smith, *Destinies: Canadian History since Confederation*, 2nd edition (Toronto: Holt, Rinehart and Winston, 1992), 338–9; 353.

9 Finkel et al., 331.

10 Strong families as the root of social stability has been a recurring theme in the face of capitalism's rise and evolution. For a discussion of this see Jane Ursel, *Private Lives: Public Policy: 100 Years of State Intervention in the Family* (Toronto, Women's Press, 1992); Kari Dehli, 'Women and Class: The Social Organization of Mothers' Relations to Schools in Toronto, 1915–1940,' PhD dissertation, U of Toronto (OISE), 1988.

11 Elaine May, *Homeword Bound: American Families in the Cold War Era* (New York: Basic Books, 1988), 10.

12 See Jane Ursel, *Private Lives, Public Policy,* and Allan Moscovitch and Jim Albert, eds., *Benevolent State: The Growth of Welfare in Canada* (Toronto, Garamond, 1987).

13 Finkel et al., 426–7.

14 Len Scher, *The Un-Canadians* (Toronto: Lester, 1992), 8.

15 Scher, 9.

16 Philip Girard, 'From subversion to liberation: Homosexuals and the Immigration Act 1952–1977,' *Canadian Journal of Law and Society* 2 (1987), 3.

17 Girard, 4.

18 I quote from a speech made by Senator J.J. Hayes Doone in New Brunswick, in 1949; cited in Senate, *Debates*, 8 May 1952, 186.

19 Senate Special Committee on Salacious and Indecent Literature, *Report*, 1953, p. 246.

20 In Ontario, evidence of citizen activity around the issue of obscenity is most easily found in the correspondence files of the Attorney-General, who regularly received petitions, resolutions, briefs, and letters calling for government action to curb the circulation of indecent materials. For one

example, see Archives of Ontario, RG 4-02, file 91.7, 1956. Further evidence can be gained from briefs presented to the Senate Special Committee. See the *Proceedings* of the Senate Special Committee on Salacious and Indecent Literature.

21 Canadian Preparatory Committee, International Conference in Defence of Children, Submission to Senate, Special Committee on Salacious and Indecent Literature, *Proceedings* (25 June 1952), 161.

22 Christian Social Council of Canada, Brief Presented to the Senate Special Committee on Salacious and Indecent Literature, *Proceedings* (17 June 1952), 77.

23 For a discussion of the evolution of mass-produced pocket books and the various technologies that made it possible, see Janice Radway, *Reading the Romance* (London, Verso, 1987), ch. 1.

24 Margaret Culkin Banning, 'Filth on the Newsstands,' *Reader's Digest* (October 1952), 148.

25 Banning, 150.

26 For a discussion of *Playboy* and the construction of the 'new' masculine ideologies in the 1950s, see Barbara Ehrenreich, *The Hearts of Men: American Dreams and the Flight from Commitment* (New York: Anchor, 1983).

27 Paul Guay, President of Press and Cinema Services (Canada's equivalent to the League of Decency in the United States), Ottawa Archdiocese of the Catholic Church. Brief submitted to the Senate Special Committee on Salacious and Indecent Literature, *Proceedings* (3 June 1952), 10.

28 Letter to Attorney General Dana Porter from a 'citizen' in Stoney Creek, dated 8 November 1955. Archives of Ontario, RG 4-32, 1955, #25.

29 'Notes taken at a meeting on 24 February 1956, during which a delegation representing a number of [Ontario] civic and religious groups presented a brief to the Attorney General re: salacious literature,' Archives of Ontario, RG 4-02, File 91.7.

30 B.C. Provincial Congress of Canadian Women, Submission to the Senate Special Committee on Salacious and Indecent Literature, *Proceedings* (11 February 1953), 41.

31 Letter to 'Ontario Government Censorship Bureau' [which did not exist; letter was directed to the Attorney General],' 20 June 1949, Archives of Ontario, RG 4-32, 1949, #270.

32 James Gilbert, *A Cycle of Outrage: America's Reaction to the Juvenile Delinquent in the 1950s* (New York: Oxford, 1986), 3.

33 Martin Barker, *A Haunt of Fears: The Strange History of the British Horror Comics Campaign* (London, Pluto, 1984), 6.

34 Kathy Peiss, *Cheap Amusements: Working Women and Leisure in Turn of the Century New York* (Philadelphia, Temple, 1986).

35 Tereska Torres, *Women's Barracks* (New York, Fawcett, 1950). While published by a New York company, the book was printed in Canada. There is a copy of the novel, with marginal notes by the Crown attorney, on file with the court transcripts.

36 Torres, *The Converts* (London: Rupert Hart-Davis, 1970).

37 Torres, *Women's Barracks*, 5.

38 George Cummings, Preface to *Women's Barracks*, 3.

39 It's important to remember that the cover itself may have been considered grounds for the obscenity charge. For the most part, the magazines that were charged alongside *Women's Barracks* contained what we would today consider to be 'cheesecake': pictures of posed women, smiling or sultry, in bathing suits. The photos in the magazines were not much more sexually explicit than the novel cover. Examples of the magazines are filed with the court transcripts. Archives of Ontario, RG 4-32, 1953, #830.

40 Judge A.G. McDougall, 'Reasons for Judgment, re: *Tragic Ground*' (22 November 1952), *Regina v. The National News Company Limited*, Archives of Ontario, RG 4032, 1953, #830.

41 *The Queen v. National News*, 16.

42 Torres, *Women's Barracks*, 81.

43 Torres, *Women's Barracks*, 45.

44 See Nikolas Rose, *Governing the Soul: The Shaping of the Private Self* (London: Routledge, 1990).

45 John D'Emilio, *Sexual Politics, Sexual Communities: The Making of a Homosexual Minority in the United States, 1940–1970* (Chicago: U of Chicago P, 1983), 16.

46 Alastair Macleod, as told to June Callwood, 'How Do You Know You're Normal?' *Chatelaine* (June 1959), 38ff. See also Valerie Korinek's chapter herein.

47 'Guiding principles in the presentation of the subject of venereal diseases,' 1. Appended to C.C. Goldring's report to the Management Committee of the Board of Education, Toronto, 13 May 1948; Toronto Board of Education, Sex Education File.

48 For a discussion, see Mary Louise Adams, *The Trouble with Normal: Postwar Youth and the Construction of Heterosexuality* (Toronto: U of Toronto P, 1997).

49 For discussion of the 'ideology of maturity' as it was applied to adolescents in the American context, see William Graebner, 'Coming of Age in Buffalo: The Ideology of Maturity in Postwar America,' *Radical History Review* 34 (1986): 53–74.

50 A.G. McDougall, 'Judgment re: *Women's Barracks*,' 22 November 1952; Archives of Ontario, RG 4-32, 1953, #830.

51 'Magazine distributor convicted,' *Ottawa Evening Citizen*, 22 November

1952; 'Davies and O'Grady disagree on value of *Diamond Lil*,' *Ottawa Evening Citizen*, 17 October 1952.

52 'Barracks story is not obscene, witnesses claim,' *Toronto Globe and Mail*, 9 October 1952; 'Snicker market,' *Toronto Globe and Mail*, 17 October 1952.

53 Brief submitted to Dana Porter, Attorney General of Ontario, on behalf of the Periodical Distributors of Canada, 9 February 1954; Archives of Ontario, RG 4-32, 1954, #26.

54 Brief submitted to Kelso Roberts, Attorney General of Ontario, on behalf of the Periodical Distributors of Canada, 1 October 1957; Archives of Ontario, RG 4-02, file 105.5, 1957.

55 Memorandum from Attorney General Kelso Roberts to file, 8 October 1957; Archives of Ontario, RG 4-02, file 105.5, 1957.

56 Letter to W.B. Common, Q.C., Director of Public Prosecutions, Department of the Attorney General, from R.K. Laishley, Q.C. [lawyer for American News], 8 November 1955; Archives of Ontario, RG 4-32, 1955, #793.

57 Letter to W.B. Common from R.K. Laishley, 8 November 1955.

58 Judgment from trial in St Paul, Minnesota, 16 June 1953; quoted in Torres, *Women's Barracks* (11th printing, 1955) inside front cover.

6

'It's a Tough Time to Be in Love': The Darker Side of *Chatelaine* during the Cold War

VALERIE J. KORINEK

In the May 1954 issue of *Chatelaine*, John Clare, the magazine's editor, published one of the few editorials that he wrote for the magazine. Titled 'It's a Tough Time to Be in Love,'[1] the editorial mused about a young couple he had witnessed holding hands on the newly opened Toronto subway. Noticing the woman's engagement ring, he speculated on what the future would hold for the young lovers, particularly in a world plagued by 'ill omens.' 'Small wonder' Clare wrote, 'we felt cheered that instead of diving for the subway as for a bomb shelter and riding off in different directions forever, our young lovers were holding hands.' But, according to Clare, 'because the stresses and strains and jolts of life today do make this a tough time to fall in love, they need a little help.' (The help in question referred readers to one of the magazine's feature articles that month, by Reverend Earl Lautenslager, which was a reprint of an address he had given to the School for Brides and Grooms at Howard Park United Church in Toronto.) Clare concluded on an optimistic, though apolitical, note: 'It always was a tough time to fall in love. Wars, depressions, economic booms and atomic bombs will always be incidentals compared to such fundamentals as love, marriage and the raising of families.'

Clare's view of the fundamentals of women's lives and, commensurately, of women's magazine content, where marriage and family are primary and all else falls from view, was and is one of the key myths of the content of women's magazines, and women's popular culture.[2] This focus upon the private world supposedly unites all heterosexual women and serves as the stimulus for the products advertised in women's periodicals. Yet nothing could be further from the truth with respect to *Chatelaine* magazine during the fifties and sixties. While I have argued in *Roughing It in the Suburbs* that *Chatelaine* included a significant component of second-wave feminist material, in addition to a host of unconventional topics for a mainstream woman's magazine, in this chapter I wish to explore what Clare referred to as the 'incidentals' – the Cold War both at home and abroad. Just as Clare was out of step with the content that the other three female editors would include in their versions of *Chatelaine* magazine between 1950 and 1969, so was his belief that the women's magazine format was largely an apolitical one. First, the Cold War influenced much of the conventional material in *Chatelaine*, such as articles on suburban life, 'normative' child-rearing practices, and spousal relationships. Cold War metaphors and illusions were also invoked to magnify the significance of articles which praised conformity in gender roles and social organization, offered guides to 'normalcy,' and drew portraits of the 'safety' of the suburbs.[3]

As a number of American and Canadian historians have demonstrated, Cold War political developments and fears of the future fostered a particularly inward-looking, middle-class ethos valuing safety, conformity, and 'traditional' roles as a buttress against global political uncertainty.[4] But those uses of Cold War ideology are not the focus of this chapter. Instead, I wish to explore *Chatelaine*'s 'darker side,' in which a host of national and international political articles dealt primarily, often explicitly, with issues of Cold War politics, protagonists, and prognostications for the future. In this regard the chapter is firmly situated within the American literature that explores the 'culture' of the Cold War.[5] Ultimately, the chapter aims to answer a number of important questions. What messages did Canada's only mass-market women's magazine provide to its readers about the most deadly of twentieth-century developments? How did these articles challenge the role and purpose of women's periodicals, with their genre-defining formula of consumer advertisements, departmental features on homes, fashions and food, and romance fiction? Finally, how did readers respond to these dark portraits of the 'age of anxiety'? However, before turning to an analysis of these political articles, some contextual information about the periodical is required so that the significance of the articles can become apparent.

During the Cold War, *Chatelaine* was the primary national magazine for women. In 1958, Maclean Hunter, the owners of *Chatelaine*, purchased and shut down its only Canadian competitor, the *Canadian*

Home Journal, and from that year until the late seventies, when *Canadian Living* was launched, *Chatelaine* was the only women's magazine in the country. Readership increased significantly during the fifties and sixties, and by 1969 *Chatelaine's* circulation stood at 909,453. By contrast, the two national mass-market magazines most often referred to as the key Canadian periodicals of the era, *Maclean's* (English language) and *Saturday Night,* had circulations of 666,406 and 86,192 respectively.[6] Readers of *Chatelaine* were drawn from all areas of the country, from rural and urban communities, and included both women and men. While Maclean Hunter management and advertising executives consistently highlighted their 'prime audience' as Anglo-Canadian, middle-class, urban and suburban married women with families, the independent readership surveys overwhelmingly indicated that the periodical actually attracted a cross section of average readers, primarily from lower-middle-class and working-class backgrounds, with varying educational levels, and who were, in fact, both married and single women and men.

Throughout the fifties and sixties, advertising accounted for slightly over 50 per cent of *Chatelaine's* content.[7] The advertisements were very traditional, encouraging readers to purchase a range of North American products including food, household goods, furniture, clothing, building supplies, and cosmetics. A further 20 per cent of the periodical featured material on food, fashion, interior design, home plans, childcare, and beauty. On average about 10 per cent of the magazine's content in those decades was reserved for fiction. *Chatelaine* fiction placed an emphasis on Canadian writers, particularly in the sixties, but in most instances the fiction in the periodical was standard genre fare – primarily romances and mysteries. Despite the fact that genre fiction was a staple, there nevertheless were spoofs of women's magazines, misogynistic stories, portraits of resistant housewives, and some very mild feminist pieces. These subversive themes suggest that the role fiction played for the magazine's readers cannot simply be dismissed. The remaining 20 per cent of the content was devoted to editorials and articles. Though far from dominant, it is this material that is critically important to any evaluation of *Chatelaine's* importance. The articles and editorials were the cornerstone of the magazine – they were given the most prominent placement inside, were advertised on the cover, and were the material that generated the most letters from the readership.

Editorials in the fifties were written by all four editors: Bryne Hope Sanders, Lotta Dempsey, John Clare, and Doris Anderson. These edito-

rials covered a host of topics, including politics, feminism, philosophy
of life issues, and *Chatelaine* magazine itself. When Anderson assumed
the position of editor in 1958 (a position she held until 1977), the
editorials quickly became wryly political and feminist. Articles written
by a wide range of staff writers and freelancers covered the gamut of
the traditional topics that one would expect to read in women's magazines, including family and marriage issues, celebrities (particularly
Canadian media personalities and the British Royal Family), pop psychology, and women's health. In addition to political issues, there were
a large number of articles which featured overtly feminist topics and
themes.

Based upon close reading and a specific article database which quan-
tifies the themes, contents, and writers of each January, May, and September issue from January 1950 through September 1969, it is possible
to provide topical breakdowns for *Chatelaine* articles. Not surprisingly,
in both decades the private world of women was the most popular
topic (25/24 per cent in the fifties and sixties respectively). In the fifties,
women's health issues were the second most popular topic for articles
(13/10 per cent), but in the sixties, political issues moved from the fifth
most popular topic to the second (9/17 per cent).[8]

Political articles covered a wide range of material, including national,
regional, and municipal Canadian concerns, international politics, and
profiles of prominent politicians. One of the primary reasons for the
increase in political material was the magazine's decision, in the late
fifties, to launch a monthly page initially called 'It's your world,' written by a collection of expert journalists and politicians, including René
Lévesque, Eric Severeid, Norman DePoe, and Donald Gordon. Subsequently, the page was assigned to journalist Christina McCall, who,
initially as a freelance writer and later as an associate editor, was responsible for writing the 'Your World Notebook Page' until late 1963,
when it was quietly dropped.[9] This page, with the rather patronizing
instructions to 'clip along these lines and save,' was intended to serve
as 'background information for women interested in world events.' In
addition to this page, there were also feature articles which explored
political themes.

In evaluating how readers might have responded to the Cold War
material published in *Chatelaine*, the composition and mood of the
periodical plays a critical factor. First, the periodical was often quietly
subversive: feminist editorials might nuzzle up against advertisements
for hair colour; romance fiction often allowed distressed suburban

wives and mothers to voice their frustrations with their lot, however conventionally these stories might end; editors sometimes published humorous articles and scathing letters which spoofed, critiqued, or complained about the fare in the magazine. This wide range of material and viewpoints questioned the commonplace opinion that the content of women's magazines was merely entertainment. Second, the coverage given to unconventional fare (by women's magazine standards), such as the widely publicized editorials and articles on second-wave feminist issues and politics, set a tone that encouraged readers to expect challenging material. Not all readers applauded this unconventional fare; in fact a good number were affronted by the challenge to their traditional roles and values. However, the debate on the 'Letters' page that swirled about women's roles in society encouraged, at the very least, some *Chatelaine* readers to question the status quo. The Cold War cultural material published in *Chatelaine* was yet another element that made this an atypical women's periodical and one which bears close study if we are to understand how a mass, national audience of Canadian women negotiated the wide variety of social and political changes that came their way during the fifties and sixties.

In sharp contrast with the John Clare editorial, 'It's a tough time to be in love,' the majority of writers and editors who approached the topic of the Cold War did not view it as an 'incidental concern' for Canadian women. Instead, these writers countered the 'age of affluence' evoked by the advertisements and some editorial fare with glimpses of 'the age of anxiety' which betrayed fear and ambivalence about the future. Thematically, *Chatelaine*'s Cold War material can be divided into five categories: progress and the space age; the atomic bomb and nuclear weapons; portraits of the communist 'other'; international primers; and Canadian women's responses to the 'age of anxiety.' It is to the age of anxiety's benevolent twin, 'the space age,' that we turn first.

Progress and the Space Age in *Chatelaine*

In the pages of *Chatelaine* during the fifties and sixties, the term 'space age' appeared with a great deal of frequency in articles, editorials, the magazine's departments, and advertisements. In the latter, 'space age' was an adjective used to describe progress, and new products – ranging from aluminum cookware and multivitamins to (very late in the sixties) products like Tang (powdered orange juice). Many of these were marketed as by-products of the U.S. space program. Similarly, in the departmental features there were fashion profiles of the new 'space age' fabrics, or 'space age' interior design (in the late sixties). In the editorial material as well, 'space age' was a general code word that indicated progress, the future, and, at its most extreme, fantastical speculations about how Canadians would live in the twenty-first century.

Unlike the progress celebrated in the advertising pages, where it was equated with new products, ease of use, and increasing affluence, in the editorial and articles pages 'progress' was also problematized. In January 1953, writer Judith Robinson published an article entitled 'Progress and Mashed Potatoes.'[10] This personal commentary regarding the upcoming Canadian general election focused closely on the general emptiness of political discourse. 'Most of us can remember', Robinson wrote, 'if and when we stop to think, where progress brought us between 1939 and 1946. Most of us know something of the more dreadful prospects progress has opened since. Belief in progress as a one-way street toward the light is no longer in fashion, and there is little in that to regret' (64). Robinson urged *Chatelaine*'s readers to be vigilant about the 'evil [that] can spread under cover of jargon; of the cant phrase heard so often that it is accepted at last without thinking and applauded without waking' (64).

The catch-all phrase 'progress' was abandoned in the late fifties when the space age was officially inaugurated through the Soviet Union's launch of the Sputnik 1 satellite (4 October 1957).[11] The tone of *Chatelaine* commentary moved from wonderment to anxiety as the Western democracies tried to explain how the Russians were able to beat them into space. One of the answers was deemed to lie in the flaws of the public educational system. Given *Chatelaine*'s focus on Canadian wives and mothers, it was not surprising when, subsequently, a number of editorials and articles about education were published with the 'space race' as their primary impetus. Doris Anderson led the way with an editorial in April 1959 calling for more women scientists: 'Ever since Sputnik with its innocuous bleep-bleep thrust us into the Space Age, we have been desperately concerned about our scientific strength compared with Russia ... But no one has pointed out one important source of future scientists we have generally ignored – and that is the female half of Canada's population.'[12] Vintage Anderson, this editorial combined her feminist analysis with an analysis of Cold War politics, concluding: 'Our female brain power is presently one of the richest untapped resources. The longer we fail to make use of it, the less chance we have for survival in the Space Age' (16).

Later that year Christina McCall published her investigative report, 'How Soft Are Our Schools?,' which offered a damning commentary about the lack of educational standards and rigour, set against the backdrop of international priorities.[13] Although it was far from clear that education truly was in the state of peril that some naysayers believed, McCall concluded with this dire warning: 'Both groups (parents and educators) have a deep responsibility in education, and if our way of life is to survive, this responsibility must be met' (78).

Women's progress (or lack thereof) in national politics offered another angle on the Cold War. An article written by Ottawa mayor Charlotte Whitton offered an 'outspoken challenge for every thinking Canadian woman' to stop being 'butterers of bread, the cutters of cake, and the brewers of tea' in Canadian politics.[14] The article critiqued women for working in political auxiliaries and in the backrooms instead of running as candidates. To amplify the importance of her message, Whitton utilized the language of the Cold War. She offered this quote from Dr Harry Gideonse, president of Brooklyn College in the United States, whose 1959 fact-finding mission to Russia resulted in a report for President Eisenhower. According to Gideonse, 'the wide use of woman's abilities in Soviet Russia could well be the determining factor in the common struggle for world survival' (152). Whitton echoed his concerns, stating that this 'deadly serious' situation called for Canadian womanhood to rise to the challenge. Despite the tone of the article, the two letters published in response to it were not supportive. Martha Forrie of Scarborough, Ontario, thought Whitton's 'assessment of the position of woman in this country is just perfect. But could we hear more of how "liberated women of other lands" manage their lives?'[15] More critically, Mrs G. Collinson of Sullivan Bay, British Columbia, responded that 'intelligent, educated women are not "hardboiled" or "crooked" enough for party politics.'[16]

'Can you protect your family from the bomb?': The Atomic Bomb and Nuclear Weapons

In the January 1950 issue of *Chatelaine*, Byrne Hope Sanders's editorial, 'What's the Biggest Thing in Our New Half Century?,' explained that in a recent editorial staff meeting to debate this question 'the argument stopped by sudden consent, for we all recognized what it was: the Atom Bomb. Around the table faces grew sombre as each of us built on the theme of fear.'[17] She reported that 'attitudes of mind went like this:

Does anyone really believe we can avoid destruction? What chance is there for a future with this black threat hanging over us, as individuals, as nations, as the world itself?' Yet, Sanders was not about to conclude on a pessimistic note. Much as she had inspired women during the Second World War to conserve resources and pitch in for the war effort, she now wrote: 'Always, man's reaction to his own creative powers – is fear. We need to think more of the creative powers for good. We should listen to the experts, and the scientists, and the dreamers for a change. Let's help to abolish those Atom Bomb blues!'

This sense of optimism influenced the editorial staff to highlight Adele White's lead article, 'Let's Abolish Those Atom Bomb Blues,' which would put an upbeat spin on the deadliest of twentieth-century scientific developments. In this respect, *Chatelaine*'s perspective was no different from that of many major American magazines such as *Life* and *Time*, according to historian Paul Boyer, whose work on the cultural implications of the atomic bomb in the immediate postwar period points to periods of alternating fear and exuberant optimism about the potential of atomic power.[18] In her article White gave readers a brief history of the origins of the atomic bomb and the power of nuclear energy. 'Someday,' she wrote, 'there may be a fantastic new way of life – a completely changed world both physically and socially, with such an abundance of goods that there'll be luxury and security for all.'[19] The abundance of consumer goods was a prevalent image in advertisements and departmental fare, where it was often proffered to readers as the promised land of ease and affluence. Despite this image of unending bounty, White could not avoid concluding with this assessment of the likelihood of nuclear war: 'It's seldom that a prosperous well-fed country wants to start an all-out attack. If fear of war gradually fades out it will be because free peace-loving people have so much more to offer than the people of a warmongering country. And, in the final analysis, it will be because each one takes responsibility ... [t]o see the power of the atom is used only for material prosperity and progress. It's too good a world to blow up' (53). This is, perhaps, the most traditional way that women's magazines addressed such potentially dire topics: minimizing the dangers, stressing the positive benefits of even the most difficult experiences, and encouraging readers not to be fearful. Instead, readers were encouraged to pitch in and make the world a better place so that all could share in material prosperity. However, this middle-class complacency and 'life is good' ethos seldom appeared again in *Chatelaine* articles on the bomb.

In January 1958 one of *Chatelaine*'s most popular writers, Dr Marion Hilliard, the head of obstetrics and gynaecology at Women's College Hospital in Toronto, wrote a hard-hitting article entitled 'The Hydrogen Bomb Should Be Outlawed.'[20] In the article, Hilliard spoke bluntly about the dangers of the bomb and about the unknown dangers of radioactive fallout from the ongoing tests of bombs. 'It seems to me pathetic and stupid that we should take such great care that individual unborn children are not harmed by radiation from x-rays and, at the same time, the world powers go on exploding bomb after bomb with who knows what untold disaster for future generations.' Drawing on her medical expertise, as well as a clearly maternal feminist position (in this article at least), she concluded with a statement urging *Chatelaine* readers to act: 'As women we are the bearers and guardians of life. The world of the future doesn't even belong to us ... We have no right to contaminate it or damage it – or let anyone else damage it. It is our responsibility to protect it for the future' (6).

Christina McCall's regularly featured column, 'Your World Notebook,' profiled another side to the nuclear controversy in 1961 when she explored the debates over whether or not Canada should accept U.S. nuclear missiles and warheads. After explaining that the sole purpose of the purchase of the new CF-104 planes had been to equip them with the nuclear warheads, McCall asked the obvious question: 'So what's the fuss all about?' The fuss, according to McCall, was caused by Canadian Secretary of State for External Affairs Howard Green, who was committed to arguing for nuclear disarmament at the United Nations. Though clearly supportive of Green's stand, McCall offered this realistic assessment of his success and the outcome for Canada: 'If Howard Green or some other world statesman, fails to achieve some plan for atomic disarmament by the end of the year, Canada will probably take the American atomic warheads for her armed forces. It's generally agreed that Canada, because of her geography and the natural instinct of her people, can never become a neutral between the Russian and the American blocs. That means we'll have to arm ourselves as effectively as our limited defence budget allows, and hope that the military strength of the Western world will prevent the outbreak of World War III.'[21]

Readers' reaction to McCall's article was mixed. Mrs A.W.F. McQueen of Niagara Falls wrote to congratulate the editors 'on ... Your World Notebook. This is a real service to everyone who needs assistance in untangling the news.'[22] Mrs Ethel M. Demaine of Powassan, Ontario,

was equally enthused: 'YWN fulfills a dire need for the Canadian
woman. In my opinion it is one of the best condensations of current
world affairs.'[23] Other readers had more specific commentary about
McCall's 'biased' perspective on the topic. According to Elizabeth H.
Marsh of Burlington, 'Christina Newman's ... Notebook on Nuclear
Weapons. ... is a piece of one-eyed reporting, drawing illogical and
unfounded conclusions. Miss Newman [sic] gives only the argument
for taking atomic weapons.'[24] Equally sceptical was Ruth Bennett of
Vancouver, who believed that 'atomic weapons would not defend us;
neither does Canada need them as a deterrent power. What Canada can
do is help prevent the spread of nuclear weapons to nations not now
possessing them. If Canada accepts nuclear weapons herself, she cannot expect to be listened to if she urges other nations not to obtain
them.'[25]

The international situation became more ominous in the early sixties
as tensions between the United States and the Soviets heightened owing to a series of challenges: the Soviet downing of an American U-2
spy plane in the spring of 1960; the Bay of Pigs showdown in April
1961; and the success of the Soviet space race, epitomized by cosmo-
naut Yuri Gagarin's orbiting of the earth – the first person to do so.
According to Margot Henriksen, the final factor which ratcheted up the
tension was President Kennedy's 25 July 1961 nationally televised address to Americans urging them to build fallout shelters to protect
themselves from nuclear war.[26] In this climate, it was natural that few
Canadians could blithely carry on their daily lives without nagging
fears of nuclear Armageddon. Doris Anderson was not immune to
these fears, and in an editorial entitled 'A Gesture of Sanity and Faith'
she offered a far grimmer assessment of the world than the one that
Sanders had offered twelve years earlier. She reported that she was as
'perplexed and filled with a sense of helplessness' as others and found
herself wondering whether Canadians should 'obediently burrow ourselves into the ground like a well-disciplined ground hog' or 'to go
calmly about stocking a bomb shelter like a grim, concrete cottage?'[27]
Undoubtedly she was also taking a shot at the American media, in
particular *Time* and *Life* magazines, which had featured numerous articles and photo essays of people happily preparing for Armageddon
by building and stocking their bomb shelters. If building a bomb shelter was futile, she questioned whether it was 'realistic or even morally
right to sit apathetically by and do nothing except vaguely hope that, in
the event of the war, we are directly hit so that the hideous prospect of

coping with the aftermath of fallout is removed from us?' Anderson offered neither closure to these questions nor any simple balm to assuage readers' fears.

Not surprisingly, reader reaction was mixed. P. Walsh from Vancouver was outraged and thought that it was 'not morally right that the press of our country should not, in our people's extremity, take a more positive role against the morals of monsters who would impose nuclear weapons upon us.'[28] Sonia Puchalski of Gibsons was more supportive of Anderson's position. 'What we should do is work with other like-minded people to see that our parliamentary representatives make our wishes and opinions acted upon ... Peace is something that individuals must work for. It cannot be achieved by apathy.'[29] Unlike other North American media, *Chatelaine* seldom demonized Russia or other communist countries, and for this 'balanced' reportage they often received negative mail assailing them for not providing a truly Canadian stand on these issues (as in Walsh's letter above).

Although *Chatelaine* would continue to publish articles on Cold War politics throughout the sixties, its last article on the bomb was McCall's 1962 article 'Can you protect your family from the bomb?,' which repeated the pessimistic images of Hilliard and Anderson. While the American media had reached the saturation point with articles on fallout shelters by 1963, primarily because of the successful conclusion of the Cuban missile crisis in 1962 and the 1963 signing of an atmospheric test-ban treaty between the United States, Great Britain, and the Soviet Union, McCall's article contained graphic material about the effects of nuclear war and the likelihood of survival.[30] Geared to answering 'pressing questions' such as 'Are fallout shelters any good?'; Which parts of Canada might be attacked if war comes?', 'Is there a safe spot in Canada?', and 'What should you know about survival after an attack?,' the article offered few assurances. With the exception of residents of northern Manitoba and most of Saskatchewan, who were distant from the larger population centres in Canada, it was clear that many Canadians would be at risk. According to McCall, it was not sensation that drove this piece, but pragmatism: 'Events of the past few months have forced even the most ostrichlike optimists among us to come face to face with that horrific nightmare of this age of anxiety: the possibility of nuclear attack.'[31]

The article failed to come to any conclusion about how Canadians should prepare – it aimed to be 'objective,' and, in that spirit, there were even instructions for how to build and stock a shelter. But the gritty depictions of life in the shelter were not reassuring. 'Assuming that you were lucky enough to escape these immediate effects of the bomb and reached the relative safety of a fallout or blast shelter,' McCall wrote, 'it's no use deluding yourself that life inside the shelter would be anything approaching normal, or indeed that life once you emerged would ever be the same again ... There has been an unrealistic tendency among advocates of fallout shelters to make them look like underground picnic areas. They won't be. They'll be cramped, stuffy, stinking cages where you'll suffer the nerve tearing suspense of not knowing whether you and your family will emerge alive' (83). Despite reporting that the 'near-hysterical' Americans had pledged to spend $700 million to build community shelters, McCall noted that in Britain and France there were no plans for a shelter program. The message of this article was understated, but nonetheless very clear: readers weren't encouraged to waste their time buying prepared foods and building fallout shelters since it was obvious they would be of little utility. Instead, McCall and *Chatelaine* must have hoped that readers would find the images so frightening that they would resolve to actively work towards preventing nuclear war rather than pondering how to survive it. As these examples indicate, it was not only the feminist material, and the wide range of topics, that differentiated *Chatelaine* from American women's magazines, but also the far more pessimistic approach to the Cold War. Whether it was their reluctance to embrace the portrait of well-stocked fallout shelters, or, their failure to demonize communists, *Chatelaine* was often out of step with its crossborder competitors.

'What's It Like to Be Mrs. Gouzenko?': Explorations of Cold War 'Others'

The difference between *Chatelaine* and its American competitors was most notable in the articles that profiled 'others' – those people outside the white, Anglo, middle-class majority who were targeted as *Chatelaine*'s primary reading audience. While *Roughing It in the Suburbs* highlights otherness in terms of ethnicity, race, and class, here I want to focus on specific Cold War portraits of communist, or formerly communist, women.[32]

These portraits of communist others were not one-dimensional sketches; instead, the people appeared as complex as North Americans in their concerns, troubles, and differing perspectives. For instance, in the early fifties, Norman Smith, the associate editor of the *Ottawa Jour-*

nal, contributed a very ambivalent article to *Chatelaine* about the appeals of communism. The opening teaser for the Smith article asked 'If you slept last night in a gutter, could your heart ignore a Communist promise?'[33] The opinionated essay, based upon Smith's recent trip to India, provided insight into how difficult it was for poor countries to resist communist offers of aid. Instead of printing platitudes about Western aid and the obvious appeal of Western democracies, Smith presented a damning assessment of the selfishness of the rich nations, including Canada. 'Surely the basic fact behind the world's unrest today is that "we" have so much and others have so little. Oh yes, there is also the plotting mind of the Kremlin. But its monstrous policy feeds on the unrest and discontent and it will continue to do so. Human misery, oppression, slavery – when these pressures are absent Communism is seen to offer nothing ... If you'd seen what I saw out there I'm sure then you too would come back a little humbled, a little ashamed of our luck and our comfort and, above all, of our easy assumption that we have these things by divine right' (58, 61). The answer, according to Smith, was for Canada and Canadians to increase their foreign aid dollars, both for reasons of human rights and for the selfish motive that only in this way would future unrest be avoided.

Smith's article is useful for determining the context in which John Clare produced 'What's It Like to Be Mrs. Gouzenko?,' a revealing portrait of the wife of the famous communist defector. It was a 'women's issue' piece because it focused on the private world of the Gouzenkos and told Mrs Gouzenko's story; however Svetlana Gouzenko did not fit the stereotype of the quiet, obedient, peasant wife. For instance, when asked if she still worried when her husband was away from home, she replied, 'After what I have gone through I am not really afraid of anything.'[34] Svetlana Gouzenko was clearly an intriguing individual in her own right. Clare revealed that she came from a middle-class professional family which moved to a large apartment in Moscow when she was a child. Having studied nursing prior to the Second World War, Svetlana actively participated in war work – she was part of the civilian defence corps in Moscow, and later trained as an airplane pilot. Svetlana impressed upon Clare that she had been an integral partner in Igor's decision to reveal the story of the spy networks, and that she instructed him to make sure he had paper documentation. If Clare was looking for an interview subject who stood behind her man, was timid, or who had difficulty acclimatizing to Canadian society he was out of luck, because Mrs Gouzenko came across as feisty, independent, and clearly in favour of the greater opportunities available to children and women in Canada. In one sense this article functions in a conventional manner, detailing the home life of a 'suburban' woman, but in other respects this portrait of 'otherness' challenges some of the presumptions of the Cold War, as this former communist 'other' could be any *Chatelaine* reader's next-door neighbour (despite her anonymity and aliases). When Christina McCall checked up on the couple six years later they still had no regrets, were convinced that they had made the best move for their children, and were both working on new books about their experiences.[35]

In keeping with their mandate to present issues of interest to women, the articles that profiled the Russian and Chinese situations focused primarily on women's experiences in those countries. In the fall of 1959, Anderson and a team of Chatelaine staff travelled to Moscow to explore the situation of Russian women. 'Imagine,' Anderson wrote, 'that for all your life, you have lived in one room shared by three other people, owned a wardrobe that could be packed in one average-sized suitcase, have never worn lipstick, never owned a refrigerator, vacuum cleaner or washing machine and that you have cooked all your family's meals on a two-burner stove. Then you will have some idea of what it is like to be a Russian housewife ... But a Russian housewife has never known any other way of life, and she doesn't believe fanciful stories of the gadget happy world of North America. To her, life has never been better.'[36] While Anderson discovered that life for women in Moscow was far from easy, she did report very favourably on the maternity policies in Russia, the government-operated daycares, and the high proportion of Russian women who worked outside the home. Equally telling, she reported that the Russian woman's 'vision of us is only slightly more distorted than our vision of her' (61). Compared to the portraits of Russians in other North American media, Anderson's was relatively positive. She expressed pleasant surprise at what she observed during her stay, writing that 'in the age of anxiety, the Russians I met seemed not at all anxious. The idea that they might be hydrogen bombed seemed ridiculous to them. There were no air raid shelters in Moscow, and no feeling that they will be needed' (66).

In contrast to the relative freedom experienced by Anderson and her entourage in Russia, the trip to China was very clearly structured by the government. Journalist Marjorie McEnaney, billed as the 'first Canadian woman journalist ever invited behind the Bamboo Curtain,' offered this assessment of the lot of Chinese women in 1960: 'Judging by what I saw on all sides, it was clear that life in the new China was not easy, particularly for women. But then, it never has been easy, except for the relatively few well-to-do. Today, many of the peasant women who once devoted most of their time to hauling water, collecting firewood, grinding millet and corn and minding the children, have exchanged these duties for eight or ten hour days in field or factory, leaving daytime care of children and preparation of meals to state organized groups and institutions.'[37] When Lynn Harrington interviewed one particular woman, Chang Kwei Hsia, in 1966, she found that peasant women considered themselves liberated because 'they keep the money they earn, and their maiden names.'[38] They might be poor but in some respects, like the Russian women profiled, they were more liberated than the majority of Canadian women. After her visit to a commune outside the northern Chinese city of Sian, Harrington concluded that the communists were shrewd to recognize women's efforts: 'The Communists early recognized the loyalty they could rouse in half the country's population by freeing women from the bondage of tradition. Women had everything to gain from the revolution and are today its fieriest supporters' (78).

International Political Primers

From 1959 to 1963 the Your World Notebook (YWN) pages were the most consistent forum for international political material. The bulk of this material focused on Cold War issues – nuclear war, weapons, military, and political tensions, and so on – indicating that though *Chatelaine* was 'women's space' it nevertheless recognized that women were affected by Cold War concerns. Readership of the YWN was not as high as that for other general feature articles, judging by letters to the editors and by the fact that the column was dropped without protest in 1963. Nevertheless, it did have a readership, and it did occasion controversy. Throughout the years a host of articles were published on diverse topics, as a sampling of some of the titles indicates: 'Latin America: Trouble at Our Back Door?,' 'The Cold War Isn't What It Used to Be,' 'Norad – Can It Protect Us from a Surprise Attack?,' 'Foreign Aid: Who's Winning the Quiet War?,' and 'West Germany Goes to the Polls This Month.'[39]

The majority of YWN columns would not have been out of place in general interest periodicals directed at mixed audiences, as they did not usually stress the 'women's angle' of these issues. For instance, in the first column of the new year, Eric Sevareid, in a *Chatelaine* exclusive, contributed a column entitled 'What Will Happen in 1960?,' in which he confidently predicted: 'I can see no reason to fear any large-scale war involving the West. I would expect to see Russia as well as Western, liberal societies grow in material prosperity and internal stability and turn even more of their energies to the problems that come with prosperity and population growth.'[40]

In the spring of 1962, Christina McCall was less prophetic but more controversial in her profile of the American radical right. Her definition of the composition of the American right was brief but pointed: 'Although their platforms and personnel vary widely they have in common a fanatic anti-Communism. The "ultras" [conservatives] believe the biggest threat to the U.S. comes not from the Soviet Union, but from Communism within. Angered by the American government's inability to conclusively solve international problems, these far rightists have convinced themselves Communist subversion exists everywhere in American society – at all government levels and in academic circles particularly.'[41] McCall drew a link between anti-Semitism, both in Canada and the U.S., and the anti-communists, and pointed to key American players, including Barry Goldwater, the Republican senator from Arizona. She reassured readers that the likelihood of this movement spreading to Canada was minimal, although she did refer to the Canadian Intelligence Service, which she reported 'was mailing copies of a fanatical anti-Communist, anti-Semitic newsletter from Flesherton, ON.' Trying to end on a positive note, she quoted President Kennedy's response to these groups: 'Kennedy is probably correct in saying that the voices of extremism will be muffled in due course ... by the good sense and stability of the "American people."'

Unfortunately, both Kennedy's and McCall's perspectives were proven incorrect. In the June 1962 issue of the magazine, an irate letter arrived from Pat Walsh, the general secretary of the Canadian Anti-Communist Secretariat in Ottawa: 'I have received many letters from many of your women readers across Canada who have asked me to protest against your smear article ... I think that such an article as you wrote belies any claim to objectivity and completely discredits the magazine as unworthy of any further consideration by thousands of your Canadian readers who are in the vanguard today across Canada in the struggle to expose the Communist conspiracy.' Not content to record their dissatisfaction, Walsh issued this threat: 'If this trend continues we will organize a nationwide campaign to alert all your advertisers to the fact that your women readers are very indignant about your efforts to smear the patriotic and dedicated attempts of Canadian anti-communists to alert the Canadian public to the dire threat of the internal threat of Communism in Canada.'[42]

If McCall and the editors of *Chatelaine* were worried by Walsh's threat, they didn't show it. Refusing to take the easy road and vilify the communists, McCall continued to question assumptions about Western commitment to peace in the world, and to question the perception that only the communists were warmongers. In a column on foreign aid, she succinctly demonstrated that while Americans contributed short-term funds in emergencies, the Russians were far better in giving sustained aid to developing and poor nations, a critically important political function in the polarized international climate. Lest Canadians feel smug, she skewered Canada's record as well: 'There has been widespread criticism in the U.S. as well as in this country, of the meagre size of Canadian contributions. We rank tenth among Western countries (behind such nations as Italy, Belgium and Portugal) ... Unless Canada and all the other "have" nations shoulder their responsibilities, we may lose the vital contest of our time.'[43]

Canadian Women's Responses to the Age of Anxiety

One of the major themes that emerges from the material discussed so far is how few articles and editorials offered readers self-congratulatory pieces on Canada's role in the various political and economic Cold War controversies. If anything, the overwhelming emphasis was on how much more Canada, and by extension, *Chatelaine* readers, could do to avert a crisis. In an editorial entitled 'Refugee Year Isn't Over for Us,' Anderson decried the country's paltry contribution to the refugee crisis. 'In the eyes of the rest of the world,' Anderson wrote, 'our strongest drive seems to be directed at becoming wealthier. Our record on Refugee Year doesn't do anything to dispel this impression ... Since we are slow starters, let's be known as strong finishers. World Refugee Year can't end for us on June 30. We haven't done enough to close the book. For us, it must continue until every camp is cleared and every homeless baby has a chance at a new future.'[44] The proof for the editors that they were on the right track came from readers like Mrs J.S. Cunningham of St Mary's, Nova Scotia, who wrote: 'Your editorials have been rapidly climbing the ladder until in June you have given us the most splendid one of all ... We in Canada have so much and share so little. Here is an opportunity to show that we are not as selfish as we appear to be – or are we?'[45] Mrs Herbert S. White of Aylmer, Ontario, wrote to inform Anderson that her 'editorial was reprinted in full on the editorial page of our St. Thomas Times-Journal.'[46]

In another case, *Chatelaine* gave readers an opportunity to write and tell the editors what they would say if they had the opportunity to speak directly with Kruschev. They received replies from forty-two readers, one of whom suggested he 'drop dead.'[47] The most intriguing letters, however, were those offering insights into the mindset of Canadian women during the Cold War. From Lila Kalen, of Edmonton, came this question: 'If we concede your viewpoints, your ideals and your way of life, we would equally like the same treatment in return, without feeling that you must force your doctrines upon us. Can you make this effort to understand us and the way we wish to live?' More passionate, and patriotically Canadian, was the response of Mrs Irene Marcassa, of Timmins, Ontario, who wrote: 'I enjoy living in our Canadian democracy because my personal freedoms are the results of my personal responsibilities ... I want for myself and for my children, the right to choose our own books, our own friends, our own hobbies, our own careers, and our own philosophies and learn in the school of our own choice ... To preserve this way of life, we will even resort to war. God willing, this will not be necessary ... Neither of us may be around to see it, Mr. Kruschev, but inevitably the iron curtain will be lifted. Perhaps the Canadian housewife and even the Russian housewife will help to do it.' The goal of *Chatelaine* editors was to get readers like Mrs Marcassa involved in politics in various ways because they were confident that Canadian women had a major role to play.

Yet while *Chatelaine* supported and encouraged women's activism, they were not uncritical in their support. Carol Chapman's article, 'How Effective Is the Voice of Women?,' was upfront in its critique, stating, 'It's ambitious aim is world peace. Born out of one Canadian mother's fears of the hydrogen bomb a year ago, its membership is booming. But what has it accomplished and where is it going?'[48] The answer was ambivalent. Yes, Chapman concluded, VOW had politicized women, and got them thinking about the issues, but their letter-writing campaign and ill-conceived goals for the future (beyond lobbying) were less than clear in 1961.

In 1965, this very issue was addressed again by writer Barbara Croft. Her advice to women interested in forming pressure groups was instructive: 'Talk your subject up, by every means within your power.

Articles, speeches, discussion groups – these are the ways to influence public opinion. If you want people to read better books, to stop buying war toys, to give up drinking, you try to show them why they should do these things, and offer them a positive alternative. You don't arbitrarily cut off their source of supply. When the majority is with you, and the moment is ripe for a change, your evidence will pack enough of a wallop to bring results.'[49] Croft's message was *Chatelaine's* message – although as they would discover from their goals of politicizing second-wave feminist issues, and a host of legislative reforms (around divorce legislation, birth control, etc.), consistent publication was certainly beneficial but it often took years, if ever, for results to emerge.

Towards a Changing World Order

It should be obvious from this overview of the Cold War material in *Chatelaine* magazine during the fifties and sixties that the magazine did not shy away from political issues, nor did it seek to structure them in ways that would most flatter their readership – either as Canadians or as women. While the published material ranges from the overly optimistic world view of Byrne Hope Sanders, who strove to highlight the positive ramifications of nuclear energy, to the dismissive way in which John Clare labelled politics 'incidental' to the ahistorical concerns of women – love, marriage, and children – to the frankly pessimistic and frightening images raised by Doris Anderson, it is clear that both editors and readers were engaged with the changing world order. Much of this engagement took an educational approach, whether to reassure or, more commonly, to spur women to pursue political activism in order to avert Armageddon. Equally important, the images of the Cold War presented were not dichotomized portraits of the good capitalism of the West versus the evil communism of the East. Instead, this was a grey world, full of ambivalence. This is most evident in the portraits of the communist 'other' – a place where writers could have chosen to celebrate the democratic freedoms and wealth of the West. Instead, they offered more nuanced portraits which contextualized the lives and experiences of communist women.

For a genre of periodical associated with escapism and entertainment, it is clear that some of the most hard-hitting material offered no stereotypical images of ease, luxury, and affluence, but a frighteningly chaotic world where few 'experts' could offer any certainty about the future. In exploring this darker side of life in the fifties and sixties, *Chatelaine*'s writers and editors entered unconventional terrain for a mass-market women's magazine. Replacing the consumer ethos of the 'age of affluence' with the politicized 'age of anxiety,' they offered not only an unconventional perspective on women's lives but also an implicit critique of the advertisements, and the advertising dollars, which underwrote the entire enterprise of *Chatelaine* magazine.

Notes

I would like to thank Green College, the Canadian Studies Program, and the Critical Studies in Sexuality Program at the University of British Columbia for allowing me the opportunity to present a preliminary version of this paper in their Cold War series. Additionally, I would like to acknowledge the helpful comments of the audience in revising this paper, in particular the insights provided by Richard Cavell and Dianne Newell.

1 John Clare, 'It's a Tough Time to Be in Love,' *Chatelaine* (May 1954), 1.
2 This stereotype of the fluffy material in women's magazines, and the importance placed on placating advertisers with material that stimulated consumption, is one of the themes of Betty Friedan's *The Feminine Mystique* (New York: Norton, 1963). Subsequent to Friedan's book, a host of other commentators have built upon her message and offered successive critiques of the ills of women's magazines, culminating in the publication of Susan Faludi's *Backlash: The Undeclared War against American Women* (New York: Crown Publishers, 1991). For a more detailed overview of this literature see the introduction to my *Roughing It in the Suburbs: Reading Chatelaine Magazine in the Fifties and Sixties* (Toronto: U of Toronto P, 2000); and Dawn Currie, *Girl Talk: Adolescent Magazines and Their Readers* (Toronto: U of Toronto P, 1999).
3 Readers interested in the impact the Cold War had on *Chatelaine* material generally should consult my *Roughing It in the Suburbs*. That issue is also dealt with in considerable detail by Mary Louise Adams, *The Trouble with Normal* (Toronto: U of Toronto P, 1997); and from a different perspective, by Mona Gleason, *Normalizing the Ideal: Psychology, Schooling, and the Family in Postwar Canada* (Toronto: U of Toronto P, 1999).
4 See Elaine Tyler May, *Homeward Bound: American Families in the Cold War Era* (New York: Basic Books, 1988); Joanne Meyerowitz, ed., *Not June Cleaver: Women and Gender in Postwar America, 1945–1960* (Philadelphia:

Temple UP, 1994); Reg Whitaker and Gary Marcuse, *Cold War Canada: The Making of a National Insecurity State, 1945–1957* (Toronto: U of Toronto P, 1994); Gary Kinsman, Dieter K. Buse, and Mercedes Steedman, eds., *Whose National Security?: Canadian State Surveillance and the Creation of Enemies* (Toronto: Between the Lines, 2000); Franca Iacovetta, 'Parents, Daughters, and Family Court Intrusions into Working-Class Life,' in Franca Iacovetta and Wendy Mitchinson, eds., *On the Case: Explorations in Social History* (Toronto: U of Toronto P, 1998): 312–37; and Franca Iacovetta and Valerie J. Korinek, 'Jello Salads, One-Stop Shopping, and Maria the Homemaker: The Gender Politics of Food,' in Franca Iacovetta, Frances Swyripa, and Marlene Epp, eds., *Sisters or Strangers* (Toronto: U of Toronto P, forthcoming).

5 Canadian cultural and media historians have not as yet attempted focused studies of the cultural production of the Cold War era. Although the Cold War often functions as a backdrop in cultural histories of television, advertising, and media studies, there is little sustained analysis of how the Cold War context of international tension, nuclear weaponry, and so on, stimulated particular types of cultural production. American critical literature holds more promise on this score; for a variety of views see Paul Boyer, *By the Bomb's Early Light: American Thought and Culture at the Dawn of the Atomic Age* (New York: Pantheon Books, 1985); Paul Boyer, *Fallout: A Historian Reflects on America's Half-Century Encounter with Nuclear Weapons* (Columbus: Ohio State UP, 1998); Margot A. Henriksen, *Dr. Strangelove's America: Society and Culture in the Atomic Age* (Berkeley: U of California P, 1997); and Lisle A. Rose, *The Cold War Comes to Main Street: America in the 1950s* (Lawrence: U of Kansas P, 1999).

6 *Canada's Magazine Audience: A Study from the Magazine Advertising Bureau of Canada, Volume 1: Profile of Readers* (Originated by the Canadian Media Directors Council. Validated by the Canadian Advertising Research Foundation Conducted by ORC International Limited, 1969), 2.

7 The percentages of editorial and advertising fare are taken from my general survey database, which, among other tabulations, counted editorial and advertising content for all the *Chatelaine* magazines published between January 1950 and December 1969. For more detail on the composition of the periodical see *Roughing It in the Suburbs.*

8 Readers interested in a detailed overview of my Chatelaine General Survey Database (which includes all 240 issues examined) and the Chatelaine Component Databases (includes 60, all January, May, and September issues from 1950 to 1969), the methodology, and the range of material tabulated are encouraged to see the Appendix of 'Roughing It in Suburbia:

Reading *Chatelaine* Magazine in the Fifties and Sixties,' PhD dissertation, University of Toronto, 1996.

9 'What's New with Us,' *Chatelaine*, January 1964, 2.

10 Judith Robinson, 'Progress and Mashed Potatoes,' *Chatelaine*, January 1953, 4.

11 In a 1958 editorial, Anderson observed that 'since Sputnik shot off into space, we have had to accept almost daily, new ideas about ourselves and the universe that are stunning to all accept students of advanced physics and children. The truth, it seems, is stranger than science fiction in 1958.' Doris Anderson, 'What's Your Future – This Year and 25 Years from Now?' *Chatelaine*, January 1958, 1.

12 Doris Anderson, 'We Need More Women Scientists,' *Chatelaine*, April 1959, 16.

13 Christina McCall, 'How Soft Are Our Schools?' *Chatelaine*, September 1959, 35.

14 Dr Charlotte Whitton, 'Canadian Women Belong in Politics,' *Chatelaine*, October 1961, 150.

15 Martha Forrie, 'The Last Word Is Yours,' *Chatelaine*, December 1961, 108.

16 Mrs G. Collinson, 'The Last Word Is Yours,' *Chatelaine*, January 1962, 88.

17 Byrne Hope Sanders, Editorial, *Chatelaine*, January 1950, 6.

18 See Boyer, *By the Bomb's Early Light*; and Boyer, *Fallout*. Worth noting is the fact that Boyer's survey of U.S. cultural products seldom utilizes or provides material from the mass-market American women's periodicals, concentrating instead on the general magazines like *Time*, *Life*, and *Newsweek*.

19 Adele White, 'Let's Abolish Those Atom Bomb Blues,' *Chatelaine*, January 1950, 7, 53.

20 Dr Marion Hilliard, 'The Hydrogen Bomb Should Be Outlawed,' *Chatelaine*, January 1958, 6.

21 Christina Newman, 'Nuclear Weapons,' *Chatelaine*, March 1961, 12.

22 Mrs A.W.F. McQueen, 'The Last Word Is Yours,' *Chatelaine*, July 1961, 88.

23 Mrs Ethel M. Demaine, ibid.

24 Elizabeth H. Marsh, ibid.

25 Ruth Bennett, ibid.

26 Henriksen, *Dr. Strangelove's America*, 200.

27 Doris Anderson, 'A Gesture of Sanity and Faith,' *Chatelaine*, February 1962, 1.

28 Walsh, letter to the editor, 'The Last Word Is Yours,' *Chatelaine* (April 1962), 150.

29 Sonia Puchalski, ibid.

30 Boyer, *By the Bomb's Early Light*, 355. Recently, Margot A. Henriksen has

criticized Boyer, and others, for arguing that passivity and denial (what Boyer calls 'The Big Sleep') characterize the period from 1963 to 1980. Henriksen claims that Americans remained aware and critical, and that the 'alternative culture of dissent' provided the population with cultural products that criticized the nuclear arms race, the civilian defence strategy, and the notion of a defensive nuclear position. See 'Time Enough at Last: The Bomb Shelter Craze and the Dawn of America's Moral Awakening,' in Henriksen, *Dr. Strangelove's America*, 192–239.

31 Christina McCall, 'Can You Protect Your Family from the Bomb?' *Chatelaine*, April 1962, 30.

32 See *Roughing It in the Suburbs*, chs 7 and 8. For articles specifically devoted to Cold War 'otherness' see I. Norman Smith, 'Three Worlds,' *Chatelaine*, June 1951, 4–5; Dr Nadine Hradsky, 'Our First Canadian Christmas,' *Chatelaine*, December 1954, 13; John Clare, 'What's It Like to Be Mrs. Gouzenko?' *Chatelaine*, March 1954, 16–17; Doris Anderson, 'Exclusive Chatelaine Report on the Russian Housewife,' *Chatelaine*, February 1960, 27; Christina McCall Newman, 'Do the Gouzenkos Ever Regret Their Decision?' *Chatelaine*, July 1960, 19; Marjorie McEnaney, 'The Quiet Revolution of Chinese Women,' *Chatelaine*, September 1960, 18–20; Lynn Harrington, 'How Chang Kwei Hsia Works and Lives,' *Chatelaine*, September 1966, 44–45.

33 Smith, 'Three Worlds,' 4.

34 Clare, 'What's It Like to Be Mrs. Gouzenko?' 17.

35 Newman, 'Do the Gouzenkos Ever Regret Their Decision?' 19.

36 Anderson, 'Exclusive Chatelaine Report on the Russian Housewife,' 27.

37 McEnaney, 'The Quiet Revolution of Chinese women,' 24.

38 Harrington, 'How Chang Kwei Hsia Works and Lives,' 45.

39 Christina McCall Newman, 'Latin America: Trouble at Our Back Door?' *Chatelaine*, September 1962, 17; Norman DePoe, 'The Cold War Isn't What It Used to Be,' *Chatelaine*, January 1961, 14; Christina McCall Newman, 'Norad – Can It Protect Us from a Surprise Attack?' *Chatelaine*, June 1962, 17; Christina Newman, 'Foreign Aid – Who's Winning the Quiet War?' *Chatelaine*, January 1963, 9; Christina Newman, 'West Germany Goes to the Polls This Month,' *Chatelaine*, September 1961, 29.

40 Eric Sevareid, 'What Will Happen in 1960?' *Chatelaine*, January 1960, 14.

41 Christina McCall Newman, 'New Force in U.S. Politics: The Radical Right,' *Chatelaine*, April 1962, 15.

42 Pat Walsh, General Secretary, Canadian Anti-Communist Secretariat, Ottawa, letter to the editor, 'The Last Word Is Yours,' *Chatelaine*, June 1962, 126.

43 Newman, 'Foreign Aid,' 9.

44 Doris Anderson, 'Refugee Year Isn't over for Us,' *Chatelaine*, June 1960, 1.

45 Mrs J.S. Cunningham, 'The Last Word Is Yours,' *Chatelaine*, September 1960, 154.

46 Mrs Herbert S. White, 'The Last Word Is Yours,' *Chatelaine*, September 1960, 154.

47 'What Would You Say to Kruschev?' *Chatelaine*, October 1959, 18.

48 Carol Chapman, 'How Effective Is the Voice of Women?' *Chatelaine*, June 1961, 40.

49 Barbara Croft, 'Women's Pressure Groups: Good or Bad?' *Chatelaine*, January 1965, 22.

7

Monkey on the Back: Canadian Cinema, Conflicted Masculinities, and Queer Silences in Canada's Cold War

THOMAS WAUGH

Don't you like girls, Arthur?
Sure I like girls, but do I have to marry one? I like you, Harry, but I don't
want to marry you.
       Is It a Woman's World? (National Film Board of Canada, 1956)

I was born the year of the Berlin blockade and hence my memory of the Cold War, at least the 1950s phase of it that I would like to address in this chapter, is fairly unreliable. However, I do remember hearing about Sputnik on the way to church one morning in Brantford Ontario, and I can recall even more concretely, the news in Miss Davies's current affairs class about the DEW Line, the Suez crisis, and the Formosa bombardment. Miss Davies, an elderly spinster with rouge-red cheeks, was the best teacher I ever had. My anxiety of the time was focused less on nuclear annihilation than on her strap, though it would never be used on me of course, the perfect four-eyed, anti-athlete poet pet who loved the slides of her summer trip to Switzerland in the company of her 'roommate,' another unmarried schoolteacher. I also remember the projectionist from the Brantford Board of Education, who would turn up every once in a while and show us 16mm NFB programs of nature films and Norman McLaren cartoons; a tall, thin man in a suit, bow tie, and red moustache whom I reconstruct as a slightly eccentric bachelor.

    The point of these reminiscences is to suggest how public education, marital status, and the National Film Board of Canada interface with geopolitics in a cultural analysis of the Canadian Cold War. This analysis builds on the work done in Canada by social scientists Reg Whitaker and Gary Kinsman, literary historians Robert Martin and Peter Dickinson, and communications experts Michael Dorland and Andrew Dowler, and others who have scrutinized the development of Canadian cultural policy during the postwar period. It is indebted also to the work of American queer and feminist cultural and socio-political historians such as Allen Bérubé, Steve Cohan, Robert Corber, John D'Emilio, Barbara Ehrenreich, and Amy Villarejo, whose work is usually assumed to be applicable to the Canadian context, although in ways still to be pinned down.[1] My analysis scrutinizes a more elusive and amorphous trace than the archives of courts, cabinets, and print media that critics have tended to examine thus far, namely the cinematic imaginary of the Canadian Cold War in the period that begins at the end of the Second World War and lasts approximately to the late fifties of Suez, Sputnik, and Formosa.

There is a consensus about this period in North America among these social and cultural historians, albeit a contradictory one, and it might be summarized as follows. Both Canada and the United States saw a certain osmosis of geopolitical insecurity and gender insecurity, although predictably Canadians experienced this phenomenon differently, its version of U.S. sexual panics, paranoia, purges, and scapegoating often muted or delayed – a kind of branch plant tag-along version. Nevertheless, the reign of terror in both countries was inseparable from what Corber, following postwar sociologist C. Wright Mills, has called the postwar gender settlement or consensus, a negotiated truce brought on by postwar economic displacements. It enshrined the organization man as the hegemonic model of masculinity, replacing the cowboy and entrepreneur in the cultural imaginary and in socio-economic organization alike, and shifting the predominant ethos from production to consumption. This settlement, however, did not prevent (and may even have provoked) what Corber calls 'the crisis in masculinity,' which was resonant with conflicting models of masculinity, cultural resistances, and what Ehrenreich has called the 'flight from commitment' on the part of men resisting domestication as heteroconjugal[2] consumers. Canadians seem to have imitated only half-heartedly American modes of resistance to the white, middle-class regime of gender and political conformity as they emerged in the early postwar period, from beat culture and the artistic avant-garde to the civil rights movements, the embryonic youth revolt, and the sexual revolution.[3] On the other hand, Canadians by and large seem to have taken a back seat to no one in terms of the institutionalization of psychiatry, judging from Kinsman's chilling study of this insidious medico-scientific infrastructure of the new settlement as implemented in Canada.[4] Bolstering Kinsman's study is the primary evidence of the National Film Board of Canada itself, whose series on mental health, *Mental Mechanisms*, appeared in 1947 to great international success. Produced in collaboration with Montreal's Allan Memorial Institute (notorious with Cold War historians for its CIA-sponsored research on LSD somewhat later), the series went on to the sequels *Mental Symptoms* and *Mental Health* and kept resurfacing in various guises throughout the fifties. *Mental Mechanisms*, to which I shall return, was at first produced for professionals but struck a popular chord with lay audiences. As such it may be seen as symbolically cementing the discursive shift in the public sphere from the collective politics of the popular front and the war effort towards the individual regulation of private life, from the villainy of fascism to the villainy of controlling or distant mothers.[5] If security was the byword of Cold War geopolitical ideology in Canada, as Whitaker and Marcuse have established with their witty subtitle, *The Making of a National Insecurity State*, Dowler and others have confirmed that security was also the key to emerging Canadian cultural policy in the 1950s. But it was American mass culture, not the commies and perverts, that provoked Canadian cultural insecurity and our embrace of the fast-consolidating model of governmentality in the cultural sphere. Dowler has described this model as aimed at 'secur[ing] the internal, "metaphysical" frontier of culture' and 'repairing economic dependency in the realm of the material'; in short 'the use of culture as a disciplinary regime to ensure the development of a distinctive and therefore defensible character of the Canadian state.'[6] I am not challenging this consensus here but rather showing how the Canadian cinematic imaginary engaged with, mediated, and merged these anxieties, discourses, and issues, sometimes explicitly, often obliquely, throughout the postwar period.

In cinematic terms, this period – 1945 to approximately the end of the 1950s – might be called the last premodern phase of Canadian film history, dominated almost entirely by the activities of the National Film Board. Traditionally viewed as a kind of dark ages – in my mind to a large extent because *film noir* seems to have been the presiding stylistic influence over this chilly phase when Canadians seemed to wear winter clothes all year round and performed in morbidly didactic docudramas – this gloomy Ottawa interregnum stretched between John Grierson's originary inspiration in the heat of the anti-fascist conflict and the moment when the scarred but modernized Board emerged blinking from its pupa in the sunny Montreal suburbs after its move there in 1956.

It is especially fitting symbolically that the National Film Board should be the focus of this reflection on cinematic traces of the Canadian Cold War in its first decade. After all, founder Grierson and the Board had been among the first Canadian sacrificial victims, individual and institutional respectively, of the post-Gouzenko version of Cold War fear, desire, and censorship between 1945 and 1951, as Whitaker/Marcuse and Evans have recounted.[7] Indeed, the uneven and intermittent cinematic output that explicitly addressed the geopolitics of that period hardly merits attention otherwise. In contrast to the pioneering 'World In Action' films of the Second World War that had cemented the institution's global reputation for its cutting-edge discourse on international issues, the half-hearted postwar series of commissions for the various armed forces, the Mounties, and NATO, and a few dutiful works on such subjects as democracy in the developing world and non-military uses of nuclear energy, are hardly worth a second look. Although, as recounted by Gary Evans,[8] the NFB received a large, and secret special subsidy from the Psychological Warfare Committee to produce a 'Freedom Speaks' audio-visual program for international audiences during the early fifties, it apparently diverted most of these funds towards its own traditional hobby horses and dexterously avoided the assigned subject throughout the whole period. While a well-timed film about the Mounties or Berlin was periodically tossed as a bone to the wolves, the work of governmental liberalism went on unperturbed, either because the rank and file and producers alike had learned their lesson well from the earlier blows dealt their charismatic founder and colleagues, or because of some deep-seated resistance by artists to bureaucratic control.

One prominent exception that proves this rule is an all-but-explicit allegory of the Korean War and more generally of the arms race that was released in 1952 and became one of the most popular films ever made in Canada, an entrenched staple of both the Canadian film canon and of my old Brantford projectionist's package no doubt, though I don't remember it: Norman McLaren's *Neighbours*. In subsequent interviews, McLaren confirmed the starting point of the famous parable about fatally pugnacious neighbours as an impartial reflection on the Korean conflict between two civilizations he identified with, and he expressed amazement that he had got away with it at a time when 'peace' was a dirty word[9] – not to mention impartial views of anti-Communist conflict. It is all the more amazing when we consider that the film, unbeknownst to McLaren, was purportedly funded through the Freedom Speaks Programme.[10] These ironies may have accrued to the film because Canadians, as usual, hardly noticed it until it received an Oscar, or because politicians and bureaucrats of the time were as little gifted in film exegesis as their successors fifty years later, especially of a film as deceptively light and inconsequential as a cartoon. Besides, McLaren was the Board's most prestigious in-house artist, despite being tainted by his sympathy with China and a 'fellow traveller' background, and despite having a particular personality bent (to which I shall return); as such he was untouchable, all the more so since McLaren successfully played the grand naïf.

Neighbours is as interesting now for its treatment of Cold War gender insecurity as it was then for its brave discourse on Cold War missile envy. Indeed, the film seems to be a textbook articulation of the regimes of masculinity that arose in the aftermath of the war. Here laid out upon the screen is what has been called the 'feminist folk myth'[11] of the postwar gender settlement: women evicted from the factories into the domestic space of the nursery, crouching and hiding, and 'organization men' ensconced in the suburban public space of the front lawn, comfortable in their domesticated masculinity and corporate suits, pipe-smoking providers for the nuclear family. They are providers, it is clear: not the producers or individualist entrepreneurs of yore, seen only as passive consumers, conformist subjects of the white-collar middle-class suburban dream. But the dream is a precarious and insecure one, as flowers and fences start appearing and conflicts about territoriality and commodity acquisition explode in the escalating savagery of neighbourly violence. McLaren's parabolic logic ironically maintains the Cold War slippage between private affinities and political loyalty, but it also acknowledges the intense ideological struggle over masculinity within the postwar settlement. The settlement's exclusions and disenfranchised others are also here – if only in the form of the war-painted primitives whose guise the men take on – as are its release valves, all funneled into and at the same time disguised by McLaren's allegorical combat, abstracted by his hyperbolic and hysterical slapstick pixillation.

Deciphered in this way, *Neighbours* allows us to see with fresh eyes the NFB Cold War catalogue and identify a contradictory but rich body of work similarly concerned with gender and sexuality, and specifically with masculinity. How else, for example, can we look at another of the

Norman McLaren's 'organization men' ensconced on the suburban front lawn in *Neighbours* (1952). As much a statement about masculinity as about the Cold War? Collection La Cinémathèque québécoise. © National Film Board of Canada.

canonized Canadian works of this period, *Corral* (1954), the romantic portrait of an Alberta cowboy taming mustangs, and of a macho cameraman taming a hand-held 35mm camera, except as a nostalgic fantasy – the organization man in denial – of a model of masculinity now increasingly outmoded by proliferating suburban conformity and consumption 'down east'? A whole body of several dozen less canonical films (more in fiction or docudrama than in conventional documentary) comes into view that specifically addresses, either through denial or celebration, these newly forming models of masculinity. Some explicitly riff on the Millsian social science filtering in from the United States, offering surprisingly explicit and insightful critiques of the new regime. Take for example *The Cage* (1956), a kind of Canadian *Death of the Salesman*, in which, to quote the official description, 'a capable business man [is] caught on the treadmill of our competitive society.' This organization man in a split-level house has an existential crisis and discovers he's a 'big phony nothing.'

Other films from this cluster of works are narrativized as intergenerational conflicts or conflicts quite literally between older and emerging models of masculinity. Among this group my sentimental favourite is *A Musician in the Family* (1953), a short fiction which apparently borrows, unacknowledged, from Sinclair Ross's story 'Cornet at Night.'[12] In the film, a prairie farm boy, Andrew, is forced to choose between his agricultural heritage, figured by the gruff father who expects him to follow in his footsteps, and his musical talents, figured by his effusive, young blonde schoolteacher, Mr Phallup, who is mentoring him on the trombone, and who has no spouse in sight. This film, directed by one of the Board's small network of female creative staff, Gudrun Parker, heads a subcategory of these masculinity films that can be called proto-feminist. These films insist on an alternative model of masculinity that is neither old-fashioned entrepreneurial nor contemporary corporate, but rather is sensitive, expressive, creative, tender, nonconformist – in short, sissy. The most dazzling film along these lines came from one of Parker's scripts that she had scarcely remembered when I interviewed her, and about which I have already written elsewhere.[13] Similar to *Musician*, *Being Different*, released four years later, shows a boy, about twelve years old, struggling between the peer pressures of his jock paperboy pals and his desire to chase butterflies with new naturalist friends, which he is encouraged to do by the bespectacled Miss Davies clone who mentors him in his gender rebellion. The 'discussion trigger' format leaves the sober and stressed boy caught between hockey and butterflies and mercifully allows the ending to be unresolved – we all know what the possible endings are and none was very nice in 1957.

Parker's performing arts documentaries – 'A' list prestige productions such as *Opera School* (1952) and the Oscar-nominated *The Stratford Adventure* (1954) – can also be seen in this light. The latter contains, in addition to a delicious queer subtextual moment I have discussed elsewhere,[14] yet another vision of masculinity as artistic expressiveness. But it is also a key text in the symbolization of cultural governmentality, with its walk-on performance by Vincent Massey, then Governor General and a well-known prophet and advocate (in the 1951 Massey Report) of high cultural governmentality itself. Cultural policy and alternative masculinity thus come together here, though ineffectually; a certain grass-roots preference for *Gunsmoke* and American mass culture over the effete Canadian high culture, enthroned by the new postwar institutions, the Canada Council, the Stratford Festival, the new National Ballet and Opera companies, and the CBC (which, incidentally, was repeatedly queer-baited in tabloids in both Montreal and Toronto) was the overwhelming dynamic.[15] (The first thing that appeared on our brand new TV screen back in Brantford in the midfifties was the World Series.) Further research may gauge the extent to which governmentality absorbed artistic resistance, forestalling, for example, the development of an effectual Canadian artistic avant-garde, just as it had a hand in diverting and determining the development of a bona fide indigenous cinema industry (as Michael Dorland and his counterparts in the private sector have traditionally argued.[16])

Another prophetic film, *Howard* (1957), is a cornerstone of the Board's growing youth film genre that would come to dominate in the next decade. The story of a high school graduate torn among his various future options as they are embodied by those around him – organization man, family founder, cynic, dropout – *Howard* was the NFB's closest echo of the beat-inspired 'road movie' mythology then resonating south of the border. The film sets up specific equations between the domesticated organization man and heterosexual familial entrapment, and maps resistance to this hegemonic configuration in terms of homosocial opting out. Howard's temptation is a summer hitch-hiking jaunt from sea to sea, sleeping out under the stars with his loner best friend, George, who doesn't flirt or dance at parties and actively parodies the rituals of female heterosexual socialization. Not surprisingly, similar fantasies of male homosociality are recurring preoccupations of

Aspiring butterfly chaser George (foreground) struggling with the peer pressures of his jock paperboy friend in *Being Different* (1957). © National Film Board of Canada, 2003. All rights reserved.

Loner George tempts Howard (foreground) with his fantasy of homosocial sea-to-sea 'dropping out' in *Howard* (1957). © National Film Board of Canada, 2003. All rights reserved.

the masculinity films, whether evoked with nostalgic longing for an all-male public sphere, with the psychologizing discourse of 'phases' and 'immaturity' that the new psychiatrization would specialize in, or with the sympathetic identification and crypto-eroticism which energize *Howard*.

The issue of homosociality brings us back to *Neighbours*, which calls out in this light to be read as a version of the homosocial triangulation that structures *Howard*, each man killing first the thing his buddy loves before finally killing the thing he loves in that film's orgiastic ballet. The homosocial reading, ironically, is all the more apt when one looks at the truncated version of *Neighbours* that circulated in the fifties and sixties after complaints that the shocking segment showing violence against wives and babies made the film unsuitable for young audiences. The censored version became a parable about rivalry over a flower between apparent bachelors, which must have looked very queer indeed. In either version, the two men end up in adjacent graves, as if homosocial camaraderie had replaced heterosexual genealogy as the main principle of cemetery organization.

A large number of films spoke of bachelorhood during this period, oddly enough, despite the mythology of Cold War compulsory heterofamiliality, and they didn't need to be censored to do so. Indeed, bachelorhood is the most stressed and least coherent trope of the whole corpus, and one that spreads across the gender line. In the most anomalous film of them all, *Is It a Woman's World?* (1957), a dream fable purportedly about misogamy, Fred Davis, decked in three tubes of Brylcreem, plays a suave bachelor lawyer fighting off potential matchmakers and suitors, and must have seemed like Hugh Hefner's ideal audience for his new magazine.[17] Davis's misogynist playboy conveniently has a nightmare of matriarchal persecution and workplace gender role reversal (where male clerical staff are sexually harassed by cigar-smoking female bosses) and naturally ends up succumbing in the end, like his contemporaneous Hollywood marriage resisters, to the tender trap. *Is It a Woman's World?* was rediscovered and recycled by the women's Studio D in 1977, and repackaged for latter-day feminist audiences as the 'conventional myth that women indirectly exercise power through their ability to manipulate men through sex and marriage.'[18] But this disturbingly limited and literal reading of an unusually witty and acute proto-feminist narrative seems in denial of everything really going on on the screen, including a discreet queer joke or two that surface in the gender role reversal dream skit, and elsewhere, as in the deceptively blithe repartee Davis lets drop (quoted in this chapter's epigraph). Here is a film that needs an updated reading through a post-millennial, post-Butler filter; despite the playful and energized female performances and the unprecedented feminist camp humour of the script, its real energies articulate male anxieties about marital status, gender performance, and sexual identity.

Many of the Board's psycho-social issue films from the period are immersed in this trauma of the married/unmarried binary. The pregnant heroine of *Woman Alone* sums it all up when she blurts out histrionically 'I'm not married!,' as if this was not already fully evident to the kindly Salvation Army matron who is welcoming her to her 'home.' The ghost of Miss Davies hovers over these films' procession of singles: frustrated, hostile, rejected, and altruistic spinsters, lonely and frustrated bachelors, fey arts performers, benevolent mentors, and homosocial couples – and none quite so well lubricated and oblivious as Fred Davis. Marital status becomes a determining slant of an entire discourse on marginality. Even the two pioneering and prize-winning films about drug addiction, *Drug Addict* (1948) and *Monkey on the Back* (1956), depict substance abuse in the context of conjugal and extra-conjugal relations. Here homosociality is the conduit for infection, and conjugal relations are its principal casualty, whether through pimping, prostitution, and 'promiscuity' in 1948, or marital betrayal and breakup in 1956.[19]

Symptomatically, the first two of the Mental Mechanisms films, *Feeling of Rejection* (1947) and *Feeling of Hostility* (1948), depict the eponymous feelings in two unmarried female characters. Both films posit happy marriage as the prophylactic against emotional maladjustment, and position distant or smothering mothers presiding over crippling nuclear families (with weak or absent fathers, of course) as the cause of all trauma. The two lead characters, while not literally lesbians, do go to movies alone, and have 'complex sexual inhibitions.'[20] Fortunately, after therapy, the rejected dowdy mouse develops the skill to fend off salesmen trying to sell her unfeminine apparel (she proudly declares that she wants to see 'gayer' shoes than the practical ones first shown), and the hostile one manages a vestimentary triumph as well: progressing beyond her unreciprocated schoolgirl crush on her female schoolteacher, compensating for her own mother's distance à la *Mädchen in Ottawa*, she later acquires a smartly severe wardrobe that complements her chilly intellectual demeanour and man-hating frigidity. The narrator keeps spelling it out for us: 'These are the subtle, disguised ways in

Mädchen in Ottawa. Hostile schoolgirl develops an unreciprocated crush on her female schoolteacher in *Feeling of Hostility* (1948). © National Film Board of Canada, 2003.

which her repressed hostility for men has expressed itself. Love is fascinating but very dangerous. The danger of being deserted, the experience with her father and her failure with her mother following her second marriage, have damaged too much her capacity for love. She cannot trust men. She is also envious of them.' Not all of the unmarried are damaged goods however. On the male side the wonderfully expressive Mr Phallup is one of the most appealing and lively characters in the whole Cold War catalogue, as well as just one degree this side of swishy, while on the female side there is a whole roster of luminously sentimentalized portraits of unmarried female schoolteachers, including a 'kindly' older professor in *Hostility*.[21]

The nicest spinster of them all shows up in another film about sexual marginality called *The Street* (1957), where working-class prostitutes who hang out in a Yonge St cocktail lounge and talk Hollywood slang are led back to the pink-collar workforce and proper English by one Miss Walker, of the Elizabeth Fry Society. The knowing smile of this middle-aged and portly social worker, her patient support, jaunty perm, little beanie, and efficient chauffeuring to job interviews would convert the Whore of Babylon to the straight and narrow. Needless to say, by the end of the film the hooker heroine Kathy is well on her way back from the brink of marginality thanks to the male attentions in her new workplace – both office mentorship and heterosexual courtship coming to the rescue as Miss Walker fades into the background, her work done.

I don't mean to ridicule these films about social and sexual marginality, for I have been genuinely amazed in the course of this research at how, as the Cold War progressed, liberal social dramaturgy became bolder and more acute in its perceptions of the exclusions and margins of the postwar settlement, including those of a sexual, racial, class, generational, and social character. No wonder censorship brouhahas erupted so predictably around these films: *Drug Addict* was too compassionate for Americans, *Neighbours* and *The Street* were too frank about violence and sex, respectively, for children.[22] Of course, as Studio D was so quick to point out, the films are ultimately complicit in the 'settlement' for all their critical entanglement with it; nevertheless the films resist facile generalizations about the conformity and homogeneity of Cold War culture.

That said, it must be noted that one kind of marginality remains unmentionable and offscreen in these films, and yet, paradoxically, that marginality – namely queerness – is at the very centre of the corpus, the real monkey on the back of the postwar NFB. This monkey clings not only to all these mysterious bachelor and spinster films and other works on sexual marginality, and not only to the films about troubled masculinity and homosociality, but also to the entire corpus of psycho-social issue films that constitute the Canadian cinematic imaginary of the Cold War period. Silences in cultural imaginaries are a familiar problem, as Michel Foucault has compellingly argued:

> Silence itself – the things one declines to say, or is forbidden to name, the discretion that is required between different speakers – is less the absolute limit of discourse, the other side from which it is separated by a strict boundary, than an element that functions alongside the things said, with them and in relation to them within overall strategies. There is no division to be made between what one says and what one does not say; we must try to determine the different ways of not saying such things.[23]

This is not the place to ponder at length the historical reasons for what Corber calls the 'gay male expulsion from representation,'[24] or why it continued at the Board right up into the 1980s. It is hardly surprising that a governmental institution could not have sheltered the mini-tempests and tentative probings that Martin and Dickinson have docu-mented within modernist literary subcultures in both English and French Canada, or the avant-garde visual and literary experimentation increas-ingly visible within the United States in the postwar period, or of course the constant discourse that Eric Setliff and Ross Higgins have dissected in the lively tabloid press of English and French Canada respectively.[25] Looking at the Board's way of *not* saying queerness has already proved to be interesting in itself, but this culture of silence has further faultlines that I have deliberately left out of my analysis until now. I can't finish without probing these underground registrations of same-sex sexualities that are lurking within the NFB corpus. It is not the first time I have done so, for from the beginning my auteurist fallacy discovered in discreet and tiny closet networks more than one phallic auteur. See, for instance, my account of McLaren's *A Chairy Tale* (1957), a collaboration with his acolyte Claude Jutra, another of the closeted queer artists at the Board.[26] *Tale* is another pixillated relationship fable but this one is very pronoun-avoidant and gender ambiguous in con-trast to the gender extremist *Neighbours*. Relationship roles between the handsome, young male intellectual and the chair that doesn't want to be bottom until s/he's been top, the question of who gets the tail and who loses the cherry, all must be negotiated onscreen, and the film, rather than being about geopolitics, seems to be exactly about what it seems to be about: the couple – *all* couples.

These observations prompt another look at *Neighbours*, for like all silences, its silence is less overwhelming than is immediately apparent. In the thrall of my subtextual impulses, it is not too difficult to imagine for starters the discreet zeal with which McLaren must have manipulated his two performers into ripping their shirts off. Somewhat more significant than the beefcake, however, is the way the male-male combat in pixillated form operates less as a sparring match than as a modernist same-sex *pas de deux*, which would be repeated in *Chairy Tale*, albeit between man and ungendered chair, and yet again with a man and a woman in the two great ballet films of the late sixties and early seventies, *Pas de deux* (1968) and *Ballet Adagio* (1971), in which other types of image-processing dissect and lyricize the ritualized heterosexual mating that is the core of classical ballet. The trope is repeated for the last time in McLaren's testamentary film, *Narcissus* (1983), in which two stunning male-male *pas de deux* conclude the career of an artist most commonly and erroneously seen as an abstractionist. In this film only one of the all-male duets is the result of a special effect; the other is performed in the pro-filmic flesh. If the special effects of pixillation and, later, optical printing had perhaps been the post-production distancing mechanisms that allowed McLaren to confront his actors' torsos in *Neighbours*, and real bodies and real desire in general over the next decades, his strategy of dispensing with them at last in *Narcissus* and filming in real space and time a semi-nude male duet gives to his career the teleological shape of a fifty-year coming-out process.

The *pas de deux* is not the only link between *Neighbours* and *Narcissus*; both narratives of homosocial interaction revolve around a flower. I won't belabour the stereotype of men who feel strongly about flowers, though this and many other stereotypes are absolutely pertinent, but I would like to dwell on the particular nature of *Neighbours'* flower itself. The flower, a 3-D puppet creation, gets a little choreography of its own, flaunting its leaves and stem in a way that looks like a parodic performance of a mating dance (similar to Ann Miller's performance in Hollywood's *Kiss Me Kate* the following year). In other words, this is a very queer flower, rather camp at the very least. Indeed, one observer of the time, Adolfas Mekas admiringly called it in print a 'fairy flower.'[27] In the light of American queer art historians' explorations of the ways

Neighbours (1952) as Cold War allegory or orgiastic pas de deux? Collection La Cinémathèque québébecois. © National Film Board of Canada, 2003. All rights reserved.

configurations of camp and silences operated as an expression of resistance and criticism during the Cold War, this little flower in its own
context of silence can be seen as a full-blown icon of Cold War desire
alongside Jasper John's flags, Robert Rauschenberg's erasures, Andy
Warhol's shoes, and John Cage's conceptual silences.[28]

In the past my auteurist outing methodology has not spared McLaren's
lover of forty years, Guy Glover, with whom he shared a muralled
Ottawa apartment that had nothing to do with suburban territoriality,
and whose role as top-ranking bureaucrat and producer at the Board is
otherwise well known. Was it their collaboration and the conviviality of
their legendary Saturday night parties, so public according to Board
insiders that the term 'closet' is hardly appropriate, that made them the
object of an anonymous denunciation to the Mounties in the late for-
ties? As Whitaker notes, the denunciation 'incorporated what could
only be called malicious gossip about 'gay private parties' given by
members of the 'clique' at which [targeted NFB commissioner] McLean
was usually in attendance, and even a suggestion that McLean was
being blackmailed. Some of these innuendoes came from private film
makers whose veracity was questioned by the Mounties themselves.'[29]

It is not anachronistic to focus on the word 'gay' in Whitaker's note,
as the term was in use as subcultural argot in the postwar era with very
much its current meaning, in Anglo Montreal as elsewhere.[30] Whitaker's
note, together with its citation, offers the standard slippage in Cold War
discourse between conceptions of communist and homosexual subcultures, and becomes fairly conclusive in its implication that both queer
networks and queer-baiting were part of an overall picture that is
further fleshed out by the combination of 'malicious' and 'gossip' with
the original terms 'clique,' 'private party,' and 'blackmail.'

Leaving behind the silences that have grown up around this 'gossip,'
let us return in conclusion to textual evidence, beginning with anec-
dotal data on yet another film's production history. McLaren's one-
person floral artisanal model of animation was not to remain forever
the only one in the age of Fordism – even at the Board. Some of the
younger artists of the embryonic Studio B, heterosexuals all, started
working on a more industrial model of production – cel animation –
around the turn of the decade. Their second effort was a spry cartoon
on the history of transportation in Canada (an appropriate topic for the
year of Harold Innis's death), the industrial cartoon tradition an appropriate medium for adding parody and punch to such a deadly topic.
The cartoon became *The Romance of Transportation in Canada* (1953), but,

as Colin Low, the director, has explained to me, there was uncertainty as to how to complete the final package.[31] The traditional NFB stentorian voice-over would normally be necessary to rescue the Hollywood-style fluff for the NFB's national security mission, but what Low calls 'a straight narration' [sic], commissioned from their usually reliable commentary expert, was clearly not working with the new format and sensibility. Producer Glover, who kept his tactful distance from McLaren's work, but sometimes seems to have been involved in everything else that was going on at the Board, was in the studio that day. Glover joined in the brainstorming and came up with a new commentary, and his spontaneous reading of the text was so obviously right that it was immediately attached to a film that was to become another canonical text of the Cold War. Over a relatively slow moment in navigation history, for example, Glover's mock-pedantic voice intones, 'By the eighteenth century, fleets of bateaux (as they were called after the French *bateau*) plied an extensive lake and river system made more navigable by the construction of canals and locks,' with the affectedly obvious etymological parenthesis sending up the entire self-serious trope. This text and its eccentric voice-over constitute the perfect wry gloss on this strictly homosocial history of flouncing and pompous white men carving a capitalist empire out of a so-called wilderness; they are also clearly camp, and in fact downright sissy. Indeed, how else could the film articulate so concisely and so flippantly the insecurities that clouded discourses both of nationhood and masculinity – not to mention those of the governmental documentary – all at the same time? When one learns that the Liberal minister and hatchetman Robert Winters saw *Romance* and barked 'Who authorized that?,'[32] one wonders whether the question exemplifies the befuddlement of yet another Canadian politician confronted by arm's-length cultural activity, or whether the question reveals some more fundamental phobia.

Many of the titles I have mentioned in this chapter were produced for a new communications medium that was to become an even stronger instrument of cultural governmentality, gender hegemony, and queer exclusion than the NFB – namely television. *Howard, The Street, Monkey on the Back, Is It a Woman's World?, The Cage,* and *Woman Alone* were all part of the 'Perspective' series produced by the Board for the CBC between 1956 and 1958. (Interestingly, many of these films were scripted by Charles Israel, who departed from an apparently successful screenwriting career in the Los Angeles television milieu in 1953 for the backwoods of Toronto/Montreal, for reasons never fully explained, in

Railway workers in *The Romance of Transportation in Canada* (1953), a camp cartoon history of flouncing homosocial nation-builders. Collection La Cinémathèque québécoise. © National Film Board of Canada, 2003. All rights reserved.

order to pursue his interest in writing on social issues.)[33] Indeed, television was the Cold War medium par excellence, as Senator McCarthy himself found out, and it installed its own silences. The NFB would eventually lose the turf war with the CBC that it pursued throughout the fifties, but its precarious relationship with television became a permanent one all the same. Television did not have the same opening, or the same kind of opening, for the entangled tropes of social marginality, male crisis, and national insecurity that had become so prominent in the NFB imaginary, and thus television may well have been one of the factors extending the long silence around the monkey on the Board's back. Ironically, the new regime that gradually took over the NFB in Montreal after 1957, including the new French studio, would do little to disturb that silence. Its new technologies and aesthetics of direct cinema, *la vie à l'improviste*, preferred the surfaces of experience rather than its faultlines and undercurrents, the centres of society rather than its margins, thus relegating the docudrama style of 'Perspective' to the archives, and its spinsters and bachelors along with it. This new silence, even deadlier than the fractured silence of the first Cold War era that has been analysed in this chapter, was unfortunately to last several more decades.

Filmography

Feeling of Rejection (Mental Mechanisms series), Robert Anderson, 1947, 21 min.
Feeling of Hostility (Mental Mechanisms series), Robert Anderson, 1948, 31 min.
Neighbours, Norman McLaren, 1952, 8 min.
A Musician in the Family, Gudrun Parker, 1953, 17 min.
Romance of Transportation in Canada, dir. Colin Low, script and narrator Guy Glover, 1953, 11 min.
Corral, Colin Low, 1954, 11 min.
Is It a Woman's World? (Perspective series), Donald Haldane, 1956, 30 min.
Woman Alone (Perspective series), Julian Biggs, 1956, 30 min.
Being Different, dir. Julia Murphy, scen. Gudrun Parker, 1957, 10 min.
Howard (Perspective series), Donald Haldane, 1957, 30 min.
The Street (Perspective series), dir. Fergus McDonnell, scen. Charles E. Israel, 1957, 30 min.

Notes

I am grateful for the support of the Social Sciences and Humanities Research Council of Canada in this research, and, for a few of the research leads in relation to some of the above titles, to my research assistant Jon Davies and the students in my 2000 MA seminar in English Canadian Cinema, in particular André Caron, Éric Bourassa, and Brian Crane.

1 Reg Whitaker and Gary Marcuse, *Cold War Canada: The Making of a National Insecurity State, 1945–1957* (Toronto: U of Toronto P, 1994); Gary Kinsman, *The Regulation of Desire: Homo and Hetero Sexualities* (2nd ed. Montreal: Black Rose, 1996); Robert K. Martin, 'Sex and Politics in Wartime Canada: The Attack on Patrick Anderson,' *Essays on Canadian Writing* 44 (1991): 110–15; Peter Dickinson, *Here Is Queer: Nationalisms, Sexualities, and the Literatures of Canada* (Toronto: University of Toronto Press, 1998); Michael Dorland, *So Close to the State/s : The Emergence of Canadian Feature Film Policy* (Toronto: U of Toronto P, 1998); Andrew Dowler, 'The Cultural Industries Policy Apparatus,' in Michael Dorland, ed., *The Cultural Industries in Canada : Problems, Policies and Prospects* (Toronto: Lorimer, 1996), 347–65; Allen Bérubé, *Coming Out under Fire: The History of Gay Men and Women in World War Two* (New York: Macmillan, 1990); Steve Cohan, *Masked Men: Masculinity and the Movies in the Fifties* (Bloomington: Indiana UP, 1997); Robert Corber, *In the Name of National Security: Hitchcock, Homophobia, and the Political Construction of Gender in Postwar America* (Durham: Duke UP, 1993); *Homosexuality in Cold War America: Resistance and the Crisis of Masculinity* (Durham: Duke UP, 1997); John D'Emilio, *Sexual Politics, Sexual Communities: The Making of a Homosexual Minority in the United States, 1940–1970* (Chicago: University of Chicago Press, 1983); Barbara Ehrenreich, *The Hearts of Men: American Dreams and the Flight from Commitment* (Garden City, NJ: Anchor Press/Doubleday, 1983); Amy Villarejo, 'Forbidden Love: Pulp as Lesbian History,' in Ellis Hanson, ed., *Out Takes: Essays on Queer Theory and Film* (Durham: Duke UP, 1999), 316–45.

2 This article indulges in the neologisms 'heteroconjugal[ity]' and 'hetero-familial[ity]' in order to name the overwhelming but invisible ideological assumption of characters' positioning within heterosexual marriage and the heterosexual family, an assumption that is all but universal within narrative and specifically cinematic texts in the pre-feminist era in Canada.

3 This is not to say, of course, that later on in the sixties and seventies Canadians would not develop robust and distinctive modes of resistance to the

prevailing regime of gender, cultural and political conformity, especially in metropolitan and campus areas.

4 Kinsman, *Regulation of Desire*, 109–16, 124–5, 129–33.

5 Eric Setliff shows how Canadian tabloids subscribed to the prevailing mythologies of blaming Mom in 'Sex Fiends or Swish Kids?: Gay Men in *Hush Free Press* [Toronto], 1946–1956,' in Ian McKay, ed., *The Challenge of Modernity: A Reader on Post-Confederation Canada* (Toronto: McGraw Hill Ryerson, 1992), 164–5.

6 Dowler, 'Cultural Industries Policy Apparatus,' 338.

7 Gary Evans, *In the National Interest: A Chronicle of the National Film Board of Canada from 1949 to 1989* (Toronto: U of Toronto P, 1991), 6–17; Whitaker and Marcuse, *Cold War Canada*, 227–60.

8 Evans, *In the National Interest*, 20–6.

9 Norman McLaren, interview with John Kramer for *Has Anyone Here Seen Canada?*, transcript, National Film Board of Canada, 1978. NFB Archives, Montreal.

10 Evans, *In the National Interest*, 23–5.

11 Elizabeth Wilson and Angela Weir, 'The Greyhound Bus Station in the Evolution of Lesbian Popular Culture,' in *New Lesbian Criticism: Literary and Cultural Readings*, ed. Sally Munt (New York: Columbia UP, 1992), 97

12 Sinclair Ross, 'Cornet at Night,' *The Lamp at Noon and Other Stories* (Toronto: McClelland and Stewart, 1968): 29–45. The story was adapted for the Board under its original title in 1963, somewhat less successfully, by Stanley Jackson.

13 Thomas Waugh, 'Cinemas, Nations, Masculinities (The Martin Walsh Memorial Lecture, 1998),' *Canadian Journal of Film Studies*, Vol. 8, No. 1 (Spring 1999): 24–5, 39–40; Parker had left the Board for the private sector by the time her script was directed by Julia Murphy.

14 Waugh, 'Cinemas, Nations, Masculinities,' 23–4, 35–7.

15 Eric Setliff, 'Sex Fiends or Swish Kids?,' 158–78; Ross Higgins and Line Chamberland, 'Mixed Messages: Gays and Lesbians in Montreal Yellow Papers in the 1950s,' in Ian McKay, ed., *The Challenge of Modernity: A Reader on Post-Confederation Canada* (Toronto: McGraw-Hill Ryerson, 1992), 422–31. *The Ottawa Citizen* no doubt echoed popular stereotypes in 1949 in referring to Board employees' 'uncut hair,' shorthand for both commies and queers (as well as artists). Cited in Whitaker and Marcuse, *Cold War Canada*, 254.

16 Dorland, *So Close to the State/s*.

17 However, the only explicit *Playboy* consumer I've spotted in the 1950s corpus is the furtive raincoater who patronizes the drugstore where

Howard has an after-school job: 'Mustn't interrupt him until he's ready.
He's going to rifle through the picture and photography magazines. Have
a good look at the nudes and cheesecake. On the sly. Then when he's seen
all there is to see, he'll finally find the magazine he was really looking for.
A *Saturday Post.*' In fact he opts for Canadian content instead: *Maclean's.*

18 Official catalogue description for the recycled film *How They Saw Us: Is It
a Woman's World?*, series director Ann Pearson, National Film Board of
Canada, 1977.

19 These two unusual films are fascinating beyond their prophetic elaboration of the issue of substance abuse: their image of Toronto and Montreal
urban undergrounds is a unique audio-visual boon for historians of social
marginality in Canada.

20 Citation from a review of *Feeling of Rejection* in *The Journal of the American
Medical Association* (22 May 1948), excerpted in response-analysis document. Typescript, National Film Board of Canada Archives, Montreal.

21 'Kindly woman professor' is the descriptor of hostile Clare's 'faculty
editorial representative,' provided by an unmarried professional female
spectator in the expert feedback compiled by the Board in response to an
early version of the film, 'Criticisms of Script on "Hostility,"'p. 2, archives
of National Film Board of Canada, Montreal. The final commentary for the
film describes this character, a portly white-haired woman, thus: 'She has
been fortunate in finding someone who understands her, a wise teacher
who recognizes her limitations as well as her endowments, who helps
her, and is happy over her successes without in turn using her or making
the demands her mother made. Through her Clare gains some understanding.'

22 *Drug Addict* was refused import to the United States because of its lenient
views of addiction as deserving of treatment rather than criminalization;
The Street was withdrawn at the last minute from its Sunday 5:30 pm
broadcast slot, 27 January 1957, by CBC brass who protested that the work
(which depicted prostitutes) was 'not suitable for family viewing,' in an
atmosphere exacerbated by the recent screening of the 'Perspective' film
on interracial marriage, *Crossroads*, and a panel discussion about the
suitability of Elia Kazan's *Baby Doll* for Canadian theatres. McLaren's
version of the bowdlerization of *Neighbours* by educational film distributors in the fifties and its restoration during the Vietnam war is illuminat-
ing: 'They thought this short scene at the climax of the film robbed the film
of a lot of its guts and message, and that it should be put back. It was a
very vapid film without that ... though another reason for having cut it out
originally was that I believed in the formal structure of the film, because

I'm a stickler on a strict form, that *the film dealt with two men and a flower ...'*
Interview with John Kramer, 1978 (my emphasis). All three cases are docu-
mented in primary documents in the respective title files in the National
Film Board of Canada Archives, Montreal.

23 Michel Foucault, *The History of Sexuality* (New York: Pantheon, 1978), 27.

24 Corber, *Homosexuality*, 101.

25 Higgins, 'Mixed Messages'; Setliff, 'Sex Fiends.'

26 Thomas Waugh, *The Fruit Machine: Twenty Years of Writing on Queer Cinema*
(Durham: Duke UP, 2000), 195.

27 Adolfas Mekas, 'Excerpt from *Hallelujah the Hills!*,' in Gretchen Weinberg,
'MC et Moi (A Spiritual Portrait of Norman McLaren),' *Film Culture* 25
(Summer 1962): 46. Rounding out Mekas's profile of the animator on this
page are other suspect descriptors: 'Bashful, slim, full-eyed ... a lonely
artist ... presenting us with a world bizarre, gay, merry and charming.'
Thanks to André Caron for bringing this to my attention. Mekas wasn't
born yesterday and was a film maker/intellectual from New York, where
they knew about such things, and his brother Jonas, the high priest of the
New York experimental film scene, went quickly from denouncing in 1955
the fifth-column homos within the scene to respectfully acknowledging
their contribution eight years later. Cited by Richard Dyer, *Now You See It:
Studies on Lesbian and Gay Film* (London: Routledge, 1990), 134.

28 Cf. Jonathan D. Katz, 'The Silent Camp: Queer Resistance and the Rise of
Pop Art,' in Trish Kelly and Serge Guilbaut, eds., *PLOP! Goes the World*
(Durham: Duke UP, forthcoming). See also Cavell's introduction to this
volume.

29 Whitaker and Marcuse, *Cold War Canada*, 461 n. 7.

30 As, for example, in interviews cited in Maurice Leznoff, *The Homosexual
in Urban Society*, MA thesis, McGill University, 1954; cited by Kinsman,
Regulation of Desire, 118.

31 Colin Low, telephone interview with the author, 25 February 2001.

32 Evans, *In the National Interest*, 26.

33 Charles E. Israel (1920–1999) was scriptwriter for *The Street, Crossroads*
(interracial marriage, 1957), *None but the Lonely* (urban bachelor, 1957), and
Borderline (teen issues, 1956). In Lucie Hall, 'An Interview with Charles E.
Israel,' *Cinema Canada* 108 (June 1984): 14–18, Israel is evasive about
possible political motivations for his migration.

Coda

Communists and Dandies: Canadian Poetry and the Cold War

ROBERT K. MARTIN

I was about eight years old when my parents got a telephone call from the elementary school. Did they realize that I was likely to turn out homosexual? The evidence? I liked girls too much, and often played with them rather than joining in the boys' games. My mother reacted in anger, and went to the school to confront my teacher. She was told firmly that she should mind her own business. My father, no great virile figure himself, was troubled by the message, and tried to raise me as a boy. Father had a basket board and hoop installed against the garage, and dutifully threw a few balls in the air. It was only years later that I learned that my teacher's phone call was one of thousands prompted across the nation, by which the government meant to enforce gender norms through the family.

It was, in Lillian Hellman's phrase, a 'scoundrel time,'[1] when friends and colleagues betrayed each other, accusing them of deviant sexuality or deviant politics – the two were one in those painful days. One waited for the news, to see who had denounced or who had been denounced. There were many accusations, but the most powerful always came down to the same two things: sex and politics.

In the modernist years of the 1940s and after, the arts in North America were sharply divided between an aesthetic of the so-called natural, national, and public, and an aesthetic of beauty and artifice. This divide persisted well into the 1970s, as Helen Vendler has recently reminded us, citing the national scandal caused by the awarding of the 1973 Bollingen Prize to James Merrill; as Vendler notes, it was a scandal provoked by anti-intellectualism and homophobia. An editorial in the *New York Times* denounced the administrators of the prize, who apparently believed that 'poetry is a hermetic cultivation of one's sensibility and a fastidious manipulation of received forms.'[2] Instead of the aesthetic tradition, the *Times* called for a Whitmanesque voice, which they identified with a symbolic geography. As Vendler puts it in her summary, the *Times* 'thundered' that '[t]here is a whole world west of New Haven [the site of Yale, which administered the prize].' There are ironies in these controversies, not least of which is that the argument is about the unvoiced issues of politics and sexuality, rather than about aesthetics – words like 'fastidious' can be coded sexually without sexuality being directly addressed. No one need say that Merrill was a homosexual; it's enough to say that he is fastidious. The greatest irony is, of course, the appeal to the authority of Whitman against a homosexually inflected Eastern aestheticism. Such an argument relies on Whitman being safely categorized as a manly poet of the West, and not the tenderest lover he often wanted to be. For the *Times*, Whitman was the poet of the West and hence a poet of national expansion; poetry of those Cold War years needed to assert national identity and power, to be self-sufficient, and to be free of foreign influences. Like the modern art whose role in creating the supremacy of New York has been so well traced by Serge Guilbaut,[3] the literature of the Cold War had to be large, powerful, and masculine. This is not to make any assumptions about lived sexuality; rather, it is to assert the influence of heteronormativity – faced with the battle for the world, wasn't sexual nonconformity dangerous?

A Canadian literary scandal participated in much of the same discursive controversy as the one traced by Vendler. I have in mind the Governor General's Prize for poetry in 1946, given to Robert Finch. Finch was not present at the ceremony, since he had not been informed – perhaps deliberately – that he had won. Earle Birney was called upon to speak in defense of Finch, who was under vigorous attack at the ceremony. Birney got this role to play because he had written on Finch's work in a largely sympathetic manner.[4] For Birney, Finch's poetry is 'only rarely "precious" or merely decorative; predominantly it is poetry of the suavest subtlety.' Birney goes on, however, in ways that become treacherous. Birney asserts Finch's 'bridges of kinship with Housman,' a link that has been repeated in Finch criticism over the years. Quite apart from the fact that there seems to me to be virtually no connection between Housman and Finch, given Housman's colloquial speech, rural settings, and domination by the loss of young men, the language of Birney's comments works in ways that we can recognize as highly charged. Housman and Finch share a 'deceitful simplicity of form,' a construction that seems to say more than its surface allows. What precisely is deceitful? Is it the form or the self? What is there to be deceptive about? Birney also calls attention to the thematics of friendship in both poets, seen as an 'almost despairing groping through the long "miles from heart to head."' Birney concludes with terms that have been consecrated in the critical discourse of Canadian poetry. Finch is 'cosmopolitan,' not native (he was in fact born in the United States), and his work displays 'Gallic fastidiousness' (that word, again). French is always the Canadian other, and when this otherness is linked to fastidiousness it becomes downright treasonous.[5]

Birney's innuendo was picked up by John Sutherland, who had just taken on Patrick Anderson, accusing him of homosexuality (a charge that Anderson considered libellous). Sutherland's article on Finch in *Northern Review*[6] was so extreme that five members of his editorial board, including A.M. Klein, F.R. Scott, and A.J.M. Smith, and two regional editors, P.K. Page and Ralph Gustafson, all resigned. Although Sutherland's attack on Finch was not as personal as that on Anderson (and Sutherland even mentioned Anderson as someone more deserving of the GG than Finch), it was scornful and condescending. For Sutherland, Finch offered a poetry of platitudes, of excessive self-consciousness. His poetry was decorative (despite Birney's comment), and the conceits 'illogical and silly' (40). He is in the end no more than a 'dandified versifier.' This concept of Finch as dandy, first argued by A.J.M. Smith, has persisted to the present day; Brian Trehearne makes it the central figure of a recent study of Finch.[7] It is certainly true that there is something of the dandy in Finch, but we need to remember how slippery a term 'dandy' is and how much it belongs to a form of self-construction.

It is not surprising that Sutherland should have decided to reveal the psychology and hidden life of Patrick Anderson. The 1940s and 1950s were a time in North America when a more pragmatic and cruder version of Freudian psychoanalysis was in fashion, and it brought with it a moralizing and controlling role, especially with regard to sexual difference. Daryl Hine gives his version of this period in *In and Out*,[8] his long poem set at McGill in the 1960s, where an unsuppressed homosexuality is joined to a Catholicism left over from the fin de siècle and reinforced by a new Anglo-Catholicism popularized by Eliot. Significantly, Hine's coming out and his love affair with Hyacinth are ways of breaking away from his arrogant step-father, a psychiatrist.

The suggestion of the personal as political that we find in Hine is fully present in Anderson, who wrote as a committed communist, at least until the end of the war. If for Christopher Isherwood, 'Berlin meant boys,' for Anderson 'politics meant boys.'[9] In other words, his attraction to young men was filtered through his political goals. An early poem that shows the shape this could take is 'Armaments Worker,'[10] which eroticizes the working class. The worker is relaxing during a break, waiting for a moment of new life. The factory produces 'the weapons to reclaim a landscape, / whose green again will be a people's corn.' The last stanza of the poem sets up a paradox: 'look hard as comrade in your human strength / and soft as love on iron and its peace.' The hard metal creates a softness, in which love makes peace. The reference to 'comrade' is likewise double: it is the communist term for human relations, and it is the particular sign of male love in Whitman. This connection was also made in *En Masse*, the Canadian journal of the Labour Progressive or Communist Party, whose masthead carried a quotation from Whitman. The dilemma with which Whitman struggled was also Anderson's – how to be self-sufficient and particular and also one of all humanity. For Whitman to deny his sexuality in order to gain a larger audience was to betray his role as the poet of male love; but to announce his sexuality and his love for men was to lose any claim he might have to be a national poet. Anderson was working within the party but against its view that homosexuality was an aberrant product of capitalist society that was not found in socialism. Like American critic Newton Arvin, or even F.O. Matthiessen, Anderson devoted himself to overcoming that self-serving and misguided view.

These themes are further explored in Anderson's 'Boy in a Russian Blouse,'[11] a poem that challenges the assumption of modernism as a renewed masculinity. Instead, Anderson celebrates a form of fluid sexual identity and performance. The boy is twelve years old, just on the verge of sexual identity, in a liminal space, not yet quite male or female. His Russian blouse also points in more than one direction, evoking both the popular front and the aestheticism and sexuality of the Ballets Russes. Located in a treacherous middle ground, the boy is 'neutral.' This neutrality applies both to his body and to the clothing that covers it: 'neither male nor female, neither a shirt nor a dress.' This radical indeterminacy is sustained throughout the poem. The boy has 'almost breasts maybe,' seeming feminine, but he also has 'big boots' and a 'heavy walk,' although the boots have 'high heels and sharp toes.' While the boy's masculine movements call attention to the performance of his sexuality – his legs 'shoot out and strut' – he cannot be confined to a single gender – 'so much a bride,' 'brutal and half a-girl.'

Anderson's 'Rink'[12] similarly challenges ideas of the normal, though differently in different versions. In its later versions, 'Rink' ends with the bland and awkward line 'echoes enormously surrounding them / from caves the darker for their happy yells.' But in the original version, as published in 1945, it is quite different, the last two lines reading: 'skating on history and on young men / towards the female goal and all the girls.' The marvellous pun sets up the goal as *telos* and goal as the object of the puck. In this public ceremony, under the sign of capitalism, the boys learn not to wear Russian blouses as part of their education in heterosexuality via the national sport, hockey. These examples of Anderson's poetry vividly illustrate some of the ways in which the Cold War politicized homosexuality (and lesbianism) through a psychologism that was designed to pathologize.[13] Yet out of this pathologization emerged a politicized homosexuality, the perfect example of a Foucauldian counter-formation: homosexuals and lesbians increasingly saw themselves in political terms, as the culture was increasingly so portraying them.

Notes

1 Lillian Hellman, *Scoundrel Time* (Boston: Little, Brown, 1976).

2 Helen Vendler, 'Ardor and Artifice: The Mozartian Touch of a Master Poet,' *The New Yorker*, 12 March 2001, 100–4; this quote 100.

3 Serge Guilbault, *How New York Stole the Idea of Modern Art: Abstract Expressionism, Freedom, and the Cold War*, trans. Arthur Goldhammer (Chicago: U Chicago P, 1983).

4 Earle Birney, 'The Poetry of Robert Finch,' *Canadian Poetry Magazine* 10.3 (1947): 6-8.

5 The critical terminology surrounding Finch (including on the covers of his books) would later call attention to his fastidious nature. Apparently this is now a term of praise.

6 John Sutherland, 'Review of Robert Finch's *Poems*,' *Northern Review* 1.6 (August/September 1947): 39.

7 Brian Trehearne, 'Finch's Early Poetry and the Dandy Manner,' *Canadian Poetry* 18 (Spring/Summer 1986): 11–34.

8 Daryl Hine, *In and Out: A Confessional Poem* (1975; rpt. New York: Knopf, 1989).

9 See my article 'Sex and Politics in Wartime Canada: The Attack on Patrick Anderson,' *Essays on Canadian Writing* 44 (1991): 110–25.

10 Patrick Anderson, 'Armaments Worker,' in *The White Centre* (Toronto: Ryerson, 1946), 16.

11 Anderson, 'Boy in a Russian Blouse,' in *The White Centre*, 57.

12 Anderson, 'Rink' in *A Tent for April* (Montreal: First Statement, 1945), unpaginated; revised in *A Visiting Distance: Poems: New, Revised and Selected* (Ottawa: Borealis, 1976), 45–6.

13 This fear of secrets was dramatically brought out in Hitchcock's Quebec film, *I Confess* (1953), which conflates Catholicism, espionage, and homosexuality; the contemporary relevance of the film is acknowledged in Robert Lepage's *Le Confessional* (1995).

Contributors

Mary Louise Adams is a professor in the School of Physical and Health Education, and the Department of Sociology, Queen's University. She has published *The Trouble with Normal: Postwar Youth and the Making of Heterosexuality* (1997).

Richard Cavell is Professor of English and Director of the International Canadian Studies Centre, University of British Columbia. He has published *McLuhan in Space: A Cultural Geography* (2002, rpt. 2003).

Steve Hewitt is a lecturer in the Department of American and Canadian Studies, University of Birmingham. He has published *Spying 101: The RCMP's Secret Activities at Canadian Universities, 1917–1997* (2002), and, with Reg Whitaker, *Canada and the Cold War* (2003).

Franca Iacovetta is a professor in the Department of History at the University of Toronto. She has published *Such Hardworking People: Italian Immigrants in Postwar Toronto* (1992); *Gender Conflicts: New Essays in Women's History*, ed. with Mariana Valverde (1992); *The Writing of English-Canadian Immigrant History* (1997); *A Nation of Immigrants: Women, Workers, and Communities in Canadian History*, ed. with Paula Draper and Robert Ventresca (1998); *On the Case: Explorations in Social History*, ed. with Wendy Mitchinson (1998); *Becoming a Historian: A Manual for Women and Men*, ed. with Molly Ladd-Taylor and Edmund Akaba et al. (1999); *Enemies Within: Italian and Other Internees in Canada and Abroad*, ed. with Roberto Perin and Angelo Principe (2000); and *Women, Gender, and Transnational Lives: Italian Workers of the Worlds* (2002).

Gary Kinsman is a professor of sociology at Laurentian University. He has published *The Regulation of Desire: Sexuality in Canada* (1987), its second edition, *The Regulation of Desire: Homo and Hetero Sexualities* (1996); and is co-editor of *Whose National Security? Surveillance and the Creation of Enemies in Canada* (2000).

Valerie J. Korinek is a professor of history at the University of Saskatchewan. She has published *Roughing It in the Suburbs: Reading* Chatelaine *in the Fifties and Sixties* (2000)

Robert K. Martin is Professor and Director of Études Anglaises at the Université de Montréal. He has published *The Homosexual Tradition in American Poetry* (1979) and its second, expanded, edition of the same title (1998); *E.M Forster: Centenary Revaluations*, ed. with Judith S. Herz (1982); *Hero, Captain, and Stranger: Male Friendship, Social Critique and Literary Form in the Sea Novels of Herman Melville* (1986); *The Continuing Presence of Walt Whitman: The Life after the Life* (1992); *Queer Forster*, ed. with George Piggford (1997); *American Gothic: New Interventions in a National Narrative*, ed. with Eric Savoy (1998); and *Roman Holidays: American Writers and Artists in 19th Century Italy*, ed. with Leland S. Person (2002).

Thomas Waugh is Professor and Director of the Programme in Interdisciplinary Studies in Sexuality, Mel Hoppenheim School of Cinema, Concordia University. He has published *Hard to Imagine: Gay Male Eroticism in Photography and Film from Their Beginnings to Stonewall* (1996); *The Fruit Machine: Twenty Years of Writings on Queer Cinema* (2000); *Out/Lines: Underground Gay Graphics from before Stonewall* (2002).

Reg Whitaker is Distinguished Research Professor Emeritus, York University, and Adjunct Professor of Political Science, University of Victoria. He has published *Drugs and the Law: The Canadian Scene* (1969); *The Government Party: Organizing and Financing the Liberal Party of Canada 1930–1958* (1977); *Federalism and Democratic Theory* (1983); *Double Standard: The Secret History of Canadian Immigration* (1987); *Federalism and Political Community: Essays in Honour of Donald Smiley*, ed. with David P. Shugarman (1989); *Canadian Immigration Policy since Confederation* (1991); *A Sovereign Idea: Essays on Canada as a Democratic Community* (1992); *RCMP Security Bulletins: The Depression Years*, ed. with Gregory S. Kealey (1993); *RCMP Bulletins: The War Series*, ed. with Gregory S. Kealey (1993); *RCMP Security Bulletins: The Early Years, 1919–1929*, ed. with Gregory S. Kealey (1994); *Cold War Canada: The Making of a National Insecurity State, 1945–1957*, with Gary Marcuse (1994); *The End of Privacy: How Total Surveillance Is Becoming a Reality* (1999); and *Canada and the Cold War*, with Steve Hewitt (2003).